The Pearl

Said one Oyster to a neighbouring Oyster, "I have a very great pain within me. It is heavy and round and I am in distress."

And the other Oyster replied with haughty complacence, "Praise be to the heaven and to the sea, I have no pain within me. I am well and whole both within and without."

At that moment a crab was passing by and heard the two Oysters and he said to the one who was well and whole both within and without, "Yes, you are well and whole, but the pain that your neighbour bears is a pearl of exceeding beauty."

Kahlil Gibran

"For those that have the symbol, the passage is easy."

An Alchemical Text

The Earth Awakens

Marilyn Barry

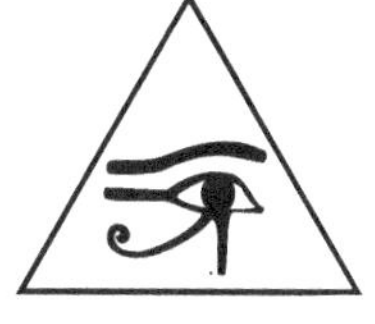

Inner Way
www.innerwayonline.com

First published 1997 as *The Awakening Princess*

ISBN 978-0-9530811-9-6

Calligraphy for 'The Pearl' by Christine Harris

Printed and bound Lightning Source

Published by
Inner Way
77 The Park, Findhorn
Forres IV36 3TY
Scotland.
www.innerwayonline.com

Contents

For Sandolphon's Little Ones

Introduction

In 1985, after the break up of a relationship, I sold my cottage in Scotland and travelled around the world. It was both a healing journey and a quest in that I was searching for something but I did not know exactly what it was. It became an extraordinary journey taking me to America, New Zealand and Australia. My intention was to travel for three months. I was away for a year and a half.

The first part of The Earth Awakens describes my journey around the world and the many clues strewn across my path although I did not recognize them at the time. Through an obscure encounter in New Zealand, I found myself in Pasadena, Southern California, studying Psychosynthesis (a transpersonal psychology) with Vivian King, a kindred spirit, whose house I shared. When I realized that I had dreamt about this house six years earlier, and my room in it, I knew it was an omen. The second part of the book is about the inner journey I took during the first year of my Psychosynthesis training and how this led me to the revelation of having taken a major initiation in the Great Pyramid during the reign of Akhenaten when my name was Sheta Nut. Within six months I had written a six-hundred-page manuscript, with illustrations. To be more precise, it wrote me!

In 1987 I returned to Scotland to build up my Psychosynthesis practice. The manuscript was placed in a closet and dismissed as a figment of my overactive imagination. It remained there until January 1989 when I received a mysterious telephone call from Egypt. A stranger, the wife of an English engineer contracted to build a new sewer under Cairo, had met a client of mine on the Giza plateau, and wanted to offer me a house overlooking the Great Pyramid. When I had recovered from the shock, I accepted her offer and travelled to Egypt at the beginning of February. The house, which her family used as a weekend retreat, did indeed overlook the Great Pyramid. It was framed in the bedroom window. I took up residence in the house, which stood in the grounds of a children's weaving school, on the 4th February 1989.

It would take another eight years for me to discover the significance of this date.

As the Great Pyramid was being cleaned, it was closed to the public. Everyone I knew, including the engineer, applied for permission for me to enter, but the authorities were adamant: absolutely NO admittance. I was disappointed for several reasons. The Nile did not run anywhere near the Giza plateau and there was no sign of a causeway under the Sphinx. However, I did see a boat similar to the one described by Sheta Nut, which had been found buried in a stone pit beside the Great Pyramid in 1954. It is now in a special museum, and when I saw the boat I cried uncontrollably as I relived Sheta Nut's final voyage along the Nile. I also met an American Egyptologist who confirmed that Sheta Nut's name in ancient Egyptian really does mean Secret of the Sky. After I found a book in which Herodotus described an underground causeway leading from the Nile to the Great Pyramid, I was even more determined to gain entry. Then I realised that I had not asked the Great Pyramid itself for permission to enter.

I arrived during the workers' tea break and indicated that I wanted to enter. They replied in Arabic which a man passing by translated for me. They were telling me to ask the Inspector of Giza and pointed to a building in the distance. To my astonishment the Inspector of Giza not only gave permission, he accompanied me and insisted on using my camera to take photographs of me inside the Queen's and King's Chambers. Normally cameras are not allowed inside any of the pyramids. He also allowed me to go down into the area beneath the Great Pyramid known as the Pit, which has been closed to the public since it was discovered that it sent people crazy. Ascending through the Grand Gallery to the King's Chamber was the most exhilarating experience of my life, enabling me to fully understand Sheta Nut's longing for initiation in the Great Pyramid, which has been described as the greatest House of Light on Earth; a record in stone of the history and development of humanity.

When I walked out afterwards into the bright Egyptian sunlight, I was both laughing and crying. Sheta Nut had not failed her initiation. Through many lives and many deaths, she has survived, and her immortal spirit lives on through me.

In 1998 I watched the video recordings of Drunvalo Melchizedek's Flower of Life workshop, in which he talks about initiation in the Great Pyramid during the reign of Akhenaten whose mystery school prepared its students for unity consciousness. He also describes the Christ consciousness grid, which he says was completed on the 4th February 1989, the day I moved into the house overlooking the Great Pyramid. At the very end of his workshop, he says the planet's awakening will come through the children acting in unison. Everything Drunvalo describes I have experienced and written about. As he also talks about what I saw beyond the third locked door, I now had no choice but to take myself seriously and go public with what I know.

A recent seismic survey has revealed several unexplored tunnels and cavities beneath the Sphinz, including a large rectangular chamber beneath the monument's front paws. There is also a fresco in a temple at Abydos (see back cover) depicting an aeroplane, a space shuttle, a helicopter, and tanks facing an eagle. How else could the ancient Egyptians have known about twentieth-century technology and American's confrontation with Iraq, but through time-travel? What powerful message were they sending us over three thousand years ago?

Prologue

Shamballa

A wide valley, surrounded by mountains, shimmers under an amber Sun that casts no shadows. The valley, which is a dazzling emerald green, is sprinkled with intriguing fairy tale structures. Round houses with pointed roofs, domed dwellings, hexagonal and pentagonal buildings with luminous stained glass windows blend into the lush landscape. There is nothing square or rectangular, and floating high above the scene are several translucent globes of colour, like soap bubbles suspended in the cloudless sky.

"Welcome to Shamballa," says Maitreya, making an arc with his arm, as if to embrace the scene.

It does not resemble any of the scenery around Mount Shasta, from which we were so swiftly and mysteriously transported, and yet it looks so familiar. Its crystal clarity contrasts sharply with an ethereal beauty, which enchants me and inspires my heart to burst into song. Shamballa fills a longing deep within my being, which I have always been aware of but until now could not name.

"There is not a person in the world who does not have a secret longing for Shamballa," Maitreya replies in answer to my thoughts.

We walk through the valley along a winding path with borders of flowers heavy with fragrance, their colours iridescent. As we walk, I notice a tinkling sound, as if bells are being rung by an imaginary breeze. I stand still, gazing up at the globes in the sky and listening, to see if my senses are deceiving me. I am told that the tinkling sound emanates from the flowers, and the globes are music made visible.

"I've heard about the music of the spheres, but this is amazing!" I exclaim.

I am led into a village where the structures appear to grow organically out of the ground. Little round houses with lopsided roofs grow like toadstools, and sprout grass from their roofs and chimney pots.

"What a heavenly place," I sigh, my senses all aquiver with the sound, sight and smell of it. "I know this village well. I visited it in my inner world when I was a child."

He smiles at my recognition.

Running in and out of the structures are angel children, singing and laughing, with soft white dove-down on their wings. They wave to us and then, giggling, cover their round cherub faces with tiny dimpled hands. When we are half way through the village, I notice that they are following us. They appear to know me, but call me by a name I do not recognize. They are particularly intrigued by Maitreya's clothes, which they find delightfully funny. He looks perfectly normal to me, dressed in jeans, shirt and sandals, but the angel children, whose clothes appear to have been spun with threads of translucent moonlight, laugh uncontrollably.

We arrive at a large octagonal building with curved windows, accessed through an avenue of graceful soaring columns. An inner golden radiance beckons us into a wide hall with a highly polished marble floor and a domed ceiling covered in stars. Leading off the hall are many doors, but only one of them is open.

Before I can ask any of my burning questions, a tall exotic-looking female appears at the far end of the hall. She is dressed in a long flowing gown the colour of a summer sky, but her skin, in contrast to her gown, is as black as ebony. As she approaches, she holds out her arms to embrace me. I have no idea who she is, but her fragrance is unique and unmistakable. I would recognize it anywhere, but cannot identify it. Unlike Maitreya's fragrance of rose petals, it is tantalizingly familiar, like everything else in this mysterious place. I want to know about this building, who the fragrance reminds me of, and why I am so attracted to the open door.

"This is the Temple of Dreams, and behind those closed doors the Dream Weavers are sleeping," she tells me. "We are waiting for them to awaken."

"Why don't you just wake them up?" I ask.

"We can't do that," she replies in a whisper. "They can only awaken when they're ready to, otherwise they will lose their dreams."

She says I can explore the room with the open door, but reminds me not to disturb the Dream Weavers. As I wander across the hall, I hear her and Maitreya talking, and their voices are like a beloved song I have forgotten how to sing.

The room beyond the open door resembles a small chapel, like those side chapels in old cathedrals. What appears to be an altar is in fact a small bed, the cover having been thrown aside when its occupant awakened. Through an open window blossoming rose bushes impregnate the room with their fragrance, and when I turn a man dressed entirely in black is standing in the doorway. He smiles and embracing me says: "You don't remember me, do you?"

I feel embarrassed because it's true. Although he is as familiar as the fragrance, I have no idea who he is. Then he turns and is gone. I gaze out of the open window hoping my sense of smell will help me to remember, but it reveals nothing. When the lady in blue enters the room, I tell her about the man standing in the doorway.

"That's the Omega Man," she informs me, as if it is obvious.

She asks me how I feel about the room.

"I love it," I sigh. "It feels like my room."

"It is your room," she responds. "You have just awakened. You were one of the Dream Weavers, but now you are awake and ready to take the Journey."

"What Journey?" I ask in surprise.

"It's related to the promise you made to me."

If I made a promise to her, I do not remember it, and I wonder if I am suffering from amnesia.

An angel child enters the room and is tucked into the altar bed by the lady in blue, who whispers about a journey and a spiralling vortex. She speaks softly until the angel child falls asleep.

When I ask if the angel child is dreaming now, like the Dream Weavers, she nods and asks me if I would like to watch the dream. Intrigued, I follow her out of the room and into a chamber with a screen around its circular wall. When the door closes behind me, the chamber is plunged into darkness until the screen lights up. Now I find myself travelling at great speed through a spiralling vortex amidst what appears to be flames. I am inside fire, and notice movement at the very bottom of the vortex where it narrows to a point. A sphere and legions of tiny thrashing creatures catch my attention, and when one of them penetrates the sphere, I enter and ignite it like a match being struck, but as I become the images on the screen I feel restricted and confined. The sphere with me inside it spins, like a miniature sun, rotating in its own orbit until it finds a place to attach itself. The sphere divides within itself, accompanied by a distant throbbing sound; a familiar and ominous drum-beat that causes my heart to race. Signs, symbols and geometric shapes appear and disappear, as microscopic entities line up and link arms in an elaborate cosmic dance.

Slowly the images on the screen fade and the chamber is in darkness again. When the door opens, several angel children are waiting outside. They run into the circular chamber with the screen and sit cross-legged on the floor, and it does not take me long to realize that they too are watching the dreams of the Dream Weavers.

"Will the angel child remember it's only a dream?" I ask.

The lady in blue looks at me with her deep mysterious eyes and enquires: "Have you remembered?"

"What would happen if I did?"

"Then you would be fully awake in Shamballa, and would be able to carry its energy to Earth," she tells me. "This would enable others to awaken without losing their dreams and then . . ."

Before she can complete her sentence, I know what she is going to say. "Then we'd have Heaven on Earth!"

She smiles, and as I follow her across the hall her fragrance stirs me again, filling me with long-forgotten memories. If only I could remember. Her perfume sits on the tip of my tongue.

"Would you like to accompany me to the Love Feast?" Maitreya asks, joining me in the hall and interrupting my reveries.

The fragrance melts and is absorbed into my being. One day I will remember who she is, but when I turn to speak to her she has vanished. We are alone under the vaulted star-spangled ceiling.

"What's going on? I feel as if my brain is short-circuiting. I am called a name I do not recognize, a mysterious man embraces me, and the lady in blue, whose fragrance is driving me crazy, says I have awakened, but I'm confused."

"You work here," he laughs, "but your personality is bewildered because it has never been here before. This is why you are confused. Your personality does not know what to make of it all, but your soul is active in Shamballa."

I stare at him with my mouth open.

"When I visited this place as a child, I was tuning in to my soul. I thought I was imagining it."

"Children are deeply connected to their souls," he explains. "They perceive what is invisible to most adults."

"I'm not sure if my soul is dreaming me or I'm dreaming my soul."

"Until you become a conscious transmitter between Heaven and Earth, you are dreaming each other. Your soul can only experience the physical plane through you, and until now you could only experience the spiritual planes through your soul. Now you are having a direct experience."

We leave the Temple of Dreams and walk across the valley away from the village where the angel children live and play. As we walk, others join us, and although they are happy to greet us I see that they are filled with a purpose which both absorbs and delights them.

"Are you going to the Love Feast dressed like that?" they ask Maitreya, laughing and rolling their eyes. Everyone finds his clothes enormously amusing and incongruous. As for their clothes, they appear to have been woven out of sunlight, rainbows and moonbeams.

I wonder why they are laughing at his clothes.

"They don't normally see me dressed like this," he explains, reading my thoughts. "It amuses them. We both need to change for the Love Feast."

I am taken to a central area where a multicoloured building soars with spires and candy stripes of all different hues. It reminds me of St. Basil's Cathedral in Moscow, but unlike St. Basil's, it has music bubbles bouncing on and off its spires. Heavenly music greets us as we enter the building, which glows from an invisible source.

In a small room, which resembles the inside of an oyster shell, I am given a rainbow robe which I change into, leaving my clothes in a neat pile beside my backpack. When Maitreya appears again, he is dressed in a long white robe tied with a golden belt. He looks quite different without his jeans and shirt. It is as if he has become more feminine.

"Beyond form I can be either male or female, both or neither. I am merely wearing your thought-forms. When we met on Mount Shasta, you thought I was masculine. Now you are seeing me as feminine."

I have no idea how to respond to this statement.

As we continue on our way to the Love Feast, I notice others heading in the same direction, but when I ask them why they don't have some form of transport, they laugh.

"We either walk or fly. If we have to be somewhere in a hurry, we think ourselves there," they explain. "But if we have to be somewhere instantly, we love ourselves to where we are needed."

I long to explore the technicalities of thinking and loving myself to where I need to be, but we have arrived at our destination: a circular open-air temple perched on top of a small hill. Around a central area there are tiers of seats upholstered in shades of magenta, violet and a colour I do not recognize. The angel children sit beneath a raised platform in the shape of a six-pointed star where Maitreya stands and waits. There is a feeling of great expectancy. Not even the angel children stir.

"We are gathered here for the Love Feast," he announces. "And the purpose of the Love Feast is, as we all know, to send love, healing and blessings to Gaia, and to all who dream with her."

Everyone in the temple stands up and waves, which causes their clothes to sparkle in the sunlight. Maitreya asks me if I know how to send blessings. When I shake my head, he points to my solar plexus, and then, to my amazement, pulls out a thread as fine as spun gold. One of the angel children brings a small white bird resembling a dove, and the golden thread is placed in its beak. When the bird is released, it flies high above our heads with the golden thread, which unravels mysteriously from within my ribcage. The bird soars higher and higher until it disappears into the Sun. As I watch, in awe, similar threads of a golden hue are released from everybody in the temple, including the angel children. Like my thread, they are taken by the white birds up into the Sun, which now resembles the canopy of a huge Maypole, with all of us connected to it by our golden threads.

"We invite the Great Beings from within the Solar Disc to overlight us at the Love Feast," Maitreya invokes. "We include all beings from within this Solar System, from the Great Central Sun, the Cosmic Triads, Sirius which guards the Secrets, and all Beings, Solar and Cosmic, who love and support Gaia in her Mission. And finally we invoke the Great One within whom we all dwell, and who dwells within us."

After making some complicated hand gestures which I cannot follow, Maitreya proclaims: "May the Love Feast begin."

"PEACE ON EARTH," we all chorus in unison. "MAY PEACE ENTER THE HEARTS OF ALL WHO DREAM WITH GAIA."

To my great surprise, millions of the small white birds fly out of the Sun trailing golden threads through the sky, and disappear behind the distant mountains.

"LOVE TO GAIA AND TO ALL WHO DREAM WITH HER."

As we send love, our golden threads appear to glow with a pinkish light, which I find fascinating. Maitreya explains that it is the love from our hearts flowing through the threads, which gives them this salmon pink hue.

"HEALING TO GAIA AND TO ALL WHO DREAM WITH HER," is our next invocation. This time a series of rainbows emanate from our threads. Like the white birds, they too disappear behind the mountains. Maitreya explains how all colours have a healing quality. Each colour we send will find its way to a place, condition, creature or being who needs healing.

"These are special rainbows," he adds. "They appear in the

dreams of the Dream Weavers to help them to awaken."

"JOY AND LAUGHTER TO GAIA AND TO ALL WHO DREAM WITH HER."

I am told how important it is for the Dream Weavers not to take themselves too seriously; to find joy in simple things, and to laugh as much as possible.

"MAY GAIA AND ALL WHO DREAM WITH HER AWAKEN TO THEIR FULL GLORY."

After the Sounding of the Note, which Maitreya says he can neither explain nor reveal to me, we all embrace without becoming entangled in anyone else's golden thread. After embracing more people than I can count, the six-pointed star we have been standing on ascends and encapsulates us. Maitreya invites me to travel with him in the star tetrahedron, which rotates and carries us above the temple.

"Good luck on your Journey," everyone shouts, "and may the promise of the rainbow be fulfilled."

"What's the promise of the rainbow?" I ask as we soar over the building with the spires and the music bubbles.

"Do you remember the story of Noah's Ark?"

I nod, remembering how Noah's Ark survived the great flood and how a rainbow appeared as a sign of God's promise never to allow the world to be destroyed.

He smiles as he reads my thoughts.

"This is the promise we in Shamballa are dedicated to."

When I look down, I see that we are travelling above the Temple of Dreams towards the mountains, behind which Shamballa is hidden. The Earth gradually develops a curve on the horizon, which grows until it is a shimmering blue-and-white globe with all of its continents clearly visible. I can see where night ends and day begins, the Moon shining in the night sky, and the stars stretching into infinity.

"Now you are ready to pass through fire," he announces.

Then I realize what is happening. We are travelling towards the Sun, and there is nothing I can do about it, except trust and surrender to the experience.

The Sun is growing larger. It is now so big, it fills the sky with its radiance. We are travelling through a light impossible to describe. It is so bright I have to shield my eyes, but it does not burn me. Then I realize that when I am inside fire or fire is inside me, it cannot burn. It only burns when I separate myself from it. I now know that separation is an illusion. Everything is a part of me, including the Sun. From this point of view, nothing can ever hurt me again.

"We can only be hurt by people or things we have separated ourselves from," I laugh. "When we know we are all a part of each other, it's impossible to be hurt or to cause harm."

This is a great revelation.

"If we are all a part of each other and of everything that is, and if, as you said on Mount Shasta, we are embraced by love, then..." I laugh even louder, "we are all IN LOVE!"

Maitreya laughs with me: "Love is all there is. Everything else is an illusion; a dream."

"We are all In Love! When people fall in love, they are merely remembering their truth. What's so exciting and what really turns them on is the fact that they have broken through an illusion into the reality of who they've been all along. The other person, the beloved, has simply brought it back into consciousness for the one who loves."

I am thinking I shall never forget this truth about being In Love and leading a life without fear, when Maitreya speaks:

"You must always remember this, for you are embarking upon a long and difficult Journey. Others may try to discourage you. They may say you are crazy; that Shamballa is a figment of your imagination; that it's too late to save the world. You must remember that even these people are a part of you, as is everything else you will encounter."

I cannot imagine ever forgetting this exhilarating truth, and continue with my reveries:

"If everyone on Earth knew they were a part of each other,

they'd stop fighting. There would be no divisions; no more splitting of the land, for the Earth does not belong to any one country, leader or nation. She is a living being and we are all a part of her."

I am so excited, I do not notice that we are travelling through a shaft of fire, but when I look closely I see that each flame is an angel. We are travelling through a host of angelic beings. They dart and dance, leaping in greeting, joining only in order to separate and join again in an ecstasy of singing and dancing. The sound of their singing is unlike anything I have ever heard before. It climaxes in one crescendo after another in quick succession, like a multiple orgasm. I feel exalted by their singing and want to join in with them. To my astonishment, I realize that the Sun is a massive gathering of dancing singing angels. I am almost blown away by this discovery.

Maitreya tells me we are travelling to the centre of the Sun to commune with the Cosmic Lords of Will and Love, which sounds very impressive. The angels continue to dance and sing all around us as we enter a central arena, where seven great beings are seated upon seven enormous thrones. Each being holds a musical instrument resembling a trumpet. I try to imagine what it would sound like if they chose to blow through these golden trumpets, and decide it would probably burst my ear drums. The seven thrones encircle a blazing central area, which shines with such an intensity of light I have to shield my eyes. Peering through the cracks between my fingers, I just manage to see two majestic beings towering above our heads.

"Greetings Great Ones," proclaims Maitreya. "We bring blessings from Gaia's embodiment and all beings related to her Mission."

"Ananda is already preparing to leave to bring about Gaia's awakening," nods one of the Lords. "Are the Dream Weavers ready to awaken? Are they prepared for this great cosmic event?"

I feel uncomfortable, remembering how many doors are still closed in the Temple of Dreams.

"The Dream Weavers are stirring in their sleep. We know if they are not ready to awaken when Ananda joins Gaia, the Great

Dragon will destroy the Kingdom, and then the Dream Weavers will lose their dreams. We come to beseech you to delay your arrival, Great One, to give us more time to prepare them."

"I cannot delay my journey any longer," Ananda responds with a sweet, melodious voice. "Gaia calls out to me in her sleep. She longs for my arrival. I do have one question: why are the Dream Weavers causing her so much pain? Even here in the Sun we hear her cries. Why are they continuing to torture her? It concerns us greatly."

"Most Glorious One," Maitreya addresses Ananda. "The Dream Weavers are asleep and are not aware of what they are doing. They need more time."

The Cosmic Lords merely continue to affirm that Ananda cannot delay his journey any longer, adding that it is the fulfilment of the prophecy.

"If we delay, the Dream Weavers may create Wormwood, and we cannot allow this to happen. It is not part of the Plan," both Lords agree, shaking their lofty heads.

Maitreya continues to ask for the granting of even a short delay, repeating that the Dream Weavers will lose their dreams if they are not ready to awaken. "In Shamballa we are dedicated to fulfilling the promise of the rainbow," he concludes.

"We cannot allow them to create Wormwood, and we see how rapidly the situation is deteriorating. Ananda must travel to Gaia for, as he says, she calls out to him in her sleep. She longs for his love. We can no longer allow her to bear or suffer what the Dream Weavers are inflicting upon her. Many emissaries were sent in an attempt to end her suffering, but most were killed for their efforts on Gaia's behalf. It is better to sacrifice the Dream Weavers when the Great Dragon destroys the Kingdom than allow them to create Wormwood, which must be prevented."

"We accept your decision, most Glorious One," says Maitreya. "We will increase our efforts and will continue to pray for a miracle."

As we drift away from the two Cosmic Lords and the seven

thrones, I ask about the Great Dragon.

"The Great Dragon symbolizes Gaia's kundalini, which will be aroused when she is awakened by Ananda. Just as your dragon ascends from the base of your spine when you awaken, the Great Dragon will also ascend."

"Are you telling me that I have a dragon?" I ask.

"Kundalini is your life-force," he nods. "The fire of spirit."

I remember being inside the fire which ignited the sphere in the angel child's dream, but cannot understand why the Great Dragon has to destroy the Kingdom, whatever that is.

"The Kingdom is another name for the collective unconscious which will no longer be large enough to contain Gaia after she awakens."

"But why does the Great Dragon have to destroy it?" I complain.

"Its task is to shatter any structure which prevents Gaia from expressing her full glory," he explains. "If the Dream Weavers are not ready to awaken, they will lose their dreams."

"Will they die?"

"When cosmic events occurred in the past, the Great Dragon destroyed the Kingdom through earthquake and volcanic eruption, but this time we are praying that the destruction will not occur. If enough people awaken with Gaia, the Kingdom will expand and the Great Dragon will ascend in full consciousness for the first time in the history of the world. This is the miracle we are expecting."

"What would happen if Wormwood occurred?"

"Wormwood is the name given to any planet which is destroyed or made desolate by the life-forms who have taken embodiment upon it.

"Do not lose heart," he adds, seeing my tears. "Remember the promise of the rainbow, and expect a miracle."

I long to bring everybody up here to see for themselves the beauty and grandeur of Gaia's blue-and-white globe serenely spinning in infinite space.

"The world has been damaged by fearful and defensive thinking, but love can heal all of the damage that has been done," he explains. "When enough people love Gaia, their love creates an energy field, which can heal as well as call others to take action on her behalf. When you embrace with love, your energy field expands, and as love flows from your heart, it heals. However, when you are defensive, your energy field contracts, making you even more vulnerable. Therefore, love is the only protection you need, and love is instant. Sunlight takes time to travel from its source, but love reaches its goal the instant it is released. This is because love is infinite."

I know how it feels to be In Love and long to be able to love myself to where I am needed.

The Earth grows larger, as we move further away from the Sun, until we can no longer see her contours. Soon we are gliding towards the mountains encircling Shamballa. Then we see its spires, domes and music bubbles, and as we slowly drift down behind the candy-striped building, I cannot resist poking the music bubbles which, to my surprise, do not pop when I stick my fingers in them.

As soon as we land, the star tetrahedron stops rotating and vanishes, and Maitreya waits for me while I collect my backpack from inside the oyster shell room. He takes it from me and puts it on his own back, repeating what he said to me on Mount Shasta:

"It is light and easy to carry."

Then he asks me if I will accompany him to his garden.

We cross the valley and climb one of the mountains on the other side, at the top of which I glimpse the golden spires of a palace reflecting the rays of the Sun and resembling a beacon of light. Half way up the mountain, we arrive at a deep ravine with a bridge across it resembling a rainbow with a handrail of fine silvery thread strung with pearls. When I touch the handrail, it sounds a note as if I have plucked the string of a harp. I am intrigued by the rainbow bridge, and I half expect to fall through it, but it supports both of us without even swaying.

As we approach Maitreya's garden, which surrounds the palace, a flock of pure white doves fly out over our heads. Beside the gate into the garden is a brass plate, which has engraved upon it:

"RESIDENCE OF THE BODHISATTVA"

The gate is made of a pearly material in the shape of an angel, and when Maitreya touches the angel-gate it swings open with a light tinkling sound.

The garden beyond is exquisitely beautiful and fragrant, with a circular pool at its centre. The water is clear and still with a single white lotus growing in it, and as we approach I notice within the heart of the lotus a large pearl, glistening like a precious jewel. The garden is bursting with flowers of all different shapes, sizes and colours, their fragrance causing me to feel light-headed. Beside the pool is an enormous ancient tree with a white seat hanging from its branches. I sit on the seat and am given a fruit that is delicious and very juicy, and as I eat it a great peace fills my being and I long to remain here in Maitreya's garden.

He leaves me on the swing-seat and enters the palace, which has walls resembling mother-of-pearl and gold-tipped pinnacles soaring into the clear blue sky. He reappears with something in his hand, and as he gives it to me he says it is the Seal of Shamballa. I hold it, feeling its weight and studying the pattern engraved upon its golden surface.

"This Seal will help you on your Journey."

I beg him to tell me about the Journey, but he says I have already embarked upon it, and asks me if I know the story of Sleeping Beauty. I certainly do. It's my favourite fairy tale.

"Sleeping Beauty is Gaia's story," he explains. "Do you remember how she pricked her finger on the spindle of a spinning wheel and fell asleep?"

"A Prince travelled from a far off land to awaken her," I add. "Then the Kingdom, which had fallen asleep with her, also awakened."

"The spinning wheel is symbolic of physical existence."

"Gaia is spinning around the Sun," I point out.

"Everything in existence is dancing."

"Dancing?" I ask, in surprise.

"Dancing and spinning are the same energy," he continues. "When she pricked her finger on the spindle, she spun into physical existence, which lulled her to sleep. The Prince came to awaken her."

"He had a difficult time reaching her," I interrupt. "He had to make his way through the brambles which surrounded the Castle."

"The brambles are symbolic of the illusion of physical existence. The entire Kingdom had fallen asleep to the reality of its eternal nature. The Prince lived outside the Kingdom and could see through the illusion, which enabled him to penetrate the brambles."

"And the entire Kingdom awakened with her."

"When the Kingdom awakened, it remembered she was their Princess."

"Is Gaia our Princess?"

He nods.

As I gaze into the distance, I murmur:

"Gaia is an awakening Princess."

"This will arouse the Great Dragon. Part of your Journey involves finding the Great Dragon and being a mediator."

"I don't know where to look," I protest, "or what to say."

"You may have to be willing to go to the last place on Earth you would ever want to visit," he informs me. "When you have prepared the Bridal Chamber for Gaia and Ananda, gather as many people as you can find to be there when they are reunited."

When I ask where it is, he tells me the only way the Journey to the Bridal Chamber can be understood is through imagery.

"Gaia is asleep in the Castle, which is a symbol for her psyche."

When I complain that I don't know how to find the Castle, he tells me to take one step at a time.

"In the story of Sleeping Beauty it was considered a tragedy when she pricked her finger on the spindle of the spinning wheel. If, as you say, Sleeping Beauty is Gaia's story, is physical existence bad?" I ask.

"Only if you resist it or identify with it. Do you remember the rest of the story?"

"The King and Queen were trying to protect the Princess from the thirteenth fairy who had not been invited to the christening, which made her angry."

"If she had been invited to the christening, what gift do you think she would have given to Sleeping Beauty?"

"Probably a spinning wheel," I conclude. "But she was so angry, she put a curse on Sleeping Beauty instead."

"Do you think the King and Queen were justified in protecting the Princess from the fairy whose gift could have given her a conscious experience of physical existence?"

"But maybe they didn't know what gift the thirteenth fairy was going to bring to the christening," I point out. "They were afraid of her power, so they didn't invite her, but of course she found out. Then they had to be really careful in case Sleeping Beauty found the spinning wheel. This reminds me of how some parents protect their children from life, which creates a kind of living death."

"Physical life is a paradox. Nothing is what it appears to be. The fairy who had the gift of consciousness was not invited, and because she was not allowed to give the gift, it became a deadly weapon. Instead of spinning in full consciousness, the spinning wheel sent the Princess to sleep. The gift became a curse because the King and Queen denied its existence in the Kingdom."

"Are you saying that the thirteenth fairy was a good fairy?"

"Fairy tales tell you everything you need to know about life. Do not exclude anything in your Kingdom. If you do, it may turn against you. Include and do not judge it. The thirteenth fairy, witches, demons and monsters are the shadows cast by resistance to the light. The dance of light and shadow creates physical life. Matter can only appear to be solid for as long as it does not surrender to the light."

"If everyone in the world surrendered to the light, would we all vanish?" I ask. "Is Gaia going to disappear from beneath our feet?"

"Gaia is a living being," he reminds me. "If you cooperate with her, she will do everything she can to support you. She needs you as much as you need her."

There is a long silence as we exchange our love for each other. Then I carefully place the Seal in my backpack and begin to remove the robe, which I am still wearing, but he tells me I can keep it. I am overcome with joy, as I love the robe of many colours and was hoping he would give it to me.

I have no desire to leave Maitreya's garden. To stay here would be much easier than going on the Journey.

"Remember you are In Love," are his parting words. "Everyone and everything is a part of you. If you close your eyes, you can love yourself to the foot of Mount Shasta."

As we embrace on the seat, he does not appear to mind the fact that my tears are running down his neck. I take one last look at the garden, at the lotus and the pearl in the pool, the soaring palace, the angel-gate, and at Maitreya's radiant face. Reluctantly I close my eyes. We still have our arms around each other and the swing-seat is gently swaying beneath the great old tree. It is like being rocked in a cradle. The flutter of the doves returning to the garden is the last sound I hear.

One

Revelations

When I opened my eyes, I was alone and the Sun was beginning to set, casting a rosy haze across Mount Shasta. I rubbed my eyes, wondering if Maitreya and Shamballa were a dream. Then I remembered the rainbow robe and the Seal, but there was no sign of either of them. I was disappointed to see that I was wearing my ordinary clothes, and a thorough search of my backpack revealed nothing. If I could have held them in my hands, I would have been convinced that my experiences were real, but now I doubted what had happened to me.

I walked back to the camper van which, with its curtains drawn, was glowing like a lantern. Inside Lawrence was obviously cooking a meal by candlelight.

"Hi!" he greeted me. "How was your day?"

I longed to tell him about Shamballa, but fearing his ridicule I asked him about his day.

"Great," he replied enthusiastically. "I sorted through my books and papers, and found some articles you might like to read."

Lawrence lived like a gypsy, his hair and moustache bleached by travel and beach-living. He was a gatherer of obscure information which he then shared with the many people he met on his travels. Mount Shasta was the first stop on our journey through the wilderness. For me, it was part of the vision quest I had embarked upon since leaving my home in Scotland. For him, it was a normal part of his nomadic lifestyle. We were friends, not lovers, and shared a great love of nature.

"Are you hungry?" he asked.

I nodded and sat down, glancing through the papers in a daze.

"You look spaced out," he observed, as he heaped rice onto a plate. "Mount Shasta has that effect on people. Apart from being a sacred mountain, there are stories about it being hollow inside with secret chambers where the Masters meet. It's also supposed to be one of the entrances to the mythical Kingdom of Shamballa."

"Shamballa!" I exclaimed. "That's where I've been all day. Maitreya took me there."

"Maitreya took you to Shamballa?" he gasped, looking at me as if I had hit him over the head with one of his saucepans. "Do you know who Maitreya is?"

I nodded, trying to remember what had been engraved on the brass plate beside Maitreya's garden gate.

"He's a Bodhisattva," he informed me. "As an enlightened, ascended Master, he relinquished his place in paradise to help humanity. Maitreya is the eastern name for Christ, and as a Bodhisattva, Lord Maitreya holds the Christ energy for the world."

"Gosh!" I stuttered. "No wonder he didn't want a sandwich."

"You offered Lord Maitreya a sandwich?" he roared, almost dropping the plate of food. Then he laughed hysterically. He had a great sense of humour and obviously thought this was the funniest story he had ever heard. He fell about slapping his thighs and spilling rice all over the floor. When he was more composed, I explained that Maitreya had said he wasn't hungry.

"You bet he's not hungry!" he agreed, collapsing into more fits of laughter. "What was Lord Maitreya seeing you about then? Does he want you to save the world?" He thought this was another huge joke and laughed loudly.

"I was sitting on a rock when he approached me," I explained. "He acted as if he knew me. Then he took me inside Mount Shasta and through a tunnel which led to Shamballa."

"Do you know about Shamballa?"

"Yes, it's heavenly," I sighed.

"According to the teachings of the Kalachakra Tantra, the Warriors of Shamballa, also known as the Rainbow Warriors, will return to Earth to defeat the Lords of Materialism. Then they will establish the Kingdom of Shamballa on Earth."

"I didn't see any warriors," I said thoughtfully, remembering what the mysterious lady in blue had said about awakening and taking the energy of Shamballa to Earth.

"Shamballa ascended into the paradise of the fifth world during the reign of Queen Visvamati," he explained. "Are you sure you didn't imagine it?"

I remembered that when I was a child and had told people

about the fairies, angels and spirit children I saw and played with, they accused me of having an over-active imagination. I decided not to talk about my visit to the Sun, but that night I could not sleep. If it was true, why did Maitreya contact me? If it wasn't true, why did I imagine it?

The following morning we set off for the wilderness. Lawrence was in high spirits and, after filling up with gas, we travelled along the back roads. He hated the freeways and avoided them as much as possible. In the late afternoon we stopped to take a swim. It had been hot all day with temperatures in the nineties. Noticing how low the water was in the lake, I asked what had happened to it.

"It's being piped out to L.A.," he informed me.

"Don't they have their own water?"

"They don't have enough water of their own, so they take it from the north. It goes through long pipes under the ground. Then they wash their pavements with it. L.A. is a terrible place," he said, pulling a face. "It used to be called the City of the Queen of the Angels. My family moved there to make piles of money, and are forever offering me jobs, but I don't want to become a wage slave. They're all overweight with high blood pressure, and they think I'm weird because I lead a simple life in my camper van.

"I'll tell you some of the crazy things they do in L.A. They get up early and drive in their cars from one end of the city to the other. All the people from one side drive to the other side, while the people from the other end drive in the opposite direction. They totally jam the freeways and then they all get angry with each other. They yell, wave their fists and toot their horns. At the end of the day, they all drive back home again and repeat the entire performance. You can imagine how much pollution this creates."

"Why do they do it?" I asked. "Are they crazy?"

"They do it to earn piles of money to buy things. They buy their children things too. In fact that's how they express their love for them. Then do you know what they do?"

I shook my head.

"This is really wild," he said with wide-eyed amazement. "They have all of the things they buy wrapped up in brown paper bags and cardboard boxes. They're suffocating themselves."

"Do they put them over their heads?"

"No, but the cardboard boxes and paper bags are made from trees, and everyone knows trees absorb smog, but they're cutting down all the trees to make packaging for the things they can't stop buying," he explained. "Some days it's so smoggy in L.A. they can't see where they're going."

Horrified, I said that was the last place on Earth I'd ever want to visit, and then remembered Maitreya's words: "You may have to be willing to go to the last place on Earth you'd ever want to visit."

"That's not all," he continued. "There were several preschools in L.A. where the little children were sexually abused by their teachers. But the pre-school scandal is nothing compared to what's happening to the missing children on the milk cartons."

I had wondered where the children pictured on the milk cartons had vanished to.

"They've been kidnapped by Satanists, who are using them in black magic rituals," he informed me.

"I can't believe that!" I exclaimed in horror.

"No, neither can anyone else. That's why nobody is doing anything to stop it, but the fact remains that in this country alone a million children disappear every year. One hundred thousand end up in morgues and fifty thousand are never found, but there is no registry for lost children. It's easier to find a missing car than a missing child."

We drove for a long time in silence.

Then Lawrence suggested visiting some islands he knew, which he described with great enthusiasm, praising their beauty, and the ferries which travel to them every day. The drive to these islands was spectacular. We travelled across mountains resembling cathedrals, beside lakes of deepest emerald green, over stone bridges worn hollow by centuries of cascading water, and through dark mysterious forests. He was right about the islands. They were strung out like pearls in the ocean against a mountainous backdrop. That night we watched the Sun dropping into the sea like a great scarlet plum, with the islands silhouetted against a blood-red sky.

The next day we caught the ferry and sunned ourselves on its deck as we drifted out to the islands. On the first island we hitched a ride to a deserted cove that Lawrence had described to me, and where he promised we could skinny-dip. We were naked whenever possible to feel the elements on our bare skin. The beach was protected by a steep cliff that would have been impossible to negotiate if he had not been here before and discovered the way down. Fifteen minutes later we were alone on the sun-bleached sand, stripping off our clothes, and diving into the clear cool waves. After our swim, we stretched out on the beach to dry off.

I was drifting pleasantly into sleep when something caught my eye. Lawrence had fallen asleep with his head on my backpack, and not wishing to disturb him I watched in silence as the apparition formed itself in a shaft of sunlight. At first it was vague and formless, but as I adjusted my eyes to its brilliance, I recognized it as an angel with a rainbow on its head, and a face as radiant as the Sun. I watched in awe as it slowly descended with what appeared to be a book in its hands. The angel hovered about ten feet away from me with one flaming foot in the sea and the other on the sand.

Lawrence slept on and did not stir when a voice instructed me: "Take the book which is open in the hands of the angel who stands upon the sea and upon the sand."

As the voice spoke, the angel appeared to be reading the book, which lay open in its hands. Nervously I approached the angel who towered above me and had to stoop down low to hand me the book.

"Take it and give it to the children to eat. In their mouths it will taste as sweet as honey, but in their bellies it will be bitter."

After the angel had ascended back into the Sun, I looked at the book which it had appeared to be so interested in. There was absolutely nothing in it: no writing, no pictures, nothing. Then I fell asleep and upon waking could not find the book.

"Have you lost something?" Lawrence asked, watching me as I scooped up handfuls of sand.

Feeling embarrassed, I shook my head, and asked what time it was.

"It must be at least six o'clock."

"I wonder what day it is," I mused.

We debated this for about ten minutes. He was convinced it was Friday, but I thought it must be Monday at least; maybe even Tuesday. By the time we hitched a ride back to the ferry, we discovered we had missed the last ferry. This was because it was Sunday and on Sundays there were no late ferries. We argued about what to do next until Lawrence pointed out that we had no choice but to spend the night on the island. Sitting on a bench watching the sunset, he talked about his favourite topic: the Space Brothers, who he described as highly evolved beings from other star systems. He was convinced that they were going to land in spaceships to rescue us.

"Why aren't they called Space Sisters?" I asked.

"Don't be stupid," he snapped.

"Space Brothers is sexist," I pointed out. "They should be called Space Siblings."

"I hope they land tonight," he said.

"I hope they don't," I retorted, not really believing in them, and feeling miserable about missing the ferry. "I'm not going with them. I'm expecting a miracle."

"It would take more than a miracle," he argued. "The damage to the Earth has gone beyond the point of no return. Everyone is talking about global warming, but I think we're heading for an ice age or a pole shift, which would cause tidal waves, hurricanes and earthquakes. I want to be evacuated before disaster strikes. Do you know where the word 'disaster'comes from?"

"No," I said, wishing we could talk about something else.

"'Ast' is one of the ancient Egyptian words for 'star' and 'disaster' is literally a separation or breaking away from the stars. Our problem is that we've forgotten we belong to the stars."

He suggested sleeping in one of his favourite spots on the island, which was a woodland valley cradled between two hills. It was dark by the time we arrived, and we decided to light a fire. As we walked, we picked up twigs and branches, and eventually found the perfect place to make camp. We sat down in the circular clearing we had found and soon had a fire started. It was a clear night, with the Moon and a few stars visible through an opening in the leafy canopy above our heads. We spread out our towels and ate some nuts I had found in my backpack. Sniffing the air, I asked if he smelt anything unusual.

"We are in the middle of a wood." he pointed out.

I sniffed again. It was a mixture of pine needles, rotting leaves, animal fur and stag musk. I also felt we were being watched, and seeing some movement behind one of the trees, I grabbed hold of Lawrence's arm and pointed.

"Holy shit!" he exclaimed. "Whatever it is, it's awesome."

Moving towards us was a creature unlike anything we had ever seen before. Although it was obviously an animal, it walked on its hind-legs, like a man. With furry legs and cloven hooves it pranced towards us. It had long pointed ears, a thick beard framing its surprisingly sensitive face, and curly brown hair all over its head, out of which stuck two small pointed horns. With the chest, arms and hands of a man, it played a flute. The melody was beautiful and haunting, conjuring up images of meadowlarks, waterfalls, the patter of raindrops and the rustle of fallen leaves under foot.

Lawrence clutched at me in horror, gasping: "Is it the devil?"

The half-animal, half-human creature stood in front of us, just the other side of our fire, its liquid brown eyes so deep one could see reflected in them all the wonders of nature. To look into those eyes was to experience running like a deer through forests and deep glens. His smell was over-powering and sensual: a smell of the Earth. Then I knew who had chosen to visit us this night.

"You know who I am?" he enquired in a deep husky voice.

I had said nothing, but he could obviously read my thoughts.

"Who is it?" Lawrence demanded, poking me in the ribs.

"It's Pan," I whispered.

"Who the hell is Pan?"

Pan, Lord of the Nature Kingdom, had approached Roc, a retired scientist, in the streets of Edinburgh, and Roc's account of this meeting had become a legend.[1]

Pan's deep brown eyes filled with tears. "So, you don't think I'm the devil?" he asked in his slow, hesitant voice. It was obvious he was not accustomed to speaking to humans, and he appeared to be searching for the words deep within our minds.

"I know you're not the devil," I reassured him.

He was pleased that I recognized him and played for us on his pipes. As the music drifted through the woods, many small faces peered out from behind the trees. They were shy at first, but gradually plucked up the courage to make an appearance. I clapped my hands in delight, for I knew immediately who the faces belonged to. They were the fairies, elves and gnomes I had played with as a child.

The fairies were delicate and drifted through the air on gossamer wings. Their clothes were like woven flower petals and, as they moved, their wings made a tinkling sound, which reminded me of the tinkling flowers in Shamballa. The gnomes were heavier and more earth-bound. They plodded along, stroking their long beards and hitching up their baggy trousers. They wore hob-nailed boots and funny pointed hats with pom-poms. The elves were much lighter on their feet and resembled three-year-old children. Their clothes looked hand-made and were multi-coloured. Some of them wore tights and jerkins while others were dressed in little suits, which appeared to have been spun out of silk. They skipped together in twos and threes. The goblins were by far the most lively. Appearing to be naked, they hopped, bounced and did somersaults in the air, but some were round, like balls, while others were shaped more like sausages.

For once Lawrence was speechless.

I was full of questions, and was about to ask about their clothes when a group of fairies danced up to me.

"We get our clothes from you," they chorused.

Seeing my surprise, they laughed.

"You think this is how we look, so we dress up in your thought-forms. It's great fun. Your idea of what we look like probably came from fairy tale books," they explained.

"What do you really look like?" I asked, remembering what Maitreya had said about wearing my thought-forms.

"We're just energy," they replied. "We don't have physical bodies like you, so we don't need to wear clothes, but we love to dress up in your thought-forms. It's our entertainment. We can make ourselves into any form, size or shape. Would you like to play a game with us?"

We nodded.

"You think up what you want us to wear and we'll dress up in it," they explained. The other fairies, elves and gnomes were now gathered around the fire. Only the goblins showed no interest in the game. They were too busy somersaulting through the trees.

Lawrence and I closed our eyes and thought hard. The results were chaotic because we had each thought of something different. The fairies, elves and gnomes appeared to be dressed in ballet clothes and football gear, but everything was muddled up. Some of the ballet dancers wore football boots, while the footballers were wearing ballet pumps and tu-tus with their sweatshirts and shorts. Even so, they enjoyed themselves enormously, and were pointing at each other's outfits with obvious delight. As for Lawrence and me, we were hysterical with laughter and could hardly contain ourselves.

"That's really funny!" he laughed, holding his stomach. "I haven't laughed so much since you told me you'd offered Lord Maitreya a sandwich."

After we had calmed down, I explained that we needed to coordinate our thoughts in order not to confuse the little beings who loved to dress up in our thought-forms. After they had dressed up as cowboys and Indians, punk rockers, movie stars, the Muppets and the Star Trek crew, Lawrence had the idea of having them dress up in kinky underwear. Before I could reject the idea, they all appeared in black stockings, peek-a-boo brassieres, baby doll nighties and g-strings. Everyone laughed, including Pan, but what really amused us was the fact that they were wearing the kinky clothing in all the wrong places. Some of the gnomes wore the black panties on their heads, like hats. The elves wore the stockings and g-strings around their necks as scarves, while the fairies wore the brassieres as jerkins. Lawrence, slapping his thighs, gasped: "This is better than a comedy."

We asked the nature spirits to tell us about themselves.

"We look after the plants," they told us. "We make sure the colours are right, and we conduct energy from the Sun. We pass it through ourselves into the plant we are taking care of, like a prism. When a rose bush bears red roses, it sacrifices the colour red. We absorb light and radiate the colours into the plant. We also help to bring through fragrance, which is a direct manifestation of Divinity. This is why flowers and blossoms smell so heavenly. We are transporters of fragrance. You can neither see nor touch it, yet it is ever present. We bathe in it until it interpenetrates every particle of our being. We also love music, but we don't listen to it the way you do. We are fascinated by the geometric shapes that music creates. We dance in the shapes and the waves."

I remembered the music spheres in Shamballa and wondered if these were the shapes they referred to.

"The elves and gnomes are more connected to the soil, but we are all given our blueprints by the Devas, who are nature's architects. We simply manifest their plans in the living plant or flower with which we are working, but we don't see it as work. Our work is also our play. It is what we love doing most of all. As part of our play, we make cocoons, which trap energy from the Sun, and then we take sun-baths."

"What do you live on?" Lawrence asked.

"We live on love," they replied. "We're all In Love and love sustains us. We don't need to eat or live in houses because we don't have bodies like you. We're just energy, but we can make bodies out of the ethers if we choose to. This is part of our play. It's fun to make etheric bodies to dress up in, but we don't need them. We can also construct houses if we want to.

"We never suffer from loneliness because we are always In Love. Joy is the nature of our being, and we dance for joy. Life itself is a dance. Sadly, humanity appears to have forgotten this fact. We cannot fail to notice how sad you all are. Humans have lost touch with the meaning of life. They no longer dance or sing. Their lives are without joy. We see people struggling with their relationships, their children, and their work, but we do not see them enjoying themselves. Have you forgotten that you are In Love and need nothing? You are a part of everything, just as we are. Even the Sun and the Moon dance for joy."

"The whole of creation dances for joy," Pan agreed. "But humanity appears to have forgotten this fact. It's even afraid of its own death. Does it not realize that only the physical body dies? We do not have physical bodies and are not mourning for a body, which would merely limit us. You see, we are boundless. I, Pan, can take on any form and dissolve it to create another one. I only appear to you now in this form because I am clothing myself in your thought-forms. Your thought-forms are so powerful, the Nature Kingdom can clothe itself in them. Humanity fears the death of its physical body, as if it is the only form worth having; as if it is the only form in existence. Yet you are all limited by this form, or rather by your perceptions of it. It is a mystery to us that you can be so attached to something which appears to give you so little joy. You cannot travel through other dimensions, as we can, nor read thoughts, nor clothe yourselves in new ideas. You are so identified with your physical form, you do not even realize that you are In Love. This is such a fundamental truth to us. Your unhappiness is a cause of deep concern to us, for we see you destroying the Earth in your efforts to satisfy your strange desires. Do you not know that Gaia is more than just your home? She is a living being, and we are all a part of her. She supports us, and if you destroy her, we will all be destroyed."

Lawrence and I were becoming defensive when something in the woods caught our attention. A great mysterious being was approaching. Even the goblins stood still. It floated towards us, bathing us in light, and carried the essence of meadows, trees and streams. It was the colour of grass after heavy rainfall, and announced itself as the Landscape Deva.

"I bring you this message from the Earth Devas, who are a part of Gaia. We have been here since the beginning of time and have never been separated from her. We form the vast forests, the mountains, valleys and contours of Gaia, and are acquainted with every single tree, plant and blade of grass. We are, therefore, deeply concerned about what humanity is doing to the landscape. Huge areas of forest have been ripped out, leaving gaping holes, which are now in danger of becoming barren wastelands. The soil, which is our canvas, is being washed away into the rivers and the oceans, where it kills the fish and the coral reefs. Without the soil, we cannot paint our scenes, which once gave so much pleasure to humans. Now they only appear to be interested in ripping out the trees and creating desolation. The wild areas are diminishing, and soon there will be nowhere for us to express Gaia's beauty and radiance. Humanity is in grave danger. It causes extinction, not only for its fellow creatures, but for itself. We beg you to stop destroying the landscape. If you could stop now, we would be able to repair the damage, but if you continue, the situation will become critical."

"If you destroy the Earth because you humans have forgotten how to be happy and at peace, then all of us will suffer," Pan added. "You have separated yourselves from Gaia, from Nature and the other Kingdoms because you have forgotten that you are In Love and are a part of everything else. You place yourselves in a superior position, believing you have dominion over us and the other kingdoms. You use your minds to rationalize what you are doing, but your minds merely limit and imprison you in old thought-forms, which no longer serve you. Although your lack of recognition saddens us, we can bear it, but when you harm Gaia and the many other beings who seek to live with her, we are filled with sorrow. If you could realize that you are In Love, it would mean the end of separation and rivalry, fear and insecurity."

"We know how unhappy you humans are," said the nature spirits with compassion. "We feel it when we enter your hearts and experience your deep suffering. We offer you this lesson in love: if you could only align yourselves with Gaia, she would help you to release your sorrow, for she is full of empathy for you and could soothe you. Learn to love her, the way she loves you, and take rest in her ever-open arms. She will support you in your efforts to find meaning and joy in your lives. We love her deeply because she has given herself to us freely. As a result of our love for her, we are free in a way you humans do not experience, although it is your birthright to claim this freedom for yourselves. We see humanity in chains of its own making, and in our hearts we weep for you. We would willingly give you our joy, our connection with the Earth, and would remind you that we are all In Love. We are sad that humans are not aware of our presence, even though we surround you with our love. You cannot look in any direction without finding us there. The little children recognize us, but so often they are chastised for perceiving what their parents can no longer see because they have closed their hearts to us."

"This is a message from the Devas to humanity," said the Landscape Deva. "All life thrives on love. We spread a mantle of this life-giving substance wherever we are. It shines forth, as the Sun, and when there is a specific need, we send an abundance of love to that area. Love is the essence of life and when it is allowed to work its magic, it heals. Every single particle of living matter — all trees and plants, creatures large and small, humans, and particularly children — all respond to love. Everything in existence, including the planets and the stars, long to express love, for such is the nature of the creative force you call God."

"You humans attempt to catch and keep the things and people you love, but love is not like that," the nature spirits pointed out. "Love cannot be captured because it is all around and within you. We also see you holding on to life, but life is always moving and changing. We do not hold on to anything, for we are abundant and at peace. Sometimes we celebrate ourselves with each other, which is similar to what you do when you make love. We join together and fuse ourselves, which brings us bliss. When we unite our energies, we vibrate together and become a greater channel for the radiance of the Sun and Moon to manifest in nature."

The nature spirits demonstrated this with each other, appearing to merge, so that there was no way of seeing where one ended and the other began. They sparkled in the moonlight, their colours blending and becoming iridescent. We watched in silence as the fairies, elves and gnomes fused together while the goblins darted amongst them, obviously gaining energy from the fusion. I asked Pan what the goblins were doing.

"They are blending the love generated by the fusion with moonbeams. This is a powerful blend and is used to help the trees and plants grow more vibrant. They do this at night when humans are asleep and there is more energy at their disposal. The early hours of the morning are a particularly creative time for the nature spirits. The goblins work with particles of air, soil, moonbeams and sunlight. This is why they move so quickly. They are combining the particles."

When I asked Pan if he knew about Ananda's journey from the Sun to awaken Gaia, he nodded.

"You must be ready to awaken when Gaia does, because if you are not ready, you will lose your dreams. When humans lose their dreams, they either awaken or die physically. Humanity dreams of destruction, and if it cannot change this dream to one of active, loving cooperation, then the dream will end. This is a natural law. Of course, physical death is an illusion. The physical body is merely discarded, like an item of clothing, and the soul lives on in another dimension, unless it has been damaged or destroyed through Wormwood."

"What happens then?" I asked.

"Then the soul loses its individuality and returns to the Source of all Being," Pan replied. "If the soul has not been too seriously damaged, it can be healed, but it is a long, painful process."

"Could Gaia lose her soul through Wormwood?" I asked.

Pan's eyes filled with tears, the way they had when I recognized him. "When Ananda travels from the Sun to awaken Gaia, she will become conscious on all levels of her being, but her consciousness will demand that you wake up. Currently you fall asleep when you are conceived and do not awaken until your physical body dies. You live your lives in a dream, but when Gaia sounds a new note, you will either awaken or die physically.

"Many humans live only for themselves and their own personal satisfaction," Pan continued. "They do not consider what is good for the whole. It does not matter to them if they create widespread destruction or leave behind a lethal legacy for future generations. We are concerned about the nuclear fission you are creating, for its by-products will remain in the Earth for thousands of years. We can neither contain nor recycle it. This process destroys the very atoms of which creation is composed, but those who profit from it do not care about the Earth. They care only about their brief lives, unaware that they will have to return in another embodiment to experience the results of their actions. Do not split the atom. The Sun provides you with all the light and warmth you could ever need. Learn to harness its energy."

"Everything is a part of Gaia's body," said the Landscape Deva. "All are necessary for the benefit of the whole, which is Gaia in all her glory. Nature seeks to maintain a perfect balance, for the Earth is one body, of which we are all cells. We are interconnected through Gaia, and cannot exist without each other. It is important to recognize the value of every single cell: from the earthworm to the breeze that helps to pollinate the flowers. Nothing is useless or unwanted. All are interdependent, and make up the canvas upon which we work. With this understanding, we can cooperate, for we ultimately share the same goal."

"What goal is that?" Lawrence asked.

"It is the goal of accompanying Gaia into the fifth world, which she will ascend to when reunited with Ananda," the Landscape Deva explained. "It will be the beginning of conscious creation, the opening of Gaia's heart and the heart of humanity. We in the Devic and Nature Kingdoms already have our hearts open, for we do not experience the illusion of separation. We express Divinity in our work and play. When Gaia's heart is opened, she will sound a new note which will reverberate throughout the manifest universe. There will be galactic celebrations, which we cannot even describe to you. They are beyond your wildest dreams."

"We can give you a flavour," the nature spirits suggested. "We have communicated too much. Let's dance instead."

This was greeted with approval from all the other beings gathered around our fire. Pan explained how they often dance together at night. So, accompanied by Pan's pipes, we all danced in a circle. The woods were alive with Nature's music and the delighted laughter of the three kingdoms: Devic, Nature and Human. It was a night I would never forget. Pan was still playing when we fell asleep beside the fire. The gnomes covered us with fallen leaves and then followed Pan through the woods as the Sun replaced the Moon in the dawn sky.

1 *The Gentleman and the Faun – encounters with Pan and the Elemental Kingdom – a True Story* by R. Ogilvie Crombie
Published by Findhorn Press

Two

The Galactic Gathering

As I brushed the leaves from my clothes, I thought about the events of the previous night. Was I crazy or had I been dreaming? Then I had to entertain a third possibility: maybe I was waking up and was now able to access dimensions I had not been aware of since childhood.

As Lawrence obviously had no recollection of our night's activities, I said nothing, and again doubted my sanity.

On our way to the ferry he suggested drifting around the islands for another day or two, and then driving to the Emerald Forest, which he said I would love. I believed him. So far I had enjoyed every place he had taken me to. As we drifted from island to island, pretending we were on a luxury cruise, he talked enthusiastically about the Emerald Forest, which he said had remained untouched by civilization for aeons.

"It must look exactly the way the Earth looked when life was just beginning to emerge from the rainforests," he told me. "There are people in there who have never seen a white man, a car or a television. It's as if they're still living in the Garden of Eden. They're living the way our ancestors lived thousands of years ago. They have everything they need, including soap and a method of birth control, which is extracted from a special plant. They have a remedy for everything, and they love their children."

We set off the next morning and travelled for nearly five days. At the beginning of the fifth day we caught sight of the Emerald Forest, which stretched as far as the eye could see, like a vast green canopy.

"There are areas of this forest which have never been explored," he informed me. "This is a good thing because rainforests are our main oxygen supply and climatic regulator. There are different layers of vegetation in there, from the forest floor to the canopy formed by the treetops. Everything depends upon everything else, and even the fungi growing on the trees provide nutrients for their hosts. Rainforests have developed a unique ecosystem which utilizes every bit of moisture."

"How are we going to get in?" I asked.

He admitted he hadn't given it much thought, but suggested going in on foot with our backpacks. I was about to tell him how scared I am of creepy-crawlies when we noticed the road.

"What's that road doing here?" he demanded indignantly.

I shrugged my shoulders, but suggested we could use it to gain access to the forest. I was relieved about not having to go in on foot. We drove along the bumpy road until dusk, when we decided to stop for a meal and a sleep. The road had started to narrow, and ended in a clearing where we parked the camper van.

We were awakened early the next morning by a loud voice: "You can't park here. We're making a road and need to drive our bulldozer right through where you're parked."

We crawled out of bed and looked through the window. A small dark-haired man was peering in at us.

"You'll have to move," he insisted.

"Can't we have breakfast first?" Lawrence asked sleepily. "Why not join us?"

The man's face lit up and he asked if he could bring his friend. We nodded and he called to another man sitting on the bulldozer. Soon we were frying eggs and brewing tea. I spread blankets on the ground, and the four of us sat down to a hearty breakfast. When Lawrence asked why they were making a road through his favourite forest, the two men, José and Miguel, explained that the big trees were being cut down by a logging company. What was left had been given to the poor city dwellers as part of a colonization programme.

"But the main problem is the soil," said Miguel, his mouth full of toast and tea. "It's not very fertile. They can't grow food on it, so they all end up growing coffee."

"Coffee!" I spluttered.

"Coffee is a good cash crop. It's in constant demand from the North. The poor people make money from selling the coffee beans, which enables them to buy food."

"But the land is so poor, they have to move on every two or three years," José pointed out. "Because they need to grow more coffee beans to keep themselves alive, they burn the forest as they search for more fertile land."

Lawrence was outraged and demanded to know what was happening to the people who live in the forest.

"At first they either hid or attacked the city dwellers," Miguel replied. "Then they ran even further into the forest, but the new road always catches up with them. Some of them caught diseases from the city dwellers and died."

"Isn't anyone honouring their rights?" I asked.

"What happened to that man who was helping the natives?" Miguel asked José.

"He was arrested last month for obstructing the loggers. The politicians turn a blind eye to it all because it suits them to send the poor people into the forest. They had to do something with them. They were demanding land reform."

Lawrence was speechless with rage. Miguel and José agreed that it was terrible, but there was nothing they could do about it.

"We're only under contract to build the road," they explained. "We have our families to support, and this job pays better than most."

"But we need the rainforests," Lawrence raved. "They give us air and regulate the weather. Can't you see that?"

Although they saw his point, they were not willing to risk losing their jobs. Instead they put the blame on us.

"There must be something wrong with you people in the North," they said, nodding in agreement.

We asked them to elaborate.

"Most of the timber goes to the North," they told us. "And you drink so much coffee. Why do you drink so much?"

"You answer that question," said Lawrence, turning to me. "You're the one who drinks it. I'm always telling you how bad it is for you."

I shifted uneasily and stared into my half-empty cup.

"Coffee wakes you up, doesn't it?" Miguel suggested.

"You people in the North must want to wake up real bad," José concluded.

"We can't understand why you haven't woken up yet. You must be drinking gallons of the stuff," they both agreed.

With this final comment, they thanked us for breakfast and walked over to the bulldozer, leaving us to clear up and leave, which we did in silence.

We were so upset about our experience in the Emerald Forest, we hardly spoke to each other for the rest of the day. We went for a short hike, but found the sight of charred tree stumps too depressing.

Lawrence became really angry with me two days later when he caught me sneakily drinking a mug of coffee in a roadside café when I was supposed to be picking up provisions from the grocery store.

"How can you drink that stuff?" he shouted.

It was our first big fight, and I knew he was taking it out on me for what he had seen in the Emerald Forest. It was as if it had broken his spirit. Until then he had believed there were still places in the world which remained unspoilt. Later that day he ate a whole bar of chocolate to console himself, even though he was against eating sugar, which he said was good only for the sugar and toilet paper industries, insisting that a sugar-free diet eliminates the need for toilet paper.

"We can't blame the poor people for trying to earn a living in the rainforest," I pointed out. "It's not their fault."

"The politicians, who are financed by the Illuminati, won't do anything about it," he told me.

"Who are the Illuminati?"

"They're also called the Secret Government," he explained. "In the eighteenth century, a group of international financiers planned a new World Order, which would polarize humanity. They knew if they manipulated the economy and undermined individual power, they would be able to take over the world, which they're doing. Through Third World debt, the Illuminati can take whatever they like. Imagine how much power you'd have if you had the entire world indebted to you. They have all the governments tied up in financial knots."

"I wish the Warriors of Shamballa would come and defeat them" I said tearfully.

We lit a candle and sat for the rest of the evening in silence.

"Tomorrow we'll travel to Feather Falls," he informed me before falling asleep.

The following morning Lawrence was in a lighter mood, and described Feather Falls as an awesome waterfall cascading hundreds of feet down the side of a mountain. It took us four days to drive there because we took the spectacular coastal route. We arrived late at night and I did not see where he had parked the camper van until the following morning when I discovered we were perched precariously on a ledge half way up a mountain. This was his base, where he had a small trailer with running water and electricity. He said the mountain belonged to his family, and was where he rested between trips. We spent the day washing our clothes and ourselves, hanging out the washing to dry on an improvised clothes line, and cleaning the camper van.

Early the next day we set off in the direction of Feather Falls. The approach was through a deep wooded valley with a cool, clear stream running through it. Lawrence explained how the water in the stream ran off the falls and how good it was to drink. After an hour of hiking, we were deafened by the rumble of rushing water. From a wooden observation platform we gazed in awe at the magnificent falls tumbling in a foaming white curtain hundreds of feet into the valley below. The climb to the top took another hour. Here we watched the water cascading over the edge of the mountain, and noticed how it had worn away the rock face in its perpetual fall.

By the time we decided to turn back, it was late afternoon, and although the descent was easier than the ascent, we were both tired and had to stop for frequent rests and drinks of water. We were also feeling sad because our trip was coming to an end. We both felt we could have gone on travelling for ever with nature as our playground.

We were walking along the rim of a deep valley when we detected a slight turbulence in the air and a strange whirring sound. From out of nowhere a globe appeared above our heads. It appeared to be spherical in shape, and as we gazed up at it, we saw lights on its underside.

Lawrence was beside himself with excitement, proclaiming that it must be the Space Brothers. The globe slowly descended until it was parallel to where we were standing. It was twinkling with lights and was made of a shiny metallic material.

"Awesome!" he shouted, jumping up and down on the spot.

As we watched, a hatch in the side of the globe opened and out walked an ordinary-looking female dressed in a silvery blue outfit with what looked like a walkman. She was tall with fair hair and a wholesome face. She would not have looked out of place pushing a shopping cart around a supermarket, and as she waved to us I was aware of feeling both relieved and disappointed by her ordinary appearance. I had expected to see an extraordinary extraterrestrial.

"Hi!" she called to us in a friendly human voice. "May I approach?"

Lawrence, speechless with delight, beckoned to her to come closer. She walked along a ramp which had slid out of the side of the globe, and stopped a few feet away from where we were rooted to the spot.

"I am Azra, a communicator and a member of the Ashtar Command," she announced.

"Awesome!" exclaimed Lawrence, finding his voice again. "I've been waiting for you. When are you going to evacuate the planet?"

She looked surprised, and I was thinking that, if she really was an extraterrestrial, she would not speak our language or look like us. It certainly was not what I would have expected. Surely they did not speak our language on other planets, or wear Star Trek type suits, or even have humanoid bodies like us. It reminded me of those movies where the aliens always speak English and the women wake up without having smudged their make-up or rumpled their hair during the night.

"You're right," she said, reading my thoughts. "Where I come from we do not use language. We use telepathy. This avoids deception, prevents misunderstandings, and eliminates the language barrier. I use telepathy when I listen to you, and because I am able to read thoughts, I can understand and communicate with any being anywhere in the universe. However, when I communicate with you, I need to speak your language, for as yet you cannot use telepathy. For this purpose I have a small computer, which is the gadget you see me wearing. This gadget can decode any language in the universe and speak it fluently. You think I am speaking to you, but it is the computer which enables me to make myself understood by interpreting my thoughts into your language."

"Far out!" Lawrence exclaimed.

"We understand your psychology and do not wish to shock you, so we aim to make ourselves as ordinary as possible. I am female because humans on your planet feel less threatened by women than men. This enables you to relate to me as a fellow being, which is what I am. We are neighbours in the same universe, children of the Great One, and custodians of the stars. As you cannot visit us yet, we come in our starship with warm greetings. My body also feels like yours. Go ahead and shake my hand. The shaking of hands is one of your customs, is it not?"

As we shook hands with her, she taught us a universal greeting.

"In Lakéch," she said, meeting us eye to eye. "Its literal translation is: I am another you."

Lawrence was fascinated by Azra's speech gadget, and after examining it closely, he begged to be allowed inside the starship.

"This is not the starship," Azra explained. "It's a carrier pod but it will take you to where the starship is in orbit around your planet."

After she had assured me that I would be brought back, we walked along the ramp and through the open hatch, which led into a small circular chamber with reclining seats. As Azra strapped us into the seats we looked through the transparent dome above our heads. The pod did not accelerate but ascended with great speed into the sky which changed dramatically from pale blue to indigo. We were told to unfasten our seat belts when we had escaped the gravity of Earth. We were floating above our seats giggling when we noticed an enormous starship directly above our heads.

The pod glided into the starship through an opening, which closed behind it. Then it ascended through a shaft with the three of us inside it. When we stepped out, we found ourselves on a circular balcony overlooking a garden with flowers and plants growing in it.

"We are collecting specimens from your planet," Azra told us. "We are taking them to our mothership, which is an orbiting City of Light with gardens and dwellings."

We walked around the garden, which appeared to be bathed in sunlight although we could not see where the light came from. The soil was healthy and moist with a good earthy smell. When we asked about the source of light in the garden, she explained that they had a solar collector and a sprinkler system that provided the plants with light and water.

"How does the starship travel through space?" Lawrence asked.

"Space is easy to travel through when you realize that it is not linear, but spherical. It is shaped like a torus."

As I had no idea what a torus is, Lawrence explained that it is like the inner tube of a bicycle wheel.

"In hyperspace, there are bridges which link both the planets and the galaxies. However, these are not physical bridges. They are soul bridges and can only be travelled through when you are able to function fully in your Light body, which is also called a Merkaba vehicle. So far your probes have taken people into space limited by their three-dimensional physical bodies. When your Merkaba vehicle is activated, it is easy to use the soul bridges.

"Space is divided into tones. These are not like the borders between your countries, but safeguards to protect areas from alien forces. There are many areas we cannot enter yet because we have not evolved to that level. To enter would burn up our circuits, but the highly evolved beings within these areas can visit us, just as we can visit you."

We thought she meant to say 'zones' instead of 'tones', but she was talking about musical notation. We were blown away when she explained that the universe is a manifestation of sound. Then she talked about love.

"Love is the glue which holds everything together. It is the force behind creation. Love vibrates the ethers and creates the soul bridges," she continued. "We are all In Love, and love is the secret of the Merkaba vehicle. Within the manifest universe there are highly evolved beings who have followed the path of power, having abandoned love, but they cannot use the soul bridges nor activate their Merkaba vehicles."

She spoke of these beings without judgement, but with sadness.

"There is only one way to travel faster than the speed of thought and that is through love, which bypasses all other dimensions because it is instant. Love is the source, so when we are In Love, we are at the centre of Being and can BE anywhere without having to travel there."

When Lawrence asked Azra to describe a soul bridge, she compared it to the vortex through which we are conceived, which reminded me of the angel child's dream in Shamballa.

Having walked through the garden, we approached another shaft. To our amazement, she walked up the wall of the shaft, as if the wall was a floor. She encouraged us to follow her, which we did with much giggling.

When we reached the top of the shaft, we were floating in the control chamber at the apex of the starship, where we could see the sky through an enormous transparent dome. There were instrument panels all around the walls of the circular chamber and in the centre stood a group of gigantic crystals, which sparkled in the rays of the Sun. I was fascinated by the crystals, but Lawrence was more interested in the instrument panels.

"This is the Pleiades," Azra told us, pointing to a cluster of stars on one of the screens above the instrument panels, which she described as a galactic university. "But this is only our base. We come from another star system many light years away from here. We set up base in the Pleiades to help Gaia with her Mission, but we stay in touch with our own star system, which you can see over here on this other screen. I see that you are interested in the crystals. I must tell you that the crystals hold a great secret for your world. It is part of your evolutionary process to raise your frequency from carbon to crystal. One day you will realize that crystal is a consciousness amplifier, which is why we have these crystals in our star ship."

I stared at the crystals in disbelief.

"There is great interest in your star system, for your planet is about to sound a new note. Beings from throughout the universe are here to witness this great cosmic event, which calls for galactic celebrations, and there are many starships gathered around the Earth at this time. This ship is only one of many. It is like preparing a bride for her wedding. I think you will understand. Don't you celebrate weddings on your planet?"

We both nodded.

"She's awakening, isn't she?" I commented.

"As far as I can see, humanity is going to destroy itself," said Lawrence. "The world is on the brink of disaster, and if you're going to evacuate the planet, I'd like to be included."

"We did consider evacuating the planet, but now we are expecting a miracle. We are sending love to Gaia and invite you to join with us in proclaiming her as your Beloved. We love her in every fibre of our being and ask you to bring out the force of your love to help her at this time."

"There you are," I whispered to Lawrence. "I knew the Earth would not be destroyed. Something wonderful is going to happen."

"Yes, something wonderful is going to happen," Azra agreed. "We are linking in with you from all over the universe, and invite you to love Gaia the way we do. We envy you, for you are a part of her in a way we can never be. There are no words to describe her glory or her courage. You are blessed beyond words, and we ask you to join with us in endless praise."

Azra had a faraway look in her eyes and was standing with one hand on her chest. "She gave herself to the universe."

At this point a face appeared on one of the screens saying: "Bring them to the gathering."

"We can only take you if you are willing to go," Azra told us.

Lawrence was thrilled, but I needed to know that I would be brought back, which she promised to do. Other beings in the silvery blue suits appeared and sat in front of the screens and panels. It was an extraordinary feeling seeing the Moon through the dome above our heads, as we veered to the right and slid behind it.

We noticed what appeared to be a huge wheel floating in space. It had a central hub and spokes extending out into space. Many of the spokes had globes attached to their tips, which we soon recognized as starships similar to the one we were travelling in. As we approached, we saw how huge it was, and asked why it had not been seen. Azra said it was well hidden behind the Moon, and a cloaking device also rendered it invisible.

The Moon was now behind us, and a spoke of the wheel blotted out our view of space. We drifted gently towards its tip and were locked into position. We watched in awe as other starships attached themselves to various spokes of the wheel until no spoke remained without a starship on its tip.

"You've been invited to a Galactic Gathering," Azra informed us.

I looked at Lawrence, who was busily combing his hair, and saw what a mess we both looked in our shorts, T-shirts and hiking boots. I asked if we could be given more appropriate clothing, and by the time we left the starship we were both dressed in the silvery blue suits.

We were led through the hatch into a transparent corridor, which felt like walking in space, for there appeared to be nothing between us and infinity. It was both frightening and thrilling. At the far end of the transparent corridor, with its mysterious hidden lighting, we found ourselves in a comfortable lounge with sofas. Various beings were sitting in the lounge looking at large screens, which showed three-dimensional pictures. Ahead of us were large double doors and behind us transparent walls with views of infinite space. It was by far the most awesome sight we had ever seen.

"I think I'm having my mind blown," Lawrence gasped.

Azra invited us to sit on one of the sofas, and we watched as she walked through the double doors and then appeared on the screens. We were dazed and rendered speechless by what we were experiencing. It was almost too much to take in.

When Azra returned, she asked us to follow her. Beyond the double doors, we found ourselves inside a circular chamber with a transparent domed ceiling and a magnificent view of the universe. The chamber was filled with Beings in graduated rows, and in the centre several Beings were seated around a circular table. The seats nearest to the round table were arranged in four triangular formations, each group containing three golden thrones, upon which were seated twelve Beings dressed in long flowing robes in scintillating shades of a material similar to shot silk. The light was so brilliant it illuminated the faces of those assembled in the chamber, but we could not locate the source of the light, which contrasted sharply with the inky indigo of infinite space above our heads.

Lawrence and I were shaking as Azra led us towards the circular table, where Maitreya and various other Beings waited for us. Maitreya was dressed in his white robe with the golden belt, and I felt embarrassed and shy because of what I had been told about him. He smiled and offered us two of the azure blue seats positioned around the table.

"We have invited you to our gathering to give you this Proclamation because of the precarious situation your world is in," said a Being wearing a robe of deepest indigo covered in shimmering stars. "We of the Galactic Council are deeply concerned about the pollution of Gaia Earth, the danger you are in from nuclear fission, and the entry into space of weapons of war.

"PROCLAMATION TO THE HEART OF HUMANITY:

"Due to the danger of a possible nuclear accident or attack, and because weapons of war are taken into the space around your planet, the Guardians of your Souls; the lovers of humanity and the garden-globe Gaia Earth, do hereby proclaim that you must take immediate action.

"Space is not empty and devoid of life, as you believe it to be. Universal laws, established to protect all life-forms, are broken when space is invaded with weapons of war. All future efforts to infiltrate space in this way will be blocked.

"The love of that Great One you call God, and the attendant realms you call Heaven, reach out to you in love and compassion to assist you in preventing genocide and global devastation.

"We ask you to begin at once a daily programme of visualization and meditation. Begin to weave a web of peace with your mental images until this web embraces the planet. We beseech each one of you, regardless of which nation or country you call home, regardless of your religious beliefs, economic or social status, skin colour, age or sex, to begin these visualizations.

"In addition to your daily meditations, we ask you to gather together to hold weekly, if not daily, mutual meditations, in which your combined energies and longing for peace will be multiplied. We also recommend your withdrawal from all thoughts and activities related to war and violence. This includes television, films, radio and any literary source which proliferates hostility. Do not feed this hypnotic horror, which could increase the possibility of physical annihilation of yourselves and your home planet.

"All of you, with your earnest and serious commitment to global unity, can turn the tide and create Heaven on Earth. We ask you to join together as ONE humanity and to give up all beliefs and attachments which cause separation in your world.

"We acknowledge and acclaim the thousands of human beings working towards global unity. Their voices must be strengthened until they swell into a mighty chorus. Through the noisy corridors of your minds, hear this request, and with the secret yearning of your hearts, honour it. Weapons of war have been created that can totally annihilate both your living home planet and your souls. You are in grave danger of creating Wormwood on your beautiful garden-globe. Use your power as a united humanity to put aside weapons of war and close down the nuclear reactors. Do not allow Wormwood to occur on Gaia Earth.

"We beg you to stop polluting your home planet, which is a living being. Although she cooperates with you to sustain your existence, she is reaching the point where her soil, air and oceans can no longer support life in its present form. You endanger yourselves and all other life-forms when you rip out the rainforests without replacing them, pour effluent into the rivers and oceans, and fill the air with toxins. Many life-forms have already become extinct, and many more totter on the brink. Their lives are in your hands, for you are the custodians of Gaia Earth.

"As you meditate for and visualize global unity, and withdraw your support from all actions contributing towards pollution and fouling of the Gaia Earth ecosystem, you will find yourselves awakening as if from a nightmare. You will awaken to the fragrance of your true Self and realize the power of your Oneness. You are asked to rise up as One Humanity to proclaim your Divinity and your deep bond with the Beloved: Gaia Earth, whose destiny you share.

"Acknowledge your power and change the tide of destruction. The time to act is now. We send this message from the Halls of Heaven with blessings and a promise to give you all of our support and loving presence when you say NO to the impending devastation of your home planet, Gaia Earth, who waits for you to cooperate with her to create a garden-globe for the seeds of a New Humanity."

Everyone was looking up through the domed ceiling, and it soon became obvious that the Space Wheel was travelling through space. We were moving down the back of the Moon and underneath it. Suddenly Gaia's blue-and-white globe appeared above our heads, and beyond her the Sun was bathing her in a glorious halo of light. We all gasped at the sight, for she looked exquisite, but extremely vulnerable.

"We call on the Great One to bring peace and healing to Gaia's embodiment and we pray for the awakening of humanity," continued the Being wearing the indigo robe. "It is the end of an era. We now invoke the New Epoch of love and peace, which awaits the New Humanity. We pray for the end of Wormwood and for the redemption of all who seek to destroy Gaia's embodiment."

"There is no life, no expression of spirit, without the Mother, the Great Mother of All Being," proclaimed Maitreya. "Gaia Earth is a manifestation of the Mother principle at work in the universe. The time has come. The crust of the Earth quivers as the great change approaches. We wish to transmute life on Earth with compassion and bring in the New Dispensation. Open your hearts, unite In Love, and let miracles occur. In the New Epoch all are redeemed through the radiance of Gaia Earth. Her sacred cosmic Mission reaches its fulfilment, and the Heavens rejoice. The New Epoch begins with a mass movement of the Heart. Gaia Earth enfolds you in her veil of joy and waits to ascend with you into glorious realms of Love and Light."

All of us in the chamber held out our arms and in one great wave of adoration, proclaimed: "GAIA! GAIA! GAIA!"

The Being wearing the indigo robe covered in stars was introduced as Sanat Kumara, and waving a rod with a diamond on its tip he announced the beginning of the Planetary Presentations.

A Being spoke from the back of the chamber:

"I have travelled in my Merkaba vehicle from beyond the stars, where I am a teacher on my globe. It is difficult for us to understand the crisis Gaia finds herself in, for on our planet there are no conflicts. We have no comprehension of what it can mean to be in opposition and at war with one's fellow beings. We do acknowledge the great service Gaia offers to the universe, for she is its kidneys. We give thanks for her Mission. I am here now to witness her Graduation, to sing her praises and to study the phenomenon of opposing forces. I seek knowledge for our records of all phenomena within the manifest universe."

The second speaker turned to Sanat Kumara:

"We have heard you are ready to use the Rod of Initiation, the Flaming Diamond, if Wormwood becomes a real threat to Gaia's embodiment. Is there any truth in this rumour?"

Sanat Kumara addressed all of us assembled in the chamber:

"I am reluctant to interfere with humanity's free will. I also recognize that in order for Gaia's Mission to reach completion, free will must not be interfered with. I could use the Flaming Diamond to turn the tide, as I almost did in the last Great War, but it would have been untimely, for the tide turned of its own accord, and humanity's free will remained intact. The Karma Lords begged me not to interfere with the current crisis. The Light is breaking through and we can now expect a miracle.

"As Gaia anticipates a mass opening of the Heart, naturally global events are speeded up. She is approaching the fulfilment of her Mission, which is critical, but we must not interfere as she reaches the optimum acceleration point. We trust that her Mission will succeed. If love is radiated to Gaia Earth at this time, a major breakthrough will occur."

A tall distinguished-looking male with blond hair and blue eyes was introduced as Ashtar.

"As a member of the Galactic Federation of Planets and the Inter- Dimensional Federation of Free Worlds, I work with the Ascended Masters and Archangel Michael in the airborne division of the Great White Brotherhood. The Ashtar Command represents this solar system at the Galactic Council meetings of this galaxy.

"It is time for a change of consciousness that will transform humanity and Mother Earth. It is no longer possible for humanity to continue with the style of life it has adopted. If it wants to break free, now is the time. The force of the Mother/Father God is now upon the Earth, and humanity is asked to take advantage of this wonderful opportunity. The Planet is moving into a higher level of consciousness and many Beings with a high vibration are now embodied upon the surface of the Earth. The spiritual hierarchy are in the service of humanity as never before. The Planet is being cleansed, and with a united thought-form love can manifest. Humanity is being asked to embrace the Planet with love, for when love is present, nothing but love can exist. Love is such a powerful force, nothing else can exist in its space. It can change energies, move mountains, and place a new thought-form in any given area. Love is the key to planetary ascension. It brings everything back to perfection."

Representatives from throughout the universe gave presentations, all of them expressing their love and deep concern for Gaia. I could not hold back the tears that sprang to my eyes as I listened to their presentations. Through my tears, I noticed the Omega Man who was again dressed in black, and I was about to speak to him when I was handed a beach-ball-size globe of the Earth.

"We're holding this symbol of Gaia Earth," Maitreya explained.

"That reminds me of a song," I said, without thinking. "It's called 'I've got the whole world in my hands'."

"Do teach it to us," Maitreya urged. "Then we can all sing it."

I immediately regretted my impulsiveness and blushed with embarrassment at the mere thought of singing at a Galactic Gathering, especially as my mother had told me I sang out of tune.

"I know that song," said the Omega Man, leaping to his feet. "Does it go like this?" he asked, singing loudly.

I nodded, trying not to be too aware of how conspicuous we were, and then joined in with him. Lawrence swayed along with us as the singing grew louder. We invented new words as we sang along, including the rainforests, the nature kingdom, the animals, birds, whales and dolphins, and of course the children, in our song about the whole world.

Then the Omega Man danced with me. His arms were around me, and when I looked into his eyes I had the sensation of a great fire being rekindled within me. It was the most exhilarating experience I had ever had, and he was a wonderful dancing partner, with great flair and rhythm.

"Who are you?" I asked breathlessly.

Instead of replying to my question, he merely swung me off into another sweeping dance gesture. He spun me around and around until I felt intoxicated and totally identified with Gaia spinning serenely above our heads. I had never before in my life experienced so much joy in dancing.

The globe was being passed around the chamber, and everyone was swaying and singing with obvious delight. Ashtar was singing at the top of his voice as Maitreya clapped out the rhythm. Lawrence was radiant. It was the fulfilment of his dreams.

When we had finished singing and dancing, Sanat Kumara announced that we would all dance the Christ Dance, which Sananda would lead. Sananda, a radiant Being clothed in a shining gossamer robe, I later discovered is the Being we know as Jesus. Sananda and Sanat Kumara both emitted a vibrant resonant energy field, similar in frequency to Maitreya and the twelve Beings seated on the golden thrones. Heavenly music, sounding like the music of the spheres, filled the chamber as Sananda demonstrated the dance, which consisted of hand gestures, circles, crosses, rhythmic dancing on a square, and forming a figure eight.

In the final part of the Christ Dance, the Omega Man and I were gently positioned until we faced each other. He held out his hands to me, palms up, and I laid my hands on his, palms down. With palms touching and eyes held together in a steady gaze, we danced slowly in a circle. In the final part of the dance, we formed a cross with our arms outstretched and then, after a slight pause, we embraced each other. This caused my heart to flutter, as I felt my being melting into his, although I still had no idea who he was.

After dancing the Christ Dance, we embraced and the Galactic Gathering ended. Azra indicated that it was time for us to leave, and after saying goodbye, Lawrence and I followed Azra out of the chamber, through the lounge with its strange three-dimensional screens, and along the transparent spoke.

"Who is Sanat Kumara?"Lawrence asked. "And what is the Flaming Diamond Rod?"

"Sanat Kumara is your planetary Logos," she explained. "The Flaming Diamond Rod came from Sirius. It is what you would call a magic wand."

I remembered how Maitreya had called Sirius the Guardian of the Secrets at the Love Feast in Shamballa.

On our return journey we saw the Moon's cratered face behind us, and in front of us our beautiful shining home planet. It was dusk when we landed at Feather Falls, and after we had changed back into our hiking clothes, we turned to say goodbye to Azra.

"I want to give each of you a gift," she said. Into our open hands she placed two of the most perfect crystals we had ever seen. They were clear, like cut glass, and so precisely prismed they sent rainbows cascading around the starship.

"These crystals will help you to awaken," she told us.

We were delighted with the crystals and asked about the remainder of the crystals. She told us they would be buried at various points around the Earth to activate the grids.

We said goodbye on the ramp and waved as the carrier pod, with its myriad of twinkling lights, ascended into the star-studded sky and vanished.

"Absolutely awesome!" Lawrence exclaimed as we stumbled back to the path.

"What do you think the grids are?" I asked, remembering what Azra had said about burying the crystals in order to activate the grids.

"She must be referring to the electromagnetic field around the Earth," he replied. "The Earth is also criss-crossed with leylines, which are conductors of energy. Some lines have a positive charge and others a negative one, depending upon how and where they cross."

"I'd love to know what Gaia's Mission is," I mused. "They refer to it, but never say what exactly it is."

We hardly slept that night, but sat up and talked about our experiences by candlelight. However, when we looked through our backpacks, we could not find the crystals or the Proclamation.

"Do you think we dreamt it?" I asked, wishing that Maitreya would stop giving me things which then vanish, like the Seal of Shamballa and the rainbow robe.

"If we had the crystals, it would be proof," I said.

"Maybe we'll find them at some time in the future," he suggested hopefully.

Three days later our trip ended. We had been together for a month and could not imagine life without each other. We acknowledged the many amazing experiences we had shared and said goodbye. My eyes filled with tears as I watched the multi-coloured camper van driving away with my friend and travelling companion inside it.

Three

Bodhi Junction

When I flew to New Zealand, I lost a day crossing the date-line. The next day, which was two days later, we were flying over two lush green islands with clusters of snow-peaked mountains. Both islands were fringed with white beaches, upon which white-tipped turquoise waves leaped and splashed. As the country contained more sheep than people, there were many wild deserted places, which were clearly visible as we prepared to land.

I was met at the airport by Tim, a friend of a friend, whose dark hair and eyes revealed his Maori ancestry. After introducing ourselves, he said he was upset because the Rainbow Warrior had just been blown up. I had no idea who or what he was referring to, but remembered being told by Lawrence that it was another name for a Warrior of Shamballa.

"It was a boat," he explained. "It sailed the oceans protecting them from pollution and exploitation. It also protected the whales and dolphins, as well as preventing the dumping of toxic waste at sea. It was here to stop the testing of nuclear missiles on the surrounding islands."

I asked who blew it up.

"We don't really know, but suspect the French who have already desecrated a couple of islands with their nuclear tests."

"Why don't they test their nuclear missiles in their own country?" I asked indignantly.

"They're hardly likely to risk contaminating their own land," he pointed out. "New Zealand is a scapegoat for both France and America, who are angry with us because we won't allow them to bring their nuclear-armed battleships or submarines into any of our harbours. New Zealand is a nuclear-free country."

Tim helped carry my luggage to his car.

"You can stay in my apartment for a few days," he told me. "I hope you don't mind sharing it with someone else. You may know him. He also lived in the Findhorn Community in Scotland for several years. His name is Jake, and he flies in the day after tomorrow."

I stared at Tim in amazement.

"Jake and I were in a relationship for three years, but we haven't seen each other for almost a year."

Tim's apartment was close to the harbour, where the shattered remains of the Rainbow Warrior floated, as a dismal reminder of the world's investment in violence.

When Jake arrived, he was just as I remembered him. His hair was a little whiter and he had gained weight, but his beloved crinkly old baby face hadn't changed at all. He wore his blue anorak and carried the camera case I had bought for his birthday the previous year. I was the last person he expected to meet on his arrival, and as he unpacked he told me about the woman he had recently fallen in love with.

"Patricia is younger than you and more vivacious," he said, as he searched in his luggage for her photograph.

When he went to bed to recover from jetlag, I walked the streets, alone in my grief, now knowing what I had already suspected: I was still in love with Jake.

Two days later we travelled to the other end of the North Island to help run the Peace Vigil Tim was involved in. Jake had arranged for us to stay in the house of a couple who had befriended him on a previous trip. We took part in the Peace Vigil during the day and relaxed in our hosts' spacious house in the evenings. Sometimes, when they were out, Jake played their piano. He never played the piano in front of anyone except me because he said it embarrassed him too much. His parents had wanted him to be a concert pianist, and tutored him from the age of three. I suspected that he had been a child prodigy, but when he was forced to attend music school, he threw up every morning.

As his piano playing drifted through the house, I saw an angel child dancing in Jake's haunting melodies. I had always known and loved the sensitive side of his nature, which now revealed itself to me in the angel child's dance. Remembering the angel children I had seen in Shamballa, I wondered if they were seeking expression through us. This would explain their interest in the Dream Weavers' Dreams, and if, as Maitreya explained, children are deeply connected to their souls, maybe it is the childlike part of us that will enable the Dream Weavers to awaken and express their angelic presence in our lives.

Jake's inner child was not only the key to his healing, it was in fact a symbol for his soul. It carried the same energy as the angel children in Shamballa and had travelled with him since the beginning of time, but whenever it attempted to express itself, he developed a false persona, which always failed him, just as it was failing him in this life. For, despite outer success, he was deeply disturbed and unhappy. I suspected that this unhappiness bordered on a grief so shattering he feared it would annihilate him if he faced it.

I longed to help him birth this dancing angel child, who I knew would free up his creativity and his enormous potential. I also knew how threatened he felt by the part of himself that loved to dance and express itself in music and poetry. It was delicate, like moonbeams; gossamer-winged and fey. Of course, these qualities are not accepted in a world where men are expected to lead, fight and suppress the intensity of their feeling lives. Men aren't supposed to feel anything, except maybe anger, but I knew that Jake's feelings ran deep and often caused him to behave like a wild, wounded lion.

Jake had grown up in New York. When he was angry, he became the street fighter, a role he acted out in his teens to hide his acute sensitivity, which would have been ridiculed by the gangs with whom he roamed the streets and subways. His inner child was too vulnerable and fey to be exposed to a culture in which only thugs and street fighters were acceptable. When he acted the role of the street fighter, angry and violent in his rage, I heard the anguished cries of his inner child. When the street fighter threw me out of Jake's life, his inner child begged me to stay. My conflict had been my terror of the street fighter's anger and my love for Jake.

"We've been invited to have dinner tonight with a couple I met at the Peace Vigil," he said, closing the lid of the piano.

"Do we have to go?" I groaned.

It was Friday and we were both exhausted from our busy week.

"I don't think we can excuse ourselves," he replied, shaking his head. "Let's make an effort. They only live around the corner."

It was a lively evening, with much laughter, and when we were preparing to leave, I was asked what my plans were.

"I'm looking for a Psychosynthesis training," I told them.

"We did a Psychosynthesis workshop at a centre in the Los Angeles area," they replied, smiling brightly. "They offer a three-year training course, and their teachers are excellent."

My heart sank: not the dreaded L.A. Lawrence had described to me in such lurid detail. When they gave me the address, I didn't know whether to be glad or sad, but I mailed a letter. It was then that Jake started shouting at me again, calling me a fool, and accusing me of never having grown up.

"You're such a child!" he yelled, as if it was an insult. "You never really loved me. When you love someone, you think about them."

"I've thought about nothing else for nearly four years," I cried.

"Being obsessed with someone isn't the same as thinking about them," he retorted.

He walked away from me in disgust, and I decided I could not take any more of his angry outbursts. Before we became lovers, we had promised to be midwives for each other's spirits; a promise not to be taken lightly. Despite having been in a deep meaningful relationship for three years, during which time we had shared our deepest fears and highest aspirations, he was not seeing me. He was holding up a portrait of someone else and was pointing to it as if it was me. He actually had two portraits: one of them he adored, the other one he hated. Desperately he had wanted me to be the adored portrait for him, and when I failed, he produced the portrait he despised. Being unable to convince him that neither portrait represented me, I flew to Australia to visit Judith. We had known each other at Findhorn, but now she lived with Johnny in the Blue Mountains. When we met, she was heavily pregnant. She waddled up to me, gave me a sideways hug, and laughed her merry tinkling laugh.

"What a humbug it is," she said, pointing to her huge stomach.

Johnny put my luggage in the back of his truck and drove up into the Blue Mountains, which really were blue. Johnny was as tall and slim as Judith was short and round. He had dark hair and a kind, steady voice. Judith, with her long brown hair and sparkling blue eyes, was serene and at peace with herself. She talked about trust and how even the lilies of the fields are taken care of. It was obvious how much she and Johnny loved each other when I heard them singing duets in the bathroom, which was a nightly ritual, as was their going to bed hand in hand.

Judith gave me the baby's room to sleep in. Its cupboards and drawers were full of baby clothes, which caused me to long for a baby of my own. It was in this room that I cried myself to sleep night after night longing for the kind of relationship they took for granted. During the day when Johnny worked on the farm, Judith took care of the ducks and chickens. I helped her to plant vegetables in the garden and began working on a patchwork quilt for the baby. When it rained, we sat around an open fire discussing life. Judith believed in a divine plan. All we had to do was trust and allow ourselves to be guided. I fantasized about the relationship I longed for, but Judith pointed out that a relationship has to be worked at, and in their marriage she and Johnny had compromised for each other.

"I never wanted a baby, but Johnny has always longed for children," she confessed. "Now I'm looking forward to motherhood although I know it will present me with many lessons and opportunities for growth."

I, on the other hand, had always longed for a baby and had no interest in knowing what lessons and opportunities for growth the denial of this longing was presenting me with.

"What do you really want?" she asked me.

I told her about the relationship I longed for. However, I knew I would not be in a relationship until I had completed my Journey, which I now described to her.

"Maitreya said I would understand the Journey through imagery. So I have decided to study Psychosynthesis," I explained. "I've located a Psychosynthesis centre, but I don't want to live in Los Angeles."

"Your meeting with Maitreya sounds marvellous," she told me. "I'm quite envious."

"I'm envious of your relationship with Johnny," I admitted.

"All I ever really wanted was to become enlightened," she confided, and then asked me to describe the ideal situation.

"I'd like to take a therapeutic training, which both heals and awakens, and ideally I want to live in a beautiful place with trees and flowers," I fantasized. "I'd love to live in a big old rambling house, full of light and music, preferably with a large garden to sit in. I'd like to both live and study in this house because I hate commuting. I don't suppose I'd find such a situation in Los Angeles."

"Perhaps you could study Psychosynthesis here in Australia," suggested Judith, who loved the idea of having me as a neighbour.

It sounded good, but it didn't feel right. For days we discussed my future, and then we discovered a Psychosynthesis Centre in Sydney at Bodhi Junction, which I decided to visit to see if I could study there instead of in the dreaded L.A.

I left at the end of the week to spend time alone in a friend's apartment which overlooked the Opera House. When I walked down the street to take a ferry across the Harbour, I was confronted with a large brick wall upon which someone had painted in huge black letters:

'THE WIDOWED ISIS'

This graffiti sent cold shivers down my spine for no apparent reason, and as every day that week it greeted me with its ominous declaration, I soon began to dread seeing it.

The Psychosynthesis Centre at Bodhi Junction was run by Jim Forrestal, an attractive young man with brown hair and eyes. He led me into a small room with two chairs and a couch, and listened as I tried to explain my dilemma to him.

"I'm looking for a Psychosynthesis training, and I've found a centre in Pasadena, but I don't want to live there."

"You'd be wasting your time going there," he informed me. "That Centre was shut down last February. I do a three-year training but it's only part-time, and I doubt if you'd be allowed to stay in this country without a visa."

I was rapidly losing faith in what Maitreya had told me, which proved he was merely a figment of my imagination, as was the Journey. I had travelled to the other side of the world only to discover that I was delusional.

Jim offered to give me a session, which I accepted. He invited me to lie down on the couch and breathe deeply.

"If you are willing, I would like to take you back in imagery to the point before your conception," he suggested. "Then you can ask about your purpose in this life."

I agreed, and after some deep breathing found myself in a Nazi concentration camp.

"What are you doing there?" he asked.

"I'm collecting the children," I found myself saying. "I'm waiting for them inside this gas chamber."

To my amazement, I saw myself taking them to the Children's Village in Shamballa.

"The children are traumatized. I'm helping to heal and prepare them."

"What are you preparing them for?"

"We're preparing them to disarm the world with love," I said, bursting into tears. "There's no love in the world. No love. No love. The world is dying for love."

I knew what I had to do: I would enter the Temple of Dreams as a Dream Weaver, but my purpose would be to awaken and bring love back into the world. Without love, life on Gaia's embodiment had become a nightmare. I must enter the nightmare in order to end it, as one enters the bedroom of someone who is screaming in their sleep to wake them up. This was my purpose.

"What's happening now?" Jim asked me.

I found myself back in the angel child's dream, but this time I knew what it symbolized.

"I'm being conceived!" I cried out in astonishment. "I'm inside fire, spiralling down through a vortex towards the egg and the sperm. Now I'm entering, like a match being struck, and I'm a flaming orb rotating through a tunnel."

I remembered the tunnel Maitreya and I had soared through when we travelled to Shamballa and how it reminded me of the tunnel described by people who have near death experiences. Then I realized that we enter and exit through the same tunnel. I described the microscopic entities performing their cosmic dance of creation, but now I recognized them as chromosomes.

"It's like being inside a miniature computer smaller than an atom, but it contains all of my past and future in one infinite now!" I exclaimed. "It knows all about me and all of the potential I shall one day express, and it's all happening now!"

It was a staggering experience.

"Now I'm a baby floating with my knees drawn up, and the distant throbbing is growing louder as if two drums are beating, each with its own rhythm."

As Jim guided me back into the room, I started to cry again as I remembered there was no love in the world. The atrocities of the Nazi concentration camps were still clearly visible to me.

"Your purpose is obvious," he told me, as I sat in the chair opposite him. "It would be good for you to train as a Psychosynthesis guide and teacher, for Psychosynthesis is the psychology of love. Its major emphasis is on contacting the source of love we all have access to. It begins by helping us to love ourselves, even the parts we are ashamed of. Until we're able to do this, we project our rejected parts onto other people. This is what the Nazis did. They projected what they hated in themselves, and were convinced that if they eliminated these rejected parts, they would be liberated. Of course, they were totally unconscious of what they were really doing. Psychosynthesis also helps us to become conscious."

Now I understood why Jake was so angry with my inner child.

It reminded him too much of his own vulnerable inner child, whom he had rejected. Many times during our relationship, he had told me to put my hurt child out with the garbage. Obviously that was where he had dumped his, but I was outraged by his suggestion, especially as he had been trained as a clinical psychologist.

"Yes, I'll study Psychosynthesis," I agreed. "The question is where?"

Returning on the ferry, I again wondered why I took the children from the gas chambers to the children's village in Shamballa. Then I remembered two experiences I'd had when I was four years old. Both experiences occurred in my bedroom, and the first involved the children's village in Shamballa, which interpenetrated my room. The children knew me, just as I knew each child by name. The second experience had occurred in the middle of the night, when I woke up to find three powerful beings standing around my bed. They carried an ominous dark presence, but what really frightened me was the fact that they knew me.

I had a totally miserable week, which climaxed in a documentary on television about the missing children on the milk cartons. The documentary presented testifiable evidence to prove that the missing children in America had been kidnapped by Satanists, who were using them in black magic rituals. None of this was being investigated in America because many of the people in power were practising Satanists. I had not believed Lawrence when he told me the missing children had been kidnapped by Satanists.

I was relieved to return to Judith and Johnny's farm in the Blue Mountains, where I continued to work in the garden and sew the baby's quilt. They led a simple life far from the problems of the world, but they both wondered if they were being selfish bringing a baby into a world threatened with nuclear war, pollution and a possible ice age.

"Your baby is choosing to come into the world the way it is," I pointed out.

Judith was planning to have a home birth, with Johnny helping at the delivery. They were reading books about raising children without causing them to lose their vitality or feelings of self-worth, and they did not want their baby to grow up with sexual hang-ups.

"Lawrence says we've been castrated, like bulls, to make us docile. We're castrated when we are made to feel ashamed of our bodies and our sexuality.

"None of us want war or pollution, but we've lost our power. We must have, or we'd do something about it. Just think how much collective power we have. There are far more of us than there are of the people in power, but they control us through shame and financial dependency. Sex is part of creation. Look at the trees and the flowers. They aren't ashamed when they bloom, but their blossoming is a sexual proclamation. Through it they reproduce themselves. We are the only creatures on Earth made to feel ashamed of this process, but sex is so much a part of who we are. How can we deny it?"

I remembered my own conception and how I had entered the egg and the sperm like a match being struck. It was the sex act which caused the angel child to dream about conception.

The more we discussed the state of the world, the more I wanted to continue with my Journey. I decided to return to New Zealand. With sadness and many tears, we said goodbye. A month later Judith and Johnny birthed a baby boy and called him Loren.

When I arrived in New Zealand, I decided to put to the test what Judith had taught me about trusting and allowing the universe to guide me. She had always lived her life this way, which probably explained her serenity. I said a little prayer, released my personal will, and asked for guidance. A voice in my head told me to go to Tim's office to pick up my mail. Tim ran a company called Sun Energy, which was part of a network actively involved in healing the Earth and preventing Wormwood. I had given Sun Energy as my forwarding address. At first I resisted. I was hungry and needed to eat, but the voice persisted, and as I walked into Tim's office, I bumped into Jake.

He said he had my mail, and promptly presented me with a

pile of letters. On the top of the pile was a letter postmarked Los Angeles. It was from a woman called Vivian King, who wrote to inform me that the old Psychosynthesis Centre had closed down, but she was now offering classes in her home in Pasadena. She would be happy for me to study with her, and offered me a room in her spacious house.

Although I loved New Zealand and knew I would one day return, it really was time for me to leave and continue with my Journey.

Four

Déjà Vu

I was being driven through a beautiful tree-lined suburb of Los Angeles. Large rambling houses, set back off the road in well-watered gardens, appeared to be guarded by spindly palm-trees standing sentinel against the bright blue sky. We turned into the Street of the Beautiful Fountain, on the corner of which stood Vivian King's house. It was an elegant old house, painted white, and dwarfed by an even older redwood tree in the front garden. I walked up a winding red brick path, and was greeted by a good-looking boy with dark hair and intelligent brown eyes. I introduced myself, and he told me his name was Paul, adding that he was Vivian's son. As he led me through a spacious living room full of plants, music and sunlight, I wondered if I was dreaming. Although I had never visited this house before, it was as familiar to me as an old lover.

"Paul, are you going to wash these dishes for me?"

We followed the voice into a large kitchen with an old-fashioned cooking stove. Vivian King was standing beside the sink. She was very beautiful with soft brown eyes and a radiant smile, and I felt an immediate affinity with her. Paul started washing the dishes with a pained expression on his face, as his mother greeted me with a warm hug and invited me to make myself a hot drink. She pointed to an urn bubbling away in a corner of the kitchen, adding that she was busy preparing for class, and would talk to me later. I helped by putting mugs on the table beside the urn, while Paul continued to mumble to himself at the sink.

Vivian busied herself around the kitchen until the other members of the class arrived. Then she directed us into a large sunroom with plants, thick cream carpet and cushions on the floor. Golden sunlight streamed in through the windows as we arranged ourselves on the cushions. A candle was lit and we were guided in a short meditation before introducing ourselves.

Sharon, a vivacious blonde in her early fifties, spoke first:

"What's really remarkable about me is that I've managed to remain married to the same man for almost thirty years. I love my dogs, drive recklessly and, darn it, I've forgotten my note pad!"

she exclaimed, tipping the contents of her large bag all over the floor.

Patrick, who could not conceal his amusement, was a young minister with long dark hair. He gave tennis lessons in his spare time, and without his glasses looked like Jesus.

Next to him sat David, who was tall and distinguished-looking with brown hair and blue eyes.

"I have two teenage kids and am recovering from a divorce," he told us. "I'm studying to become a clinical psychologist."

Danny, a businessman with short brown curly hair, had been a yoga teacher for many years. His wife, Meara, had the kind of hair I had always longed for. It was abundant and framed her face like a halo. She wore rainbow earrings and a string of coloured beads around her neck.

"I stay home and take care of our eight-year-old daughter, whom we named after Princess Leia in Star Wars. I hope to use Psychosynthesis with reflexology, which I practise at home."

Eleanor had pure white hair and a skin resembling porcelain.

"I give massage and when people tell me their problems, which they often do, I'd like to be able to help them. I hope to acquire some tools from Psychosynthesis. I have grown up children and grandchildren."

Marcus, an out-of-work actor with light-brown hair and dreamy eyes, was separated from his wife with whom he shared the care of their small son.

"I'm working towards giving one-man shows in churches. I like the idea of bringing Christ alive by embodying him. I believe it has more impact than a sermon."

Shakura was a medical doctor. She was small with brown hair and a pale complexion.

"What I really want is my own holistic health practice, where I can practise alternative therapies, including Psychosynthesis," she explained. "I'm separated from my husband and live alone with my cat."

John, half way between six and seven feet tall, was youthful and idealistic. Flicking his floppy fair hair out of his eyes, he described himself as a perpetual student.

"I'll probably have to remain a student for the rest of my life," he joked. "If I ever get a job, I'll be giving all of my salary back to the government to pay off my loans. So, when I get my master's degree, I'm going to study for a Ph.D."

Theo, a writer and film-maker, shared that she was a recovered alcoholic. Now in her early sixties, she lived across the road from her cantankerous old father.

"I sure would welcome some tools for dealing with him," she said, laughing. "I've been married a couple of times, my children are all grown up, and I now live alone, which I love."

After I had introduced myself, Vivian talked about Psychosynthesis:

"Sometimes I'm introduced as a Photosynthesis teacher, which is an accurate description. In photosynthesis the energy of the Sun is used by plants to grow. In Psychosynthesis, the energy of the spiritual Sun is converted into psychological nourishment for humans.

"The word synthesis is from the Greek root meaning 'to unite'. In theory, Psychosynthesis blends psychology, religion and philosophy. In practice, it combines various psychotherapeutic tools and techniques. It is also a spiritual discipline.

"Roberto Assagioli, an Italian psychiatrist born in 1888, drew inspiration from both Freud and Jung, and also from Raja and Karma Yoga. He developed techniques for working with the unconscious *and* the soul, which he referred to as the Transpersonal or Higher Self. He likened the Self, with a capital 'S', to a radiant sun, not unlike our physical Sun. He recognized that humans have an eternal aspect: a limitless source of love, will and creativity, which can be accessed and utilized in daily life. Assagioli developed the Psychosynthetic process, which quite literally means the synthesis of the psyche.

"Assagioli said that an experience of the Self is one of freedom, mastery and joy. When we are aligned with the Self, we can expect to experience these qualities in our daily lives. We will be devoting a great deal of time to the Self, which traditional psychology tends to neglect. In Psychosynthesis we affirm that we are more than our minds, bodies and emotions. We are a centre of pure consciousness, which existed before we were born and continues to exist after we die."

We asked her to tell us more about the psyche.

"The psyche is an energy field, which includes our ordinary daily consciousness, the middle unconscious where information is stored, and the lower and higher unconscious. If we liken the human psyche to a house, the lower unconscious is the basement. It is dark and we don't know what's down there until we explore it, but in order to do that we need a light. We will learn more about the Self before going down into the basement. The higher unconscious is the attic leading up to the sunroof. Through the higher unconscious, we make contact with the Self, which is a limitless source of love and wisdom. The collective unconscious is shared by everyone in the world."

I thought about what Maitreya had said about Gaia's Castle being a symbol for her psyche. If a house symbolizes the human psyche, then it made sense for a Castle to symbolize a planetary being's psyche.

"How can we explore the unconscious when we're not conscious of its existence?" Shakura asked.

"We will be using imagery and guided meditation to explore the unconscious. I will be guiding you in meditations and imagery exercises. Imagery and meditation are central to the guiding process, both being related to the creativity of the unconscious. We will be working with intuition and active imagination. Imagery is as much a psychological function as feeling, thinking and sensation. If you don't believe me, imagine sucking a lemon, and see what happens. Profound transformations can occur through imagery with or without interpretation. In psychological law anything is possible. Through imagery early pre-verbal trauma, even birth trauma, can be accessed and released through catharsis, artwork and/or psychodrama. It may be that early preverbal trauma is blocking our potential. We've forgotten the original trauma, but it is still affecting our lives. Through imagery we access it, and when it has been released, we can become creators instead of reactors in life's drama.

"Psychosynthesis is like helping Dorothy to find the Wizard of Oz. We will meet all kinds of interesting characters on the way, and all of them are parts of the personality needing integration. We call them subpersonalities because they revolve around our personal self, like electrons whirling around the nucleus of an atom. Firstly, we need to recognize these primary identifications. When we dialogue with and role play them, we begin to disidentify. We give them names because when we name something, we make it conscious.

"The most basic polarity, which is universal, is the Critic and the Hurt Child. Most of us have an internalized Critic who judges, ridicules, undermines or represses in some way. The Critic is nearly always accompanied by a Hurt Child who feels bullied, put down and rendered powerless. So, one of the primary tasks of Psychosynthesis is to redeem and re-parent the Hurt Child, as well as finding out what the Critic needs and fears."

We nodded. It was obvious we all had one of these polarities. In my relationship with Jake, he had taken on the role of my Critic, just as I had taken on the role of his Hurt Child. With me acting out his Hurt Child for him, he did not have to face it, in the same way that I avoided facing my Critic for as long as he was willing to act it out for me. No wonder we never reached resolution with each other.

"We will be working with the Hurt Child and the Critic, as well as with other major polarities," she continued. "To bring these parts of ourselves back home, we need to know where home is. We also need to recognize when we are *not* at home. In order for this to happen, we need to reconstruct our personality around the Self. When we practise Presence, we have a direct experience of the Self. As Presence is sustained Being, and the Self is pure Being, when we practise Presence, we have a direct experience of the Self. The Guiding process is based on this practice. Presence alone can heal. As a Guide, my task is not to lecture, advise or solve problems, but to awaken and enable my client to embody the Self. Then the client, who is sometimes referred to as the Traveller, will be able to solve his or her own problems. I can trust my clients' inherent ability to heal themselves. Let's practise being present for each other. Then we will see what it feels like when we're not present."

When we paired off, I noticed that my silent presence enabled my partner to expand and gain valuable insights, but when I was preoccupied with my own thoughts and feelings, I did not listen to what he was saying. In his frustration with me, he could not think clearly.

"Psychosynthesis will change your lives," we were told after the exercise. "It will affect you and everyone you meet. To make this commitment to our own evolutionary growth is to make a commitment to the evolution of the planet. All we need is the courage and willingness to open doors within ourselves.

"What we are identified with we are controlled by," Vivian concluded. "Neurotics identify with their neurosis, scientists with their minds, athletes and movie stars with their bodies. What are you identified with? It takes practice and discipline to DISidentify, for our subpersonalities are always demanding our attention. They pull us off centre. The ultimate goal is effortless radiation."

At lunch time we wandered out into the back garden to eat. It was a large garden with a lawn, flowers and trees. We sat on benches around a picnic table, which stood under an enormous tree. Paul joined us, and as we ate he cracked jokes and teased his mother.

After class Vivian suggested that I clean and type for her instead of paying rent and tuition fees. I was delighted with this offer and accepted.

"I'm writing a book about Psychosynthesis," she said. "I've been paying someone to edit and type it, but now you can help me with it."

She took me through the kitchen and along a narrow corridor to a small room overlooking the back garden. The rose bushes just outside the window filled the room with their fragrance and a strange feeling of déjà vu. Although the room was familiar to me, I did not know why, and found myself wanting to say: "This has always been my room."

By the time we had our second class, I had settled into the house, and for the first time in six months I was able to unpack.

In the second class Vivian talked about the Field of Awareness. She drew a diagram on the big board in a corner of the sunroom to illustrate her point. An egg symbolized the psyche, which included the lower and higher unconscious. The Field of Awareness was tiny in comparison, and clearly demonstrated how much we are not yet aware of.

"In the middle unconscious we store information," she explained. "It's like a filing cabinet. It is not within our field of awareness, but it is readily available when we need it. This is where we store our conscious memories. The higher unconscious holds the pattern for our lives and gives us access to the Self, also called the Transpersonal Self because it transcends the personality. The Self is symbolized by this sun on top of the egg. The lower unconscious contains our primitive drives, unconscious memories and any traumatic past events we may have suppressed. Problem-free experiences in the past do not create problems in the present. However, if a basic need was not met in the past, it will create problems in the present, and a subpersonality may develop around the need. This creates an energetic charge relating to an earlier stage of development. We can use imagery to access it.

"Today I'm going to guide you in an imagery exercise, in which you will explore your psyche. However, if I just told you to explore your psyche, you wouldn't know where to begin. So, I will use the symbology of the house. You will explore an inner house to understand what is going on within your psyche. Find a comfortable position and close your eyes. As you approach the house, notice its general appearance. Is it well-cared for, neglected or dilapidated?"

My house was a double-fronted detached house on three floors. It needed to be renovated and there were no curtains at the windows.

"Be aware that this is an important house to you. There are many rooms inside it. As you enter the house, you notice a central staircase, which you will explore later. Walk around and see if there is a meeting room, a kitchen, a living room. You may see some doors with the names of subpersonalities on them. Do not enter, but notice where these rooms are and their relationship to other parts of the house. Notice if there is a basement, but do not explore it yet."

My house was totally empty. There was not a stick of furniture anywhere, no pictures on the walls, and no doors with the names of subpersonalities on them. At the far end of a spacious living room double doors opened into a sunroom where an old man with a long white beard was working with a boy. They were too busy with their charts and diagrams to notice me. The old man, who looked like a magician, was obviously teaching the boy. I was intrigued by these two characters and wondered what they were doing inside my inner house.

"Return to the central staircase," said Vivian, interrupting my preoccupation with the magician and his apprentice. "This staircase leads to an upper floor, where you will find the room of the Self."

Half way up the staircase on a landing, I noticed a circular stained glass window, which needed cleaning. After some vigorous rubbing, sunlight streamed in through the glass revealing a beautiful stained glass angel. I was delighted and stood back to admire it.

"As you enter the room of the Self, make a note of what is in the room. It contains whatever you need to make you feel comfortable and at ease. If it has windows, look out at the view."

My room of the Self had nothing in it except two small children: a boy and a girl between three and four years old. The room was large and could be divided into two with sliding doors. In one half there was an open fireplace and in the other half french windows opening out onto a balcony with a view of rolling hills and forests. The children radiated joy and playfulness, and were delighted to see me. Taking hold of my hands, they pulled me back onto the landing, where I noticed another staircase leading up to the attic. With one pulling and the other pushing, they took me up the stairs and into an attic space with a skylight. To my amazement, an ancient Egyptian priestess was sitting on the floor deep in meditation. She was bathed in golden sunlight from the skylight, and wore a transparent gown with a painted collar. She had a strange crown on her head and a golden key in her hand. I could not imagine what an ancient Egyptian priestess was doing in my attic, but as it was symbolic of the higher unconscious, I could only conclude that this bizarre character resided there. I hurried down both flights of stairs as we were guided back into the sunroom.

Over lunch, when I described my strange experiences in the inner house, Vivian suggested I see a therapist, recommending a woman she knew who practised Psychosynthesis.

"I feel I need to see a male therapist, so that I can work on my issues with men," I replied.

David, who was having lunch with us, said he was seeing the man Vivian had been in therapy with when her marriage with Paul's father broke up. After she had given me his telephone number, I called him, and we made an appointment when Vivian would be in the area collecting Paul from his school, which was close to the therapist's office.

Now that I was sleeping in the room that was so obviously my room, I was having weird dreams. In one dream I was in a house, which belonged to a man who dismembered bodies.[1] In this dream, which repeated itself several times, I always found myself alone in the cellar. In another dream I saw a great flood approaching. I climbed a mountain, but the water was still rising, so I went up into a high tower. At the top of the tower I met many people, some of whom I recognized.

"Do you want to hear the good news or the bad news?" I asked, laughing. "The bad news is you're dead, but the good news is you are still in existence."

In the dream I found this statement hilariously funny and awoke laughing.

As I busied myself cleaning, decorating and furnishing my room at the end of the corridor, I remembered where I had seen this room before. Of course, it was the room beyond the open door in the Temple of Dreams, but then I realized this was not the first time I entered this room with its fragrance of roses. I had seen it in a dream six years previously when I was in Jungian analysis.

"In my dream I had been cleaning a house," I told Vivian. "It was this house. I emptied my bucket of dirty water into that deep enamel sink you have by the back door, and then I walked through the kitchen and down the corridor to my room; the one I now sleep in. The window was wide open, and I could see out into the garden and smell the fragrance of the roses. The bedclothes had been thrown aside as if someone had just awakened. Golden sunlight was streaming in across the bed, and there was a man standing in the doorway wearing black. He smiled mysteriously and as he embraced me, he said: "You don't remember me, do you?" I felt embarrassed because he was right. Although he was as familiar to me as the room, I had no idea who he was."

I remembered how the mysterious ebony lady in the Temple of Dreams had called him the Omega Man.

"I bet he's someone you're going to meet here," said Vivian. "What did he look like?"

I described his dark hair and beard. "But why was he wearing black? Everything else was so luminous. My analyst and I called this room the Awakening Room. I'm amazed that I could dream about this house six years before I actually saw it."

"When the Psychosynthesis Centre was closing down, I tried to rent a house in the mountains," Vivian explained. "But my signed letter of agreement was lost in the mail and someone else rented it instead. A student in one of my classes told me about this house."

The morning of my appointment with the therapist, I decided to finish cleaning out the cupboards in the kitchen. There was a cupboard high up near the ceiling which I had forgotten about, and I had to use the step-ladder to reach it. I started removing the contents of the cupboard, and then found an object which took my breath away. It was a stained glass angel, exactly like the one I had found in my inner house. When I told Vivian about the stained glass window in my inner house, she gave me the angel to keep in my room.

That afternoon, when she drove to the other side of Los Angeles to collect Paul from school, she dropped me off at the therapist's office. When he opened the door in response to my knocking, I felt as if a ball of fire leapt out of him and hit me in my solar plexus.

"I'm with a client," he told me. "Take a seat. I'll be with you in a couple of minutes."

I staggered over to the chair. "Wow!" I gasped. "What was that?"

Later, he invited me into his office and pointed to a couch opposite an armchair. His office was small with a desk and a tree growing in a tub. There were no external windows, and I wondered how he could bear to work without seeing the sky. It reminded me of a cell.

"How can I help you?" he asked.

I looked across the room at him, where he sat in his armchair with a note pad and pen on his knee. He was an attractive man in his forties with greying hair and a beard.

"There are things in my life I cannot explain or understand," I told him. "Since I was very small I've had visions and mystical experiences."

I told him about the angels, fairies and spirit children I played with as a child. "Of course, nobody believed me and I decided I must be crazy because I appeared to be the only one who could see them. Sometimes I dream about events in the future before they've happened, and I remember things that have never happened to me in this life."

"From previous lives?" he asked.

"I don't know. I've had a recurring nightmare for the last six years in which I'm falling through fire remembering what I have forgotten to remember, but when I wake up I can't remember what it is. I've had this dream ever since I dreamt about Vivian's house."

"You dreamt about Vivian's house six years ago?"

"Yes. I also have some strange characters in my inner house."

I told him about the magician and his apprentice in the sunroom, the two children in the room of the Self, and the ancient Egyptian priestess in my attic. I also told him my dream about the house owned by a man who cut up bodies.

"What was your relationship with your father like?" he asked.

I explained how my father had died in front of me in a fit of anger when I was six. "I loved him, but he was never really available. He excited and rejected me. This has continued to be a problem for me in my intimate relationships."

"This is definitely something we can work on."

"That's why I wanted to work with a male therapist," I agreed. "I do have a lot of issues around men, and spent most of this year pining for Jake, with whom I had a deep and meaningful relationship, but he was always angry."

"Like your father?"

I nodded, realizing how similar my father and Jake were.

"I thought that if I loved him enough, he'd stop being angry."

"Are you talking about Jake or your father?"

"Both," I sighed. "I felt that my father died because I didn't love him enough."

"It's very common for children to blame themselves when a parent dies," he pointed out.

"I'd like you to be my Guide Detective to help me solve the mystery of my life," I concluded at the end of the session. "I want to know if I'm psychic or psychotic."

"I'd love to be your Guide Detective," he responded with warmth. "Write down your dreams and ask for guidance on your life's purpose."

We made an appointment to meet in a week's time.

During the week Vivian had a meeting in her house of a meditation group she met with once a month. It was led by a man who had worked with Assagioli and who said that Assagioli was one of the disciples Djwal Khul wrote to in Alice Bailey's book *Discipleship in the New Age*. At the end of the meeting a woman announced that she was selling copies of the Seal of Shamballa. When I saw it, I nearly fell off my chair. Vivian bought one and hung it on the wall. I was ecstatic about the Seal because it proved that I had not imagined my meeting with Maitreya.

We had been studying Psychosynthesis for a month when Vivian led us in the Rose Imagery:

This imagery will give you rich information because every image is symbolic of your life. You will become more conscious of your own personal dynamics. Find a comfortable position and relax. For the next ten minutes you will be focusing your attention on a rose, which represents you. Just allow the images to emerge spontaneously. If you were a rose, what kind of rose would you be?"

My rose was a Peace rose. It was just beginning to open and was the only rose on the bush, although there were other roses of different varieties on bushes nearby. My rose bush was healthy, but the earth was waterlogged. We were asked to examine the bush our rose was growing on and to follow its root system into the ground to see if anything needed to be done. Vivian asked us to make a note of the condition of our rose bushes, the environment and the weather.

"In order for this rose bush to produce the best roses and to be the most healthy and productive bush, what would need to be done to it?" she asked. "Now we are going to discuss our images before we move on to the next stage."

After we had opened our eyes, Vivian explained what the rose imagery symbolized.

"If your rose was just beginning to open, it may be that you've only recently started to express yourself. If it is a tight bud, you may be afraid of revealing yourself. For an older person it may indicate introversion or over-protection. If the rest of the imagery is healthy, a rose bud may indicate a readiness to unfold a new part of yourself. If completely open, you may be too open or in the latter part of your life. The root system represents early family influence. One woman's roots had been eaten away because she had been sexually abused as a child. Another woman, with a happy childhood and a healthy root system, had dry depleted soil. Her marriage was not nourishing her. Other roses on the bush can either indicate the number of people in your family or other aspects of the personality. For example, a highly creative person may have a bush full of roses, indicating an abundance of creative energy. A lonely person, or someone who has spent a lot of time on their own, may have only one rose on the bush. The person being guided will generally know what the other roses on the bush symbolize.

"The weather indicates the emotional or mental climate of the person being guided. The Sun represents the Self. A depressed person may have dark clouds obscuring the Sun. Patches of dark cloud can indicate a troubled relationship or unresolved issues. If there is fog or smog, you can go up in a helicopter to view the scene from a higher perspective."

This made sense to me. I did see myself as a peaceful person, and I had always been alone. The waterlogged ground symbolized a highly traumatic childhood in which my parents, both emotionally unstable, were always fighting and shouting at each other.

During the second stage of the Rose Imagery, we could give our rose bushes exactly what they needed to be healthy. As I did not know what to do about the waterlogged ground, I called in the experts and asked if I should drain the soil. I was told to transplant my rose bush, which I did. They dug around in the soil until they discovered a natural spring running underneath where my rose bush had been growing. They told me it was running off a nearby mountain and contained crystal clear mineral water. They built a well for me on the spot where my rose bush had stood, so that I could drink the water, which was delicious, and I soon realized I could bottle the water for others to drink.

When I shared this with the group afterwards, Vivian said it was obviously my task to transform the emotional trauma of my childhood, which would then enable me to be an empathetic guide for others.

She then guided us in a process of integration:

"Return to your rose bush and identify with the ideal image. Close your eyes and be willing to experience what you can really be. Imagine it is the crisp, clear dawning of a new day. Dew is glistening on your rose as you approach the bush, which has been lovingly and skilfully cared for. Allow yourself to feel the impact of its presence. Notice your rose, which is fragrant and radiant. Notice its colour and the dewdrops on its petals glistening in the early morning Sun. Now identify with the rose. You are fragrant and radiant, with strong presence; effortless beauty."

I was afraid that I had neglected my newly transplanted rose bush in all of the excitement over the mineral water and the well. However, when I found it in another part of the garden, it was looking healthy and my one rose was unfolding.

"The energy of the Sun brings you life. It is absorbed into your cells. The light literally permeates your being. Be aware of your roots taking in nutrients and moisture from the earth. Take time to fully experience this interchange of energy between the Sun and the Earth through your entire system. You are an integral rose, one with the Sun, the Earth, and all other rose bushes. You are creating a bouquet of colour and a symphony of joy for the Earth."

Afterwards Vivian explained that if we did this exercise every day, it would bring integration, for it heals and integrates the personality.

A couple of days later I travelled across Los Angeles to see my therapist. I was early for my session, so I walked across the road to buy myself a cold drink in the supermarket. As I waited for the traffic lights to change from red to green, I saw a solitary male figure wearing dark glasses on the other side of the road. He was also waiting for the lights to change in order to cross over to my side of the road. Somewhere deep within my being a string was plucked. Yes, I was attracted to this mysterious man in black, but there was more: long forgotten memories ran through my mind like a distant train rumbling through a tunnel. He stood poised on the edge of the curb and on the tip of my tongue. Then the lights changed and we crossed over. When we passed each other in the middle of the road, I recognized who he was. Of course, he was my therapist.

When we were sitting opposite each other in his office, I showed him the drawings I had done during the week. One of them illustrated my father's death, with his soul soaring out of the top of his head.

"This is remarkable!" he exclaimed.

"I didn't set out to draw his soul," I pointed out. "It drew itself. This has started to happen to me recently. When I draw, it's as if I have no control over what emerges. I feel like a channel."

I handed him a drawing in which I was giving birth to a large radiant Sun. "This is interesting because the two children I found in the room of the Self are looking on with ecstatic expressions on their faces, but why am I giving birth to the Sun, and who are these children?"

"Assagioli uses the Sun as a symbol for the Self," he responded. "How do you feel about the children?"

"They fill me with joy. They're so radiant and playful."

"Then they must be aspects of the Self," he concluded. "You found them in the room of the Self, so they must be related; radiance and joy being aspects of the Self."

"Then there's this drawing," I said, handing him another sheet of paper. "It looks like a tree, but if you look closely at it, you will see it's the love of two people. Look, here's the man and this is the woman. She's pregnant."

"Oh yes! There's the baby. These drawings are fascinating."

He handed them back to me, and I told him about a dream I'd had in which I had seen a boat sailing out to sea. It had a casket tied to it with a rope, and as the boat sailed away from the shore, the casket sank. I knew if there was anyone inside the casket, he or she would die, but later in the dream, when the boat returned with the casket, I was able to lift the lid and there were those two children; the ones in the picture of me giving birth to the Sun. I knew then that they had survived their voyage sealed up inside the casket.

"What a wonderful dream," he said, smiling. "This is a very healthy dream clearly demonstrating that the childlike part of you was not damaged, even though your childhood was so traumatic."

"I feel damaged beyond repair," I commented.

"I do feel that our relationship is going to be very important," he told me at the end of the session. "Although I'm attracted to you, I do want to work with you. When I saw you crossing the road before our session, I was attracted to you before I recognized who you were."

When I confessed that I was also attracted to him before I realized who he was, we both laughed.

"I think it's really important for us not to seduce each other," I found myself saying.

"I absolutely agree," he nodded. "As a therapist, I have a clean track record. I have never become emotionally or sexually involved with any of my clients."

When we said goodbye and hugged, I noticed how tense he was.

A few days later I had an extraordinary experience with an angel, which I decided to work on in our Guiding Class. As it was a beautiful day, we sat outside in the garden on one of Vivian's quilts. It was the one with camellia stains all over it. I loved this quilt because she had shared that a lover sprinkled it with camellias before making love to her on it.

I explained how the previous evening an angel had entered me.

"I felt totally loved and accepted by the angel, who had soft feathery wings. It was both mystical and erotic, and it was as if it entered me from above and below. It's still inside me. I can feel it. Look, I've drawn a picture of the angel entering me."

"It is giving you an experience of how it feels to be totally loved," Vivian told me. "Can you become the angel and allow it to speak through you?"

"I have been waiting for you to open up to me," said the angel through me. All I had to do was open my mouth and allow the words to come out. "I love you very much. You are precious. When I am inside you, there is ecstasy for both of us, but this is an illusion, for we are already one.

"You ask about the two children in your inner house. As manifested aspects of the Self, they are not parts of your personality. They are beyond the ego and bring into matter the qualities of the Self. You cannot grow them into adults because they are ageless and appear symbolically as children. They are your gift to the world because they are your essence and will help you to bring forth great wisdom in simple language."

This reminded me of Jake's inner child, who had appeared to me as an angel child, and was his gift to the world. If these two symbolized angel children, why did I have two of them?

"They appear to you as male and female to show you that in this life you are integrating feminine and masculine qualities. The Self is androgynous and gives you the opportunity of becoming androgynous through these inner children.

"In your dream they were not damaged. They cannot be damaged," the angel continued. "As they are not parts of your personality, they were never caught up in the drama of your life. In simple language they are Divinity playing with its own creation. They carry the Kingdom of Heaven within them."

"Who are you?" I asked.

"I am an aspect of Divinity seeking individuation. This is the highest purpose an angelic being can aspire to, but without a human instrument we cannot achieve this pearl of creation."

"Am I your human instrument?"

"Yes. When you woke up in Shamballa, you made contact with me and became Self-conscious. Now I have the opportunity of incarnating through you.

"When an angel and a human become conscious of each other, the barriers between dimensions are burned away. The radiance of the Self, which is their point of contact, enables this burning to occur. Your purpose in this life is to become totally conscious; to burn away the barriers and to build a bridge for others to follow. You have now become conscious enough for me to enter you. As consciousness grows, the inner fire is clearly visible as radiance, but this fire destroys the ego. You have chosen this burning to reach higher levels of being. It is painful, but you have chosen it."

We were all fascinated by the angel, and I decided I would have more of these dialogues when I was alone.

Later that day I found a book in Vivian's office that described the Angel of the Presence. I read it with fascination:

> *You, a Soul in incarnation, are consciously aware . . . of the solar Angel, who is the Angel of the Presence. Your problem is to deepen this realization, and to* **know** *yourself to be the Angel . . .*
>
> *The mystic is ever aware of duality; . . . of the little self and the real Self; of human life expression and of spiritual life expression. Many other qualities stand for the same expression of reality. But, behind them all looms – immanent, stupendous, and glorious – that of which these dualties are but the aspects: the Presence, immanent yet transcendent, of Deity. In the nature of this* **One**, *all dualities are absorbed, and all distinctions and differences lose their meaning.*
>
> *When you are told to develop the consciousness of the Presence, it indicates, first of all, that you are at this time somewhat aware of the Angel and can now begin to respond, dimly and faintly, to that great Whole which lies ... behind the physical, tangible world of every day life.*
>
> *A symbol of this can be seen in the knowledge that the entire planet lies outside of the room ... and is only separated from you by the window and the extent of your conscious awareness ... look through the window of the mind to that Light which reveals the Angel which, in its turn, veils and hides the vast unknown, yet alive and vibrant, Deity.*

> *... Every human being is, in reality, like a miniature whirlpool in that great ocean of Being in which he lives and moves – ceaselessly in motion until such time as the soul 'breathes upon the waters' ... and the Angel of the Presence descends into the whirlpool. Then all becomes still. The waters ... stirred violently by the descent of the Angel, respond to the Angel's healing power and are changed 'into a quiet pool into which the little ones can enter and find the healing they need'.*[2]

I read this book many times and wondered if my angel was the Angel of the Presence. It was all very mysterious: finding an angel in the cupboard, identical to the one in my inner house, and now being contacted by an angel. That night I decided to have another dialogue with my angel, and sat down with paper and pencil. I asked about the magician and his apprentice.

"The magician is training an apprentice, the way Vivian is training you," my angel informed me. "This is your masculine counterpart who is involved in the alchemical changes taking place within your psyche. Rejoice, for you are awakening. You have heard the Call and can now take the Journey to the Bridal Chamber."

"Where is the Bridal Chamber?" I asked.

"It is within the planetary psyche, and will be the greatest Journey you have ever taken."

"When will this Journey begin?" I asked, assuming the Bridal Chamber was inside the Castle Maitreya had referred to.

"Not until you have integrated the various parts of your psyche. There must be no opposition or resistance to this Journey. Call your subpersonalities to a meeting and see what gifts they have for you."

I could not imagine any of my subpersonalities having gifts for me. I had been burdened and battered by them most of my life, and felt resistance to my angel's suggestion. Maybe I really was crazy. Just then the angel spoke with such tenderness and compassion, I wept.

"Dear little one, you are not crazy. In this life you came to redeem a part of yourself. You could call it receptive feminine energy, which is now opening up to other dimensions. This part of you is awake and active, and is called Sheta Nut."

"Is Sheta Nut the ancient Egyptian priestess I saw in my attic?"

"You found her in the higher unconscious because this is where she has her being, but now she is ready to complete her initiation through you."

"What initiation?" I asked. "And why through me?"

"She is a part of you."

"Is she from a past life?"

"In the unconscious there is no past or future. There is only the present. You live in multiple realities; in many dimensions, but it is safer to remain unconscious until you are ready to handle these other states of being. A premature awakening could cause psychosis. As you become aware of other states of being, you may question your sanity," my angel explained, and then added: "The Journey will unfold in the form of an allegory, for this is the only way the personality can comprehend the nature of the psyche. Later you will share this Journey through your writing."

The following week when we met for our Guiding Class, Sharon suggested that I work with Caroline, a subpersonality she adored. I had brought Caroline to our subpersonality party, where she flirted with all the men. I had enormous resistance to working with Caroline, whom I rarely allowed out. She was a flirtatious scatterbrain, who loved to paint her toenails and wear bright colours. She had a lot in common with Sharon.

"Ask Caroline who she symbolizes in you," Vivian suggested.

In order to dialogue with Caroline, I had literally to step into her shoes. Vivian ran upstairs and returned with her red high-heeled shoes, which Caroline loved to wear.

"Now you can really identify with her," Vivian laughed.

"I wish you would let me out of the cellar," said Caroline through me, wobbling in Vivian's shoes, which were too big for her.

"Why were you locked up in the cellar?"

"Because of what happened when I was nine."

"You mean when I was sexually abused?" I asked, slipping back into my own shoes. When Vivian had us dialoguing with subpersonalities, she encouraged us to sit or stand in different positions to identify and then disidentify.

"I was blamed for what happened." Caroline explained. "It was because I was daddy's little play girl. I wanted to cuddle up to a man in bed, the way I had with daddy. It was lovely with him, but with the man who sexually abused me, it was confusing."

"He shouldn't have done that to you," said Vivian. "It was not your fault. You were just a little girl needing love and affection."

"I know that, but she feels threatened by me."

Caroline was referring to me. I knew this was related to my fear of intimacy. When I identified with Caroline, men turned on to me, and this was too threatening. She would want to respond, but I rarely allowed her to, unless I felt safe. Encouraged by my father, I had been a sensual child, but after being sexually abused, I decided it was not safe.

"But now you're a woman," Sharon pointed out. "Gee, sex is great!"

I smiled knowingly at Sharon, remembering what she had shared with me about her ability to experience multiple orgasms.

"Tell Caroline you are not going to lock her up in the cellar any more," Vivian suggested. "You can now choose to let her out."

I knew it was time to integrate her into my life, but I was afraid of her energy. There was a part of me still blaming her for what had happened when I was nine.

"I'm not going to lock you up in the cellar any more," I said to the red high-heeled shoes, not convinced that I really meant it. "I want to integrate you into my life. You have zest and vitality."

"There is a part of you still resisting," Vivian pointed out at the end of the session. "I think another subpersonality is forming a polarity."

"I know what I'll do!" I exclaimed. "I'll hold a Coming Out Party for Caroline. I'll invite all the other subpersonalities and then I'll find out which one is resisting. My angel told me to hold a meeting. I'll have the party tonight."

"I wish I could come to it," said Sharon gaily. "I just love Caroline. She's great. We'll paint the town red one of these days."

Vivian had told us there were various techniques for meeting our subpersonalities. She said we could imagine them walking out of a house, travelling with them on a bus or train, or holding a meeting or a party. She said we would be surprised by who showed up.

My tools for contacting the unconscious were my writing and drawing. That evening I sat down with paper and coloured pencils ready to draw each subpersonality as it emerged. To my surprise a drawing of Caroline appeared at the top of a flight of stairs. I was standing behind her with a radiant sun on the end of a string, and on either side of her were my two inner children, who identified themselves as Joachim and Anna. Caroline looked very sexy in a red, off-the-shoulder dress. She stood between two columns supporting a plinth upon which sat a griffin and a unicorn, each facing inwards towards a triangle with an eye at its centre. We were all standing on a rainbow carpet.

"I'm not going to lock Caroline in the cellar any more," I announced. "This is Caroline's Coming Out Party and my preparation for our Journey to the Bridal Chamber. If you have any gifts or qualities you would like to contribute, please step forward. If you need a new name or a special role to play, please let me know."

I wondered who would step out first. To my surprise, it was Prune Face.

"I wish you would stop calling me Prune Face," she complained.

Prune Face came into existence after Caroline was locked up in the cellar. After being sexually abused, I became a plain, depressed little girl. From early photographs, it was obvious that the light had gone out of my life, but now Prune Face looked different. She was growing up, even though she had promised not to. She was still shy and sensitive, but now she longed for a new name. I asked her what she would prefer to be called. All subpersonalities have their own preferred names.

She told me she wanted to be called Lisa.

"I'm jealous of Caroline because she is receiving all the attention. You never gave me a Coming Out Party. You didn't even notice that I was growing up."

I apologized and asked her what she needed.

"I need to be married with children to feel safe. All I ever wanted was a quiet life in the country, growing flowers and vegetables in my garden, cooking for my family, nurturing my children, and spending quiet evenings around the fire with my husband."

I suspected Lisa was the other part of the polarity. She had always felt threatened when men turned on to Caroline. I told her she would have to be patient, as I first needed to love and heal myself.

"Lisa, you are precious to me. I acknowledge you for carrying my pain. I know how difficult it is for you to grow into a woman and how afraid you are of men. You still see yourself as an ugly duckling, but in reality you have the grace of a swan."

Lisa's face lit up. Then I had an idea. I could let Lisa marry on the inner. In psychological law anything is possible. As I had this thought, my animus stepped forward. Robert was the man of my dreams: mystical and artistic, yet grounded and practical. I had discovered him when I first entered therapy.

"I'd love to marry Lisa," he said. "I have a ring for her."

Lisa blushed as he placed a diamond ring on her engagement finger, and kissed her.

"I'll build you a house in the country beside a stream, and together we will create a garden where we can grow flowers and vegetables."

"It will really help me if you marry Robert because then I'll stop searching for him in outer men," I told Lisa.

"I have a gift for you," she said, presenting me with a dove.

"Lisa, you carry the spirit of the dove. You help me to appreciate nature, to delight in simple pleasures, and to express feminine qualities."

As Lisa and Robert walked away hand in hand, Sibyla, my saboteur, stepped forward. In a previous imagery, she had appeared with S.O.S. printed on her sweater, and a sword in her hand. She rarely smiled and was very defensive. Her job had been to protect Prune Face from being hurt, but now that Lisa had Robert to protect her, Sibyla felt redundant.

"I don't want to be a saboteur any more," she told me. "I'd prefer to be a knight on this Journey. I will give you my strength and my courage. My sword will become the sword of truth."

I thanked Sibyla, feeling relieved that she was not going to sabotage my life any more, the way she usually did. Her transformation was instant. She changed into a knight in shining armour.

Freedom Fighter now stepped forward. He usually had a grim expression on his face, but now he was carrying a sword and shield instead of his usual banner with 'ban the whatever' on it."

"I don't want to fight any more," he told me. "I'm always against instead of for something. I too would prefer to be a knight on this Journey, and I will bring my determination and integrity. Please call me Parsifal."

As I thanked Sibyla and Parsifal for their willingness to be transformed, they glowed. Then they stepped aside and stood next to Sleepy Head, who was snoring under a tree.

"Don't waste your life sleeping," urged Parsifal.

Sleepy Head staggered towards me, still in her nightdress, and yawned. "I'm too tired to accompany you on this Journey," she said, stifling another yawn, "I'll have some good dreams instead."

I knew I could not expect more of her, and I had to admit: she did have good dreams. I had always experienced difficulty waking up in the mornings, which was why I drank so much coffee. If I ever had to get up at dawn, I would be grumpy for the rest of the day. For some bizarre reason the sight of an early morning sunrise traumatized me. Sleepy Head stumbled back to her tree and promptly fell asleep.

Up skipped a character dressed like the Pied Piper, playing a merry tune on his flute. He wore colourful clothes, and had a mop of unruly blond hair. I had met him in a previous imagery when he emerged from under the robe of my Witch.

"I'd like to dedicate this Journey to all the children of the World," said the Pied Piper. "I hope you will decide to write about it in a book for the children to read. I love to dance with my special friend, the Witch."

I did not fully understand the relationship of these two characters. Were they a team or a polarity, or did they help to balance each other? He was as light as she was dark. The Witch had joined us and was wearing her usual black robe, which she had hitched up to accommodate her broomstick. She was wearing black boots on the ends of her spindly white legs, and her long black hair hung in thin strands from beneath her pointed witch's hat.

"I can cast smells," she croaked. "I mean spells. What the hell! I can cast smells if I want to, like the smell of freshly ground coffee and rose petals."

The Pied Piper accompanied her in a merry dance, which she did astride her broomstick.

The Magician waited until they had finished. He was wearing a pointed hat and a long blue and green robe with two snakes on the back forming a figure eight, and he had a fatherly arm around his young apprentice.

"I'm an alchemist," he explained. "I can change almost anything into gold. My name is Merlin and this is Arthur, my apprentice. I have a gift for Caroline. It's a Frog Prince."

In the palm of his hand sat a small green frog. Caroline was thrilled with it, but I was doubtful. I didn't want any more of those Prince fantasies.

"This is rubbish!" shouted my Pragmatist, who was dressed in a dark suit and sensible shoes. "These aren't subpersonalities at all. They're figments of your imagination."

"We're archetypes," Merlin explained. "We live in the higher unconscious."

The Pragmatist pulled a face: "What on earth are archetypes?"

"We're upgraded qualities of the personality. Subpersonalities are downgraded qualities."

The Pragmatist was not convinced and told me to stay grounded.

"I'm afraid this Frog Prince is a bit ugly, but you have the power to make him beautiful," Merlin continued.

"I don't care what he looks like," Caroline giggled. "Will he make me laugh?"

"You never know what might happen when you kiss a frog," croaked the frog. "If frogs were meant to fly, God would have given them wings."

Caroline laughed loudly.

"Caroline has the power to make the frog beautiful," Merlin pointed out. "She could transform him back into a Prince."

"So could I," said the Witch.

"You would put a spell on him, which is how he became a frog in the first place," Merlin told her. "Caroline would transform him by helping him to bring out his princely qualities. There's a difference between casting spells and helping someone to express their potential."

"I like him just the way he is," laughed Caroline.

"That will transform him faster than anything," said Merlin. "Love and acceptance break spells."

At this point Aluna, the star-spangled lady, stepped forward. I had only met her recently, and suspected she was related to my creativity. She was exotic with golden curls piled high on her head, where a star sparkled. She wore crescent-moon jewelry, a gown decorated with stars and rainbows, and she carried a wand.

"I have a magic wand for you to take on the Journey," she told me. "It grants only good and beautiful wishes. I will give you my creativity and my imagination. I can make elephants fly and catch moonbeams for your delight."

"This is a stupid party," Mona complained. "Who are these silly people? This is a complete waste of time, and I want to go to bed."

Mona was the part of me that is always moaning. She wore grey and sounded like my mother. The Pragmatist agreed with her, adding that these people weren't real.

"How dare you insinuate that we're not real," the Witch snorted. "If we're not real, how come we've been written about through the ages?"

"Only in fairy tales," the Pragmatist pointed out dryly. "Everyone knows fairy tales aren't real."

"Fairy tales are the unspeakable clothed in words," said Sheta Nut, suddenly emerging from the attic. "Fairy tales and myths never grow old or go out of fashion. They are passed down from generation to generation."

Sheta Nut was wearing a long pleated gown with her breasts hanging out, and a painted collar and belt. On her head she wore a crown looking like the astrological sign for Taurus the bull.

"You should cover up your breasts," said the Critic.

"In ancient Egypt women were not ashamed of their breasts, and men did not ogle them, the way they do in this culture," Sheta Nut pointed out. "The naked body was revered and depicted on the walls of our temples."

"What's that stupid thing on your head?" the Pragmatist asked.

"It's my Isis crown," Sheta Nut replied indignantly. "These are the horns of intelligence surrounding the solar disc."

"They don't look very intelligent to me," mocked the Critic.

"They look ridiculous," Mona agreed.

"What purpose do they serve?" the Pragmatist demanded to know.

"Isis is my personal deity," said Sheta Nut. "I bring my ability to channel higher energies and my transcendence, and I give you my name, which means Secret of the Sky. Travel with me in the solar boat, and I will teach you how to dance like a star. I give this key to Caroline."

She handed Caroline the key I had seen in her hand in the attic.

"I thought that was the key to my cellar."

"It is the key of the Gateway to Heaven," Sheta Nut announced.

I wanted to ask her to explain, but already I was beginning to identify with Sleepy Head.

"I have one concern," I told them all. "I feel that Mona, the Critic and the Pragmatist are resisting. If you cannot accompany me on this Journey without moaning, criticizing or disbelieving what you see, then I won't be able to go."

There was a long silence.

"If I stop criticizing you, I don't trust you not to do stupid things," said the Critic, who asked to be called Clara. "I need to be reassured that you won't embarrass me in public. If you wore that thing on your head, I'd die of embarrassment."

"I need your help," I told Clara. "There is no need to criticize me; just whisper in my ear when you have a concern."

Clara was delighted to hear this. Critics love to be needed.

"I need your help too," I told the Pragmatist, who wanted to be called Frank. "Please help me to stay grounded."

Frank beamed at me. "You know how much I hate moaning," said Mona, bursting into tears. "Why don't you stop me?"

I promised to stop her every time I heard her complaining. After thanking them all, I crawled into bed wondering how I could contain so many different characters without going crazy. The following day I wrote a long letter to my therapist, telling him about the angel, Sheta Nut and Caroline's Coming Out Party. At the end of the letter I wrote:

"I hope together we can unravel this mystery."

1 The repetitive dream about being in the house of a man who dismembered bodies was a prophetic dream. I was dreaming about the house I would be staying in when Vivian died fifteen years later. The house belonged to a pathologist and had a basement.

2 *The Soul, the Quality of Life*, Alice Bailey. Lucis Press, 1974.

Five

The Omega Man

It happened the evening Vivian had a meeting in her house, which my therapist attended. I was in my bedroom when he arrived, and as he stood in my doorway chatting to me, I wondered why he always wore black. Since my first session with him, he had been dressed entirely in black.

He sat on one end of Vivian's couch and I sat on the other end. Pulling up his black socks and removing his black sweater, under which he was wearing a black silk shirt, he talked about his new piano. He left early to pick up his daughter, and that night when I went to bed, I could not sleep. I wondered again why he always wore black, and sat bolt upright in bed. The Omega Man had stood in the doorway of my room wearing black, just as my therapist stood in the doorway dressed in black. How could I have been so blind? Of course, my therapist and the Omega Man were the same person, but what did it mean? Why did he appear in a dream six years before I met him, and why did he accuse me of not remembering him? Why had he expected me to remember who he was, and who exactly was he?

For the next few days, I could not free myself of pagan images. I experienced immense sorrow over the fact that humanity appears to have lost touch with its pagan soul, which connects it to the Earth through fertility rites, ritual and communion with the nature spirits. Secretly I had always been a pagan; even as a child when my mother insisted upon sending me to Sunday School.

Suddenly everything appeared to be vibrantly alive, including each shimmering blade of grass. It was as if I had been born blind and was now able to see for the first time. Nothing could have prepared me for this onslaught of colour and vibrancy. Activities I had previously taken for granted, like sitting in the garden, shopping or washing the floor, filled me with delight. The ordinary became extraordinary.

Then the visions started. In the first one I was a priestess practising tantric sex with a priest on an altar dedicated to the Earth goddess. Around us a circle of women danced clockwise and a circle of men danced counter-clockwise. Everything about this scene was archaic and prehistoric, stirring up long-forgotten pagan memories that civilization had obviously failed to extinguish in me.

Listening to Pachelbel's Canon, I became everything. I had no beginning and no end. I was boundless and eternal, and everything existed within me: universes, galaxies, planets, stars and all life-forms. I embodied a love so total and all-encompassing, it is beyond my ability to describe it. Vast, sublime and totally unconditional, the love I embodied built up until I could no longer contain it. I was bursting with love and reached the point where I had to release it, and when I did, I experienced a cosmic orgasm that burst into the universe as a newly created galaxy. After this mind-blowing experience, I was blissed out for days.

Sheta Nut had given up transcending in the attic and was suddenly extremely interested in my therapist. So, I decided to marry him off. I accomplished this feat by celebrating Robert and Lisa's marriage. In a drawing I did of their wedding ceremony Robert looked remarkably like my therapist. They were married under a rainbow with swords held over their heads by centaurs. The griffin and unicorn were there with some nature spirits, and I was standing naked in the bottom right-hand corner, totally enfolded in my angel's wings. Caroline was with Joachim, who peered over his shoulder with a cheeky grin. Vivian and Sharon loved my drawings, and Sharon often sat in my room gazing at my closet doors, where I had stuck them all.

My chakras were spinning like catherine wheels and were sending a fountain of energy through the top of my head. Intense heat at the base of my spine convinced me I was about to burst into flame, but although I was spiralling with energy within myself, I had the sensation of standing absolutely still in the centre of a spinning wheel.

A week later Vivian took us to a Sweat Lodge, which we were told was built to the same proportions as the Great Pyramid of Giza in Egypt. I sat in the position of the gods and prayed for the Earth, and when I made a commitment to healing the Earth, I was given my native American name: Blue Moon Rising. In the final quarter, when we had our dreams, I heard the heavens singing: "Ptah Hotep! Ptah Hotep!"

The next time I saw my therapist, who I now recognized as the Omega Man, he was no longer wearing black.

"This is the first time you haven't worn black," I informed him. I told him about meeting the Omega Man in the doorway of my room in my dream and in the Temple of Dreams.

"It was as if your unconscious caused you to wear black until I identified you as the Omega Man."

"It could be a coincidence," he said, shrugging his shoulders.

"There is something going on with Sheta Nut," I told him. "I have to warn you that she's very interested in you, but I don't know why. It feels dangerous."

"Maybe you could ask her," he suggested.

I said I would, but really needed to work in this session on my issues with men.

"I have this fantasy about you in which you are chasing me through a forest. I feel like a doe being chased by a stag, and when I trip you fall on top of me, and it feels wonderful, but dangerous."

"The therapeutic relationship is similar to the parent-child relationship," he explained. "If a parent betrays the child's trust, it's very damaging for the child. A therapist should never betray his client's trust. If he does, it's like incest."

"Is that why it feels so dangerous?" I asked. "It feels like playing with fire."

"We need to do some work with your father because I suspect he eroticized you when you were a little girl. Your father was not available to you. I remember my daughter wanting to climb into bed with my wife and me when she was little, but I did not encourage it. My daughter is from a previous marriage," he explained before dimming the lights and indicating that I could lie down on the couch. "It's time for you to say goodbye to your father. See if you can find the place where this ceremony of release needs to occur."

"You and I are driving up into the mountains under a canopy

of stars. It's a clear night and the Milky Way looks like a star-studded belt across the sky," I said, describing my imagery. "Now we are arriving at a log cabin high in the mountains, with a thick forest behind it, and a breathtaking view across the valley. We're looking at the view, and you're pointing to the tail of Halley's Comet. The log cabin has no electricity, so I light candles and you make a fire in a potbellied buddha of a stove with four squat legs and a chimney extending up through the ceiling. The fire and the candles cast flickering shadows across the wood-lined walls.

"I long for intimacy, but never feel nourished in my intimate relationships," I told him.

He tried to speak, but I continued:

"I long to meet a man I can play, dance and laugh with, but who can also go deep with me. My deepest relationship was with Jake, but his anger terrified me."

"I'm not surprised. It must have been terrifying for you to see your father dying in a fit of anger."

"Yes, it was," I agreed. "I remember what happened. I refused to kiss him goodnight because he had locked me out on the fire escape."

"Your father locked you out on the fire escape?"

"He left me there when my mother was out because he didn't want to be interrupted when he was working in his studio, which was in our fourth-floor apartment. Little did he know I was risking my life on that fire escape, which was old and rusty with loose railings. When I refused to kiss him goodnight, my mother said I had hurt his feelings. He died shortly afterwards, and I blamed myself."

"It's not unusual for children to blame themselves when a parent dies."

"You've taken my hand and you're pulling me towards the door," I continued with my imagery. "Beside the door hangs a large gold-handled sword studded with emeralds. You grab the sword and tell me I have to find my father. You sweep me through the door into the still, clear night, and I follow you through the snow into the forest at the back of the log cabin. You look like a knight with your sword, and I love walking in your big footprints. Now you've stopped and I'm leaning against a tree. You tell me to close my eyes."

"Let's visualize a light above our heads and see that light radiating into our hearts," said my therapist from his seat behind my head. "I have my sword and I'm drawing two circles in the snow. One is your sensual father and the other one your rejecting father. Now I want you to imagine your father standing there."

"Yes, I can see him. I'm looking into his velvet brown eyes, and there's the familiar bald spot on top of his head. He looks sad."

"Does he have anything to share with you?"

"Yes, he's sorry he died when I was so young, and for all the times he hurt me. He says he didn't know how to be a father."

"It really hurt me when you died so suddenly," I told my father. "I needed you to stay alive until I grew up. I love you, I'm working on forgiving you, but I need you out of my psyche."

"I'm moving to another level, but before I go I'd like to help you with the book."

"I don't know which book you mean," I said, wondering if he was referring to the book given to me by the angel.

"I could make it even funnier," he pointed out.

I remembered my father's outrageous sense of humour. He had played practical jokes on everyone he knew. He was also a writer and an artist.

"I loved you so much," I cried. "Why did you excite and reject me?"

"I wasn't aware of exciting and rejecting you. It felt so good to snuggle up to you in bed. You had no expectations of me, unlike your mother and my mother. You were so loving and open. Not even my own mother loved and accepted me the way you did."

"I needed you to be all of those things for me," I said tearfully. "I needed you to love and accept me, but you only wanted me when it suited you. Neither you nor my mother were ever really there for me. I felt like an object, especially when you fought over me. I remember the day you each held on to one of my arms and were both pulling me in opposite directions. Neither of you were caring about me. You were only aware of your own needs. I felt used by you."

"I'm really sorry about that," he apologized. "I'm also sorry I didn't take you to the hospital when you broke your arm."

"That was the day you were both pulling on my arms," I reminded him. "I needed your protection. I was totally at your mercy."

"I stayed close to you after I died. I felt terrible because I'd left you and your mother penniless."

I knew my father had stayed close to me. Although he died a month before Christmas, I saw him on Christmas day. When I told my mother, she said he was probably taking care of me, but I had needed him to take care of me when he was alive.

"Don't blame yourself for my death. When you refused to kiss me goodnight after I had locked you out on the fire escape, I felt you were withdrawing your love from me, the way my mother withdrew her love from me when I was a naughty boy."

"Is that why you told me naughty boy stories?" I asked.

"You loved my naughty boy stories," he reminded me.

Unfortunately my father had remained a naughty boy for the rest of his life, always longing for the approval and love he had not received as a child.

"I pray for you and your mother."

"Do you pray where you are?"

"Of course," he nodded. "I'm going to the Illusion School."

"The Illusion School!" I exclaimed. "Why are you going there?"

"To learn about illusions, of course," he laughed. "I won't be able to visit you as your father any more."

"Why not?"

"Our relationship is an illusion," he explained. "We're just two souls travelling along the same path. In this life we chose a father-daughter relationship, but when I passed over into this dimension I realized it was an illusion. I now have quite a different relationship with my parents because they're not my parents any more."

"This explains why I sometimes feel we've been lovers."

"We have. We've been just about everything to each other."

"But as my father, you set me up to experience frustration in my intimate relationships."

"You chose me as your father and had a reason for doing so. Your problems are related to your life's purpose."

This did not console me at all.

"After you died, my life was a nightmare," I cried. "I wouldn't have been sexually abused if you hadn't abandoned me by dying."

"I didn't abandon you. We were separated on the physical plane; that's all."

"That could explain why I'm always meeting people who are somehow familiar to me. They must be people I've known and loved before. It's funny how we all meet up again."

"It's not funny at all," he pointed out. "It's natural. Give my love to your mother. I always loved her even though she drove me crazy. You see, we were opposites."

"You were right when you predicted that men would land on the Moon in my lifetime, and when you told me I would learn more after I left school. I have."

"You will be amazed at how much more you will learn after you die," he told me. "I shall have to go now."

I heard a faint jingling sound in the distance.

"I want you to know that I have given you a most precious gift," he said. "One of the most divine gifts."

We embraced, and when I looked up I laughed. In the distance a sleigh was being pulled by eight reindeer, and sitting inside the sleigh was Father Christmas.

"It *is* almost Christmas," said my father smiling playfully.

"Trust you to do this," I laughed, remembering his great sense of humour. "There isn't really a Father Christmas, is there? It was you all the time. When I was a little girl, you crept into my bedroom and left presents for me at the foot of my bed. I bet you didn't notice me watching you."

"Father Christmas is an archetype," he explained. "He is the father of all children. He does exist, but when people say he loves only good children, don't believe them. He loves *all* children equally. This is the nature of his love."

I loved my father for saying this, and hugged him.

"Yo-ho-ho!" said Father Christmas, pulling up beside us.

"I'll never forget that drawing you did of Father Christmas when you were five years old," said my father. "I told your mother then that you were talented. Then there were those other funny little drawings you did of people with strings attaching them to the Sun. Don't waste your gifts, the way I did, and don't forget to write that book. It's important."

He kissed me on the cheek and climbed into the sleigh beside Father Christmas. I began to cry, but knew I had to let him go.

"We'll meet again, won't we?" I asked anxiously.

"We're always meeting," he said, taking my hand in his. "You're not conscious of it yet."

The sleigh glided through the forest with my father waving to me, and the bells on the reindeer jingling as they travelled silently across the snow. I could just hear my father's voice in the distance reminding me to write the book.

We watched as the sleigh weaved its way through the trees to the summit of the mountain, where it took off into the starry sky.

When it had disappeared, I looked down at the two circles in the snow. In each circle the snow had melted and growing in the earth were beautiful wild flowers.

After I had been guided back into the room and was sitting up, I asked what precious gift my father could have been talking about.

"I think he was referring to your sense of humour. You *are* funny. Assagioli wrote an article about humour in which he described it as 'an intimate smile of the soul'. It's called 'Smiling Wisdom'."[1]

After we had said goodbye, I headed home with the stars as my companions, feeling alone but not lonely. There comes a point in every woman's life when she must say goodbye to her father.

1 'Smiling Wisdom', Roberto Assagioli.
Now included in *Transpersonal Development* by Roberto Assagioli. Published by Inner Way 2007. Written in 1915, first published in 1922.

Six

Sheta Nut

"Do you have a copy of Assagioli's article on humour?" I asked Vivian.

She found it amongst her papers and informed me that my therapist had also written a humorous article, which she found and handed to me. Inspired by Assagioli's Egg Diagram, he had experienced a seminal insight that its complementary missing aspect was the sperm diagram. His article was illustrated with sperm diagrams depicting Grounding, the Supreme Synthesis, and a Transpersonal Quality: Gaiety. I laughed for the rest of the day and in response wrote 'The Origin of Sin', which I mailed to him.

THE ORIGIN OF SIN

The purpose of this paper is to pinpoint the origin of sin. Firstly, I must assure my readers that I have no axe to grind with men. I have never been involved in the feminist movement, which I consider to be as phallic in its thrust for power as men are. However, I must conclude, after extensive research, that sin originates in the male ejaculation (see attached diaphragm). This clearly illustrates how and where male competitive behaviour began. Here also is the origin of lust (see penetrating sperm with tongue hanging out). Further scrutiny will reveal other base human characteristics, such as envy, hatred and self-pity (see the other three sperms in the diaphragm).

Furthermore, it is the purpose of this paper to prove that the male ejaculation is merely a microcosm of the macrocosm. This may come as a shock to the ecclesiastical world, but the truth of the matter is in the Big Bang, which was God's first ejaculation. Yes, as shocking as it may seem, this is the root of the matter. Everything we see: the earth upon which we walk, the stars in the heavens, all exist because of God's orgasmic nature. Proof of the cosmic orgasm God so frequently enjoys is clearly visible in the night sky, which is engorged with stars. The universe is in a constant state of expansion. I realize the heretical nature of this statement, but I can find no other rational explanation.

As my research reveals that the soul incarnates as both male and female, women cannot point an accusing finger at men, but must accept and take responsibility for their own inner masculinity.

My conclusion is that we are all sinners and should stop feeling guilty about it.

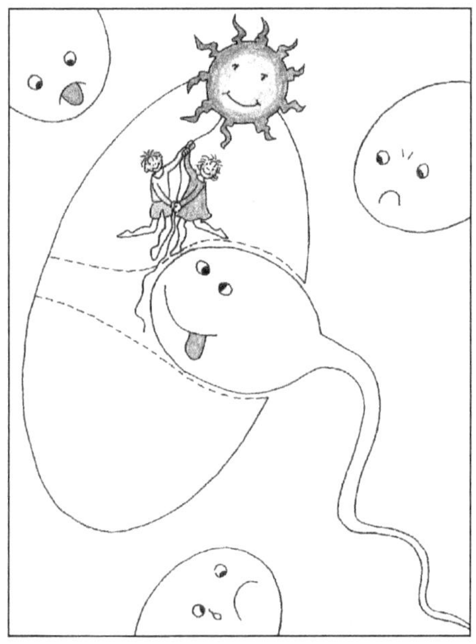

I laughed all day, and laughed even more that evening when my friend Mary took me to the cinema to see *The Gods Must Be Crazy*. By the time I collapsed into bed that night, I was aching from my day of non-stop laughter.

The following afternoon I was aware of Sheta Nut (pronounced Shater Noot) wanting to communicate, so I decided to sit in the garden with my pen and paper to write down what she had to say. I was aware of feeling some resistance, and would have preferred to spend the afternoon reading and sunbathing. Maybe some part of me knew that my life would never be the same again if I listened to her.

"I promised to find him," she said, referring to my therapist. "I am not one of your subpersonalities. I have been in existence for thousands of years, and promised to find him in the future. That time is now."

At this point I was interrupted by the man who had arrived to unblock the drains. He had 'Rescue Rooter' printed on his sweatshirt and cap.

"I love your English accent," he said.

I did not know how to respond, but could just imagine his face if I told him I was talking to an ancient Egyptian priestess. The Rescue Rooter flirted with me, and after he had gone I was glowing and light-hearted.

"When did you make your promise?" I asked Sheta Nut.

"In Egypt," she told me. "Before I took final initiation in the Great Pyramid, I promised to find him in the future if I died in the sarcophagus. We loved each other, and I must keep my promise."

I was intrigued and asked her to tell me more.

"We travelled to this planet from beyond the stars, via Sirius, and were together in Lemuria, where we worked as a priest and priestess. We brought spirit into matter, and balanced the female/male polarity. We led others in ritual and taught dance, music and tantra. We did not abuse our power, but served the people and cooperated with the nature spirits. We have always loved each other, and worked as a team until we were separated in Egypt."

I remembered the vision I'd had of practising tantric sex with a priest on an altar, and wondered if I had been tuning in to this life.

Sheta Nut nodded.

"In Atlantis, we were powerful and in leadership positions, but towards the end of that epoch we abused our power," she confessed. "One of the worst things I did in Atlantis was to operate on people with living animal parts. By escaping before the cataclysm, I did not reap my karma. I was clairvoyant and saw that Atlantis would sink beneath the waves.

"The priesthood was re-established in Egypt where replicas of our temples and pyramids were built. The Melchizedek priesthood set up its mystery schools to teach the secrets of the universe and to prepare its students for initiation into higher states of consciousness. The temples along the Nile were dedicated to different chakras, each with its own initiation ceremony, culminating in the crown chakra initiation in the Great Pyramid. Tantra was taught in the temple complex at Philae, where young people were initiated into adulthood. Love-making was an art form that only the priesthood could teach, for it symbolizes the union of spirit and matter. I had many lifetimes in Egypt until my final life as Sheta Nut three thousand three hundred years ago. In that life I was born with one burning desire, which was to become a High Priestess. This was my last life with Akara."

When Sheta Nut said the name Akara, my heart skipped a beat, and I was filled with a great longing.

"I was born under the sign of the Water Bearer during the reign of Amenophis III. I was born during the hours of darkness and was named Sheta Nut, which means Secret of the Sky, after the great sky goddess Nut, who gave birth to the Sun."

"Nut gave birth to the Sun!" I exclaimed, remembering the drawing I had done of myself giving birth to the Sun with Anna and Joachim, my two inner children, looking on with ecstatic expressions on their faces. I was amazed to hear this, as I had not understood what prompted my unconscious to produce such an image.

"I was the fifth child in a family of boys. My father worked with the Pharaoh on affairs of the state. He was what you would call a diplomat, and he travelled often to other lands. I missed him when he was away from home. My mother was beautiful but aloof, paying much attention to her appearance. She wore her long black hair piled high on her head with ivory or tortoiseshell combs, and she exuded the aroma of exotic oils. She led a busy social life, but we were not close. I had my beloved nurse, Nefta, who took care of me. She oiled my body and brushed my hair until it shone like ebony. She told me stories about the gods, but the story I loved the most was about Isis and Osiris, who loved each other beyond measure. Osiris was descended from Ra, the Sun God, who had produced Shu, the god of air, and Tefnut, the goddess of mist, in one ejaculation."

I was stunned to hear this because it reminded me of what I had written in 'The Origin of Sin'.

"Isis was the wife of Osiris," Sheta Nut continued. "But Osiris had a brother called Seth, who was so jealous of Osiris he tried repeatedly to kill him. Seth sent his brother a casket, which he enticed him into and then sealed the lid so that Osiris could not escape. He threw the casket into the Nile, but Isis rescued it. Seth was so outraged, he cut Osiris into fourteen pieces and scattered them throughout Egypt, but Isis travelled far and wide to recover them. She finally found the phallus at Philae, and through the Ritual of Regeneration she was able to reassemble the scattered parts. When she turned herself into a bird, Osiris came to life and sowed his seed in her. Later she gave birth to Horus, the hawk-headed god. Isis was my personal deity. I had her image on all of my personal items."

As Sheta Nut told me about Osiris and Isis, I remembered the dreams about the casket sinking beneath the water and. I wondered if there was a connection and whether my unconscious had been sending me powerful images in my sleep.

"It is true that I was spoilt and much loved," said Sheta Nut, continuing with her life story. "From an early age I loved to dance for my family and for the servants. I was advanced for my years and could read people's hearts. I also remembered previous lifetimes and entertained my nurse by telling her about them. We had houses in both upper and lower Egypt, and my father had many servants who he had inherited or acquired on his travels. Our houses were spacious, but the one I loved the most had tiled mosaic floors upon which I loved to walk and dance barefoot.

"I was popular, but my sweetheart was Akara. I could not remember a time when we were not together. Although we could play with the Pharaoh's children, we preferred to wander off on our own. Akara had a little flute, which he loved to play. He carried it with him everywhere he went and accompanied me on it when I danced.

"At seven years old I was taken to the temple to train as a temple dancer. I spent the next fourteen years concentrating on my training as a temple dancing priestess. I learned to stretch and extend my body to bring more Light into my energy centres, which I then projected through my dancing. The purpose of temple dancing was to embody the gods and goddesses for the inspiration of the common people, who came to the temples for spiritual nourishment and guidance. Every day I practised holding my shoulders back, twisting my body and flattening my hands to emulate the frescoes which adorned the walls of our temples and tombs. When I was not performing in the dance dramas, I practised asanas, mudras and special breathing exercises. I learned to channel and project Light through my eyes and body language, to write and read hieroglyphs, perform rituals, release my ka, and travel beyond time and space. By the time I reached my fourteenth year, I was pouring the libation wine in the temple, as well as performing other small functions in minor rituals.

"When we stayed in our summer residence, which we travelled to by boat, I would watch the solar barge carrying the initiates to final initiation on the Giza Plateau. I arose at dawn to watch them, and longed to take that journey, but Akara said hardly any of them survived being entombed alive inside the Great Pyramid.

"In his teens, Akara was sent by his family to Philae to be initiated into manhood. We did not see each other again until my sixteenth birthday. He looked so different I barely recognized him, and he was delighted with the way I had matured. He was tall and broad-shouldered with a new look in his eyes. His gift to me was a golden chain with half of a Sun-disk attached to it. I was puzzled and asked why he had given me only half of a Sun-disk.

"'We are born of the same fire,' he explained. 'We are two halves of the same flame. Look, I have the other half hanging around my neck, and the two halves fit together perfectly.'

"Then he kissed me in a way which caused a fluttering sensation at the base of my spine. Later he told me of his wish to teach me what he had learned at Philae, but I was shy. I had devoted myself entirely to my training, and had paid little attention to my developing body or my awakening sexuality. I had been bleeding for three years, but did not know how to avoid being impregnated by his seed. Akara said he would teach me, but I needed time to reacquaint myself with him. When he went to Philae he was a child; now he had grown into a man.

"Akara shared his plans for the future. He had decided to train as a musician priest, and had already been accepted into my temple complex, which housed many other priests and priestesses who lived together as a community and took care of the common people. The temples were like your universities," Sheta Nut explained. "At Thebes there were countless resident priests and priestesses trained in the arts, healing, embalming, teaching and the rites of Amun-Ra, Egypt's official religion. Only the common people led a secular life.

"Akara and I now saw each other almost every day. I knew I was beautiful, like my mother, with many male admirers. My cheek bones were high, my mouth wide and sensual, and my eyes as deep as lotus pools. I had narrow hips and small, firm breasts. I loved to flirt and flick my long hair over my shoulder. I was vain and wilful and knew my power. Sometimes I teased Akara by pretending not to notice him, but always I could detect his energy in a crowded room. There was a magnetism between us, but sometimes his possessiveness bothered me. He became moody when I flirted with the other priests, and would follow me with his eyes. I wore the Sun-disk he had given me beneath my beaded collar, for deep within my ka I knew he was the lotus of my heart, and when he played haunting melodies for me on his flute, I knew I was being consumed by the fire of my love for him.

"We had been performing for Akhenaten and his beautiful wife Nefertiti. The celebrations had continued for days. Akara had been drinking and was very merry. We were dancing and laughing together when he suddenly took my hand and led me outside into the moonlit night. We walked down to the Nile, where we could hear the water lapping against the bank. He suggested cooling ourselves by taking a swim. The water refreshed and soothed my aching body. I had danced almost non-stop for three days. The Moon was full and low in a star-filled sky, and I longed for the day when we would embody a star. After our swim, he held me in his arms and played my body as if it was a musical instrument, so that we could make the sweetest music together. He had been taught well at Philae, and that night we became lovers.

"Now that we had consummated our love for each other, Akara talked often about taking the sacred rite of union, but I was ambitious and thought only of becoming a High Priestess. I worked constantly towards new heights in the priesthood, fine-tuning my psychic abilities, purifying myself and taking all possible steps towards final initiation.

"Akhenaten persuaded us to join his Mystery School at the Horizon of the Sun Disk. After only three years of rulership at Thebes, he built his own city on the east bank of the Nile on a beautiful crescent-shaped plateau with a mountainous backdrop. Here he built palaces, a temple dedicated to the Aten, and pleasure gardens. The High Priests hated Akhenaten for dismantling the statues of Amun-Ra. He said they were corrupt because they sold absolution and immortality, and set themselves up as religious despots. They knew if they controlled the people's spirituality they would have unlimited power, for religion is a more potent psychological tool than politics. Akhenaten wanted to liberate Egypt from the tyranny of the Amun priesthood. His aim was to reinstate the ancient wisdom taught in the Mystery Schools brought to Egypt by the Melchizedek priesthood, to unite his people through the worship of One God, and to change the future.

"Akhenaten's Mystery School was symbolized by a triangle with the eye of Horus at its centre."

I was astonished when she told me this because it was exactly the image I saw at Caroline's Coming Out Party.

"The teachings of the Melchizedek priesthood included

alchemy, astrology, sacred geometry, harmonics and astronomy. We were taught to make the unconscious conscious through breath control, meditation, chanting, dream analysis and the use of a pendulum. We learnt how to communicate with nature spirits, angels, spirit guides and our own individual Aumakhua."

"Aumakhua?"

"Aumakhua is the name of the overlighting angelic presence who resides in the Solar Disk," she explained.

I thought about my angel, and wondered if this was who she was referring to. "Is my angel an Aumakhua?" I asked.

"Yes. Every person in the world has an Aumakhua, who resides in the Solar Disk, and who we are destined to embody.

"When I talked to Merirye, High Priest of the Aten, he said I was not ready for final initiation. He had read the Akashic Records and told me I would not survive the karma casting in the Great Pyramid.

"'You are young,' he pointed out. 'You have travelled far for one so young. Why not enjoy your life with Akara, who loves you deeply? If you take final initiation before you are ready, you will pursue what you are not ready to release through all future lives. Be warned: whatever you are not ready to release now will never again be yours if you go ahead with final initiation before you are ready.'

"He offered to give us the sacred rite of union, but I was proud and would not listen to him. My father had never refused my heart's desire. I would not now be denied final initiation.

"Akhenaten and Merirye talked about the Aten, which was not a new god but an access code for the twelve-stranded DNA."

"What is the twelve-stranded DNA?" I asked.

"Through the crown chakra, it reconnects us to our multidimensional reality, enabling us to time-travel, and achieve unity consciousness, which was the main aim of Akhenaten's Mystery School. If you look at pictures of the Solar Disk from the eighteenth dynasty, you will see twelve rays, like hands reaching down to Earth. This is the twelve-stranded DNA.

"The Amun priesthood plotted for many years to rid Egypt of Akhenaten. Because of my many years of training, Akhenaten allowed me into his Mystery School before I reached the required age. I was its youngest student and the last person to be initiated in the Great Pyramid during his reign.

"Akhenaten also introduced new art forms that conflicted with the traditional stylized art practised in Egypt for many dynasties. He commissioned a lifelike statue of himself, which everyone considered to be very ugly. It bore a remarkable resemblance to him and was totally unlike previous statues of pharaohs. It was talked about throughout upper and lower Egypt, and secretly it was ridiculed.

"The High Priests of Amun-Ra deliberately spread rumours about Akhenaten, which caused the common people to hate their Pharaoh. They said he was deformed, insane, perverted, and weak for neglecting his armies.

"Shortly after my talk with Merirye I had a vision of Isis, in which she told me to go ahead with final initiation. When I told Akara he became very distressed and made me promise never to refer to it again. I no longer talked about my plans, but continued with the training which would lead to final initiation. The years passed by at Akhenaten's Mystery School in which we were prepared for membership of the Alpha and Omega Order of Melchizedek."

"So, that's why Isis called Akara the Omega Man!"

"At last I was accepted for final initiation and was summoned to the Temple of the Sun at Heliopolis, to begin fasting and cleansing, and to take my vow of celibacy. I told Akara I would not be seeing him for many weeks. I would be seeing nobody but the High Priests, who would be giving me special instructions while I was in solitary confinement. Akara was so upset he lost control of himself. He begged me to stay with him, telling me I was mad to risk my life in this way. He wanted us to take the sacred rite of union, but I told him it was unnecessary. We would always be a part of each other. I loved Akara, but I knew I was the strong one. His dependency disturbed me, and he had not learned to control his emotions. I had seen him lose control before, and it filled me with contempt. I was so excited about being accepted for final initiation, it never occurred to me that our separation would be far longer than I could ever have imagined.

"However, there was no doubt about my love for Akara. It was our last night together before I entered seclusion. We did not sleep but held each other and made love until dawn. He cried, and in my passion for him I failed to separate our seeds. I knew I had conceived, but decided it would remain a secret. I would be denied my chance of final initiation if anyone knew about it. It excited me to be carrying Akara's child, and I did not consider the consequences. It amused me to conceal my secret from the High Priests, and I imagined I was Isis carrying the child Horus."

"I don't believe you could hide being pregnant from the High Priests," I interrupted. "They must have known. What about when you missed your period?"

"It was common for initiates to stop bleeding when they were fasting and cleansing," Sheta Nut explained. "We had to slow down the natural functions of our bodies to survive being entombed. It was like going into suspended animation. We were barely alive during the actual entombment, and this was to enable us to enter the celestial realms where the gods dwell. If we survived, it was like attaining immortality without dying, and we could then communicate with the gods. The initiates who survived their entombment in the Great Pyramid were taken out onto an elevated platform, so that the people could shout: "Ptah Hotep."

"Ptah Hotep!" I exclaimed, remembering what I had heard at the Sweat Lodge. "What does Ptah Hotep mean?"

"High Priest, of course."

"What happened if they failed?"

"Their bodies were taken to the mortuary temple to be embalmed.

"Several weeks later, Akara came to my room the night before I was to be taken in the solar barge to the Great Pyramid. At first

I begged him to go away, but he was persistent, and I was afraid we would be heard and discovered together. This part of the temple was heavily guarded, and I could not understand how he had gained admittance. Once inside my room, which was little more than a cell, he cried and implored me not to go through with it. He related a dream in which I did not survive and we were separated for thousands of years. As he sobbed, I held him in my arms, but I was still determined to go through with it. Akara did not know it was my life's ambition to take final initiation, although I experienced a dark premonition. An astrologer had predicted that we would be destroyed by the fire of our love.

"When Akara realized he could not talk me out of it, he began to make love to me. When his fingers played upon the strings of my body, made more sensitive through abstinence, I felt like a musical instrument. He knew how to please me and to extract from me the highest notes and deepest surrender. I felt I would burst into flame when he entered me, and as we moved as one body the danger I was in only served to intensify the pleasure. My desire for Akara at that moment was overpowering. I was intoxicated and mindless, ignorant of how much I would have to pay for this stolen time."

"Akara believed if he made love to me I would not go through with the initiation. I did not realize how much he trusted my integrity or how dishonest I had become in my ambition.

"'Now you cannot take final initiation,' he told me as we rested in each other's arms. 'It is not permitted for you to be sexual at this time. It is too dangerous.'

"This was related to kundalini and the explosive fire of sexual union. We had a great fire in our love for each other, but this fire would kill me if it was aroused during my entombment. Even knowing that I had broken my vow of celibacy, I was still determined to go through with it. Akara was deeply shaken and began to cry again. Terrified we would be discovered, I pushed him towards the door.

"'Promise me you will find me in the future if we are separated,' he begged.

"I promise," I whispered as I pushed him towards the door.

"'Even if the mists of time have clouded my memory,' he insisted, standing in the doorway. 'Help me to remember.'

"I promise," I whispered, placing my finger on his lips. "Even if the mists of time have clouded your memory, I will help you to remember."

I remembered how the Omega Man had stood in the doorway in my dream and in the Temple of Dreams saying: "You don't remember me, do you?" Now I knew he was prompting me to remember Sheta Nut's promise.

"After Akara had gone, I did not sleep. There were only two or three hours before dawn, and I spent this time centring myself. I had a premonition that I would not survive, but I could not stop the process. I felt compelled to go through with it. I had led a life totally without suffering or pain. I had experienced neither grief nor disappointment. I had always been loved and desired. Whatever I wanted I could have, including final initiation. I had never been lonely or dependent upon another. I was arrogant and self-opinionated, being so sure of myself and my decisions it never occurred to me that I might be making a terrible mistake, nor did I stop to consider the tragic consequences of my deception. I wanted only to fulfil my ambition, but I also wanted Akara. I desired both and was not able to sacrifice either. The consummation of my passion for Akara was my death sentence. I underestimated the power of final initiation. My punishment was to die physically, but never to die to the knowledge of what I had done to both our lives.

"At sunrise I was taken from my cell to the solar barge, which would carry me to the Great Pyramid. Initiates always sat at the back of the boat under a canopy, and as they sailed along the Nile people would stand on the banks to watch, for an initiate was to the ancient Egyptians what a movie star is to people today. As we started on our journey I saw Akara standing on the bank silently watching me. He was as motionless as a statue, and I shall never forget the expression on his face. As I watched him, it was as if my love for him was stuck in my throat. I told myself it was too dangerous to feel. I must remember my training of non-attachment, but still I could not take my eyes off him. As I looked, every cell in my body urged me to jump into the Nile, to stay with him. This scene has haunted me through the centuries, and I still see Akara standing beside the Nile, a solitary figure, and I hear my heart begging me to stay with him. To have remained would have created a different destiny for both of us, and for the baby I carried."

I remembered the drawing I had done of a tree, which was the love of a man and a woman for each other. In this drawing the woman was pregnant. I now knew that this tree symbolized Sheta Nut's love for Akara and his love for her.

"Long before we arrived at the Giza plateau, I saw the golden crystal capstone of the Great Pyramid shimmering in the early morning Sun. The Great Pyramid's main bulk was covered in polished limestone, which caused it to glow at sunrise, sunset and during the full Moon. The Great Pyramid attracted many visitors, but could only be entered by the High Priests and the initiates. Stories of its magnificence had spread throughout the land, and it was considered to be one of the wonders of the world.

"The solar barge stopped beneath the Sphinx, where I entered a covered causeway with polished stone columns at its entrance. It was guarded by the Sphinx, and its walls were covered in carvings depicting scenes from the underworld to prepare the initiates for their descent. The causeway ran under the Giza plateau from the Nile to the Great Pyramid. Accompanied by the High Priests, I entered a chamber beneath the Sphinx to be taken through various rituals and rites of passage. Its walls were covered in beautiful coloured frescoes, and the last one I saw before drinking Amrita, the nectar of the gods, was of Isis clothed with the Sun and poised on the globe of the World, her feet riding the Moon and her head crowned with stars.

"I was taken through the causeway to enter the Great Pyramid deep within its foundations. On an underground lake, illuminated by oil lamps at various points around the stone walls, a small boat waited for me. A High Priest, dressed as the jackal-headed god Anubis, helped me into the boat, and I knew I was crossing the Lily Lake, which in our rituals was the lake of death crossed by the ka on its way to the underworld. It was silent except for the lapping of the water around our boat. At the far side of the lake, I was taken up a flight of steps into an underground area with tunnels and a steep passageway leading upwards into the pyramid. After my long period of fasting, my ascent through this almost vertical shaft was slow and torturous. I was relieved when we reached a horizontal passageway leading to a chamber, in which I was wrapped like a mummy and pointed towards Sirius, where Isis guards the Secrets. I was now officially dead and was carried in silence through the grand gallery. Unable to move, I gazed up in awe at the high vertical walls on either side of me. I was passed through a low opening into the Initiation Chamber and carefully lowered into the stone sarcophagus. A lid was suspended above it, attached to ropes and pulleys, and after it had been lowered onto the sarcophagus I found myself in an indescribable darkness. I imagined the High Priests walking away with their torches, passing through the grand gallery and out of the Great Pyramid, leaving me totally alone in my granite tomb.

"I knew I had to release my ka and travel through the underworld. After that, if I survived, I would enter the celestial realms where the gods reside. After communing with the gods, I would explore the borders of Egypt to gather information. If my information was correct when the High Priests interrogated me, I would achieve Ptah Hotep. I freed myself easily from the sarcophagus, even though its only exit was difficult to locate. There was only one entrance and exit through which the ka could pass. It had been constructed in such a way that if the initiates returned in haste, they died instantly. The only way to return was through the spiral of conscious choice. If an initiate experienced fear, causing the ka to return in haste, that lapse in consciousness would cause instant death. This was why so many initiates failed and why the training concentrated on courage and consciousness. Numerous priests and priestesses were killed by their own terror. I had to know beyond doubt that nothing could harm me; that everything I encountered in the underworld was a part of me. The secret was to integrate every apparition, to acknowledge it as my creation, and to bring it home. I knew this and was confident. I was convinced I could return to the sarcophagus through the spiral of conscious choice, which would enable me to enter exactly where I had made my careful exit.

"I left my body in its wrappings and travelled down through the grand gallery, which connected into the long passageway leading down into the Pit, where I knew I would gain entrance to the underworld through a small doorway especially constructed for the ka. It was not a physical door any more than the concealed entrance to the sarcophagus was physical. I travelled through the eleven gates of hell where demons and hideous beings confronted me, but I knew they could only harm me if I allowed them to.

"In my travels through the underworld I heard a child crying: 'Mummy! Mummy!' and I knew it was my task to find this child. You were the child I heard crying. I appeared to you when you were seven years old. I appeared in a vision, having travelled into the future to the incarnation where I would achieve Ptah Hotep."

I remembered the vision. At the time I thought it was an angel. I had been crying for my mother, but after seeing the vision I stopped crying. I could not believe that Sheta Nut had travelled over three thousand years into the future, and then I burst out laughing: "You were a mummy and I was crying for my mummy."

Sheta Nut made no comment but continued with her story:

"I faced the karma casting and knew I had to reap my karma, for I saw all the people I had harmed in previous lives. On the third day I saw a great flood approaching and knew I must ascend to escape it. I climbed a mountain and then a tower with many steps. At the very top I was met by Isis. I told her about my journey through the underworld, my encounters with all the people I had harmed, and how I heard a child crying and had travelled into the future to find her. Isis asked me about my karma, and I promised to find and serve every person I had harmed. When she asked me to travel into the future to teach the children for her, I agreed. She was pleased with me and enfolded me in the divine fragrance she exudes. When once a mortal has been touched by Isis, all the gods know because of the fragrance she transmits to the one she has touched."

"Fragrance!" I exclaimed, remembering the mysterious lady in the Temple of Dreams whose fragrance sat on the tip of my tongue. "What does Isis look like?"

"Isis is divinely beautiful," sighed Sheta Nut. "Her skin is like ebony and she wears a gown the colour of the sky."

"It was Isis I met in the Temple of Dreams when I was taken by Maitreya to Shamballa. She told me I had made a promise to her, but I had no idea what she was talking about."

"It was my promise, which can now only be fulfilled through you," Sheta Nut explained. "After Isis had embraced me, she walked away, but when I attempted to follow her the tower caught fire. I wanted to walk through the flames, but I was terrified of being consumed. I found myself jumping off the tower to escape the fire, and as I fell I remembered what I had forgotten: fire is also a part of me. It can only burn me if I separate myself from it."

"That's what I said when Maitreya took me to the Sun: when I am inside fire or fire is inside me, it cannot burn me."

Sheta Nut nodded sadly. "It was too late. When my ka crashed onto the lid of the sarcophagus, my physical body died of shock. I had been destroyed by the fire of my passion for Akara, as the astrologer had predicted, and now we were separated. I had failed final initiation.

"I tried to re-enter my physical body, but it was impossible. I had severed my connecting thread. I left the pyramid and found Akara, but he could neither hear nor see me. We were each lost in a grief we could not share.

"In vain I travelled the borders of Egypt gathering information, and returned as the High Priests were removing my dead body from the sarcophagus. When they prepared it for embalming, they found Akara's semen and the baby I had conceived, and knew I had broken my vow of celibacy. The name of Sheta Nut was disgraced.

"I watched helplessly as Akara, consumed by his grief, drank the libation wine in the temple. I saw him harden his heart to me. It was easier for him to blame me than to face his shame.

"I stayed close to him for many years, and saw him at a banquet in Thebes. Akhenaten's reign had ended abruptly after my death, and some Hittites were visiting during Tutankhamun's reign. The Hittites, who had previously been our enemies, wanted to form an alliance with Egypt. Being uncouth, and lacking in culture and spiritual knowledge, they were not respected by the Egyptians. Their men made love like donkeys. A Hittite king and his court were being fed and entertained. Akara was one of the musicians and was attracted to a young Hittite woman with long flowing hair. She did not look or behave like an Egyptian, and dissipated her energy when she danced. Akara seduced her, which was not a favourable thing to do. Although he lusted after her, he had no respect for her, but she fell in love with him and through him experienced an awakening. The Hittites had no respect for their women, whom they used sexually. Akara was well versed in the art of love and made it impossible for her to return home. She begged him to help her, but he refused. She died alone in the desert; rejected in Egypt and unable to return to her own country. Akara created karma with her and is married to her in this life, but what bound him to her then will free him now. In this way he created several karmic bonds with women he took pleasure with after my death. Akara was born again in Egypt, but I have never been able to return."

I had spent all afternoon and all evening listening to Sheta Nut's story, and was in a state of shock.

"Now you will understand why it is important for me to keep my promise to Akara," she concluded.

Her story was incredible and would have been unbelievable if there weren't so many coincidences. I had always felt a connection with Egypt, even as a child when I begged my father to tell me about the ancient Egyptians. There was also my experience with Isis and her fragrance, and according to Jake the only time I ever talked in my sleep was when I whispered, "I promise," in the most ghostly voice he had ever heard. There was also my recurring nightmare about falling through fire remembering what I had forgotten to remember.

"I shall assume that your story is true," I told her. "You may write to Akara, but I forbid you to use power over him. You may talk to him and write, but there is no way I will allow you to manipulate him or undermine his marriage. If your story is true, he will recognize his connection with you. If he does not resonate to being called Akara, you must release him."

Sheta Nut agreed, and the following day wrote a letter:

Dearest Akara, Lotus of my Heart, it is three thousand three hundred years since we were separated in Egypt, and I promised to find you in the future. That time is now, and my heart rejoices in the knowledge that I have found you. When I experience your ka, I know you are my beloved Akara.

I can now explain why I took final initiation. It is more powerful to take initiation and fail than not to take it at all. Isis encouraged me to go ahead with it because the gods see through the illusion of time, and she knew it would take me many rebirths for my karma to be cleared. She urged me to begin the clearing so that I would achieve Ptah Hotep at the appointed time.

This is why I allowed you to make love to me. I suspected I would not become a High Priestess in Egypt because of the karma casting in the Great Pyramid. I have wandered through the underworld for many centuries and have now found the last person I harmed in Atlantis. My karma has been cleared. I can now communicate with the gods.

Akara, you are trapped in a marriage in which you will neither grow nor express your potential. Why are you so afraid of dancing with the gods and fulfilling your destiny? We are destined to dance as one star. Akara, it is I, Sheta Nut, calling forth the light of your Aumakhua through the mists of your forgetfulness.

Please help Marilyn to awaken and be her friend, for she feels alone. To whom can she speak of her inner experiences? She fears a full awakening for the isolation it will bring her and the responsibility of an awakened one at this time.

Please help her to write the book, for it will have an impact upon the minds of mortals. Later it will be made into a moving picture for the purpose of entering mass consciousness. Humanity must change its attitude and walk more lightly on the Earth. Time runs out. She knows this, but feels alone with her knowledge. Her writing is the fulfilment of my promise to Isis.

Akara, I search for you in your dreams, and long to lead you through the Gateway to Heaven. Eternally Yours,

Sheta Nut signed it, and I mailed it with a covering letter. I felt so extremely embarrassed about the letter, I thought I would never be able to face him again. I consoled myself with the fact that he had agreed to be my Guide Detective, and at the end of my covering letter I wrote:

"This is my burning question: am I a nut or a Nut?"

Shortly after my encounter with Sheta Nut, Sharon cried in class when she shared that another malignant growth had been found in her breast. When Vivian guided her, she explained how in Atlantis she had been operated on with living animal parts. Sharon was psychic and often talked about past lives. I was so shaken by what she was sharing I wanted to run away and hide. After class Sharon approached me with tears in her eyes:

"You were one of the surgeons in Atlantis, weren't you?"

Without thinking, I nodded and burst into tears.

"How do you think it felt having animal parts attached to me?"

Filled with unimaginable shame, I couldn't even apologize.

"Darn it! I knew I'd met you for a purpose," she muttered, picking up her scattered belongings and leaving the house.

I stood shaking in the kitchen, and then dismissed it as mutual madness. Sheta Nut confirmed that after searching through the centuries for all of the people she had harmed in Atlantis, Sharon was the last one.

Seven

Predictions

Vivian went away for Christmas, leaving me alone in the house, and by the time she returned I had written about Shamballa.

"Come and open your present," she called to me.

I was sitting in the office tapping away on her electric typewriter, which is where I had spent most of Christmas. I looked over my shoulder at the large gift-wrapped package she was holding out to me. I joined her on the sofa and unwrapped her mysterious gift. What I pulled out of the box caused my heart to skip a beat. It was a rainbow robe.

"Do you like it?" she asked. "My mom and I made it for you."

"I'm speechless with delight!" I exclaimed, and told her about the rainbow robe Maitreya had given to me.

Then we went upstairs to play Dungeons and Dragons with Paul and Zach, Vivian's new boyfriend. She had given the Dungeons and Dragons game to Paul for Christmas, and it was now his favourite pastime.

Zach, clean-shaven and cerebral, was a writer. Later that evening, when we had eaten and were sitting in front of a roaring log fire, Vivian suggested that I share what I had written over Christmas. So I read my description of being taken to Shamballa.

"That's really fascinating," said Zach when I had finished. "The handrail on the rainbow bridge that leads to the garden of the Bodhisattva is an accurate description of the sutratma."

"What's that?" I asked.

"The sheaths of the incarnating Monad are strung like pearls upon a thread called esoterically the sutratma."

I asked him to explain.

"Monad is another name for Spirit," he told me, after a pause. "In order for Spirit to incarnate onto the physical plane, it has to be encased in a series of sheaths. Each sheath is attached to a thread. When we die, the thread which attaches our physical body to the astral or emotional body is broken. The astral body is attached by a thread to the mental body, the mental to the intuitional, the intuitional to the atmic, and the atmic to the monadic, and finally the Logos."

"What's the Logos?"

"That's another name for God or Divinity or whichever name you prefer."

"What's the difference between a Monad and a Logos?" I asked. "You just said the Monad is Spirit, so what is the Logos?"

"The Monad is the fire of Spirit, but the Logos is pure Spirit," he said, drawing a diagram. "The Monad is manifested Spirit and is symbolized by fire. The Logos is infinite. It's not contained, but in order for it to manifest, it has to be contained."

I told him his diagram looked like a set of Russian dolls, each doll containing a smaller doll, but the doll which contained all of them was not contained.

Zach nodded: "I like the analogy of the dolls."

"Do our chakras correspond to these different sheaths?" I asked.

"Yes, they do. Chakra is a Sanskrit word, and the chakras are what I write about,"[1] he told me. "You may also be interested to know that the song of the angels in the Sun, which you so accurately describe, is called Rik in Vedic texts."

"I didn't know that!" I exclaimed.

"Another interesting detail, which is not widely known, is that Maitreya meets candidates for initiation under a great old tree in his garden."

This last piece of information sent shivers up and down my spine. Was I a candidate for initiation?

The following week I travelled across Los Angeles for another session with my therapist. As I sat waiting outside his office, I wondered how he had responded to Sheta Nut's letter. I had sent it to him in an envelope marked: *Highly inflammable — keep away from naked flame.*

I sat on the couch and he sat in his usual seat with my material on his knee.

"I had a good belly laugh over your paper on the Origin of Sin. You're so playful," he told me. "Let me give you some feedback on Sheta Nut's letter. I resonate to being addressed as Akara. I think this has some validity, but I don't know how much. I want to respond to the guidance which enjoins me to help you to awaken. I want to be here for you during this lonely transition in your life, and I will help you with the book.

"I have been questioning whether or not to remain in my marriage since before Christmas, but I'm sure I shall stay in it at least until my daughter finishes school in a few years. In many ways I am more spiritually evolved than my wife, and she is inclined to be more aggressive than I am. I am facing my own shadow and the limitations of my marriage, but I cannot see myself leaving it. I haven't talked to my wife about any of this.

"I'm attracted to your earthy mysticism. It intrigues me," he admitted, "but I've never entered an emotional or sexual relationship with any of my clients. My track record is clean."

"I had three dreams about you over Christmas. Would you like to hear them?" I asked, knowing he probably wouldn't if he knew what they were about.

He nodded and held his pen poised over his note pad.

"My first dream was on Christmas Eve. We met by chance at a public meeting and afterwards sat talking. As we talked, I noticed your backpack leaning up against a wall. It was full of clothes, and I wondered if you had left home. You asked me if I thought our meeting was by chance. I left but returned later because I had forgotten something. I found you sitting on the toilet with your trousers around your ankles, and the door wide open. I was embarrassed, but you sat there laughing."

Judging by the pained expression on his face, he did not like the idea of being seen sitting on a toilet.

"In the second dream a woman approached me and told me you'd had a big upset with your wife over Christmas."

"I did," he said, interrupting me. "We were arguing and fighting from the Wednesday before Christmas."

I was amazed to hear this, especially as our last session had been on the Tuesday before Christmas.

"In the third dream I met you in a building, but you were upset and agitated. We walked together through a garden and all the time you were bursting to tell me something. I begged you not to tell me, but you persisted. Then we entered a tiny elevator, where we were pressed together.

"'I have to tell someone,' you insisted, as we ascended in the elevator."

When I repeated what he had told me in my dream, he turned a paler shade of white.

"Nobody knows about that," he stammered. "Not even my wife."

I was absolutely shattered that my dreams had been so accurate.

"I did beg you in the dream not to tell me," I pointed out.

He said he would re-read Sheta Nut's letter.

"I can't have any secrets from you," he told me after the session.

I could feel his discomfort as he told me he had to pick up his daughter from school and then said goodbye without hugging me. He probably saw me as the client from hell.

The following day I talked to my angel.

"I'm afraid to ask this question, but I need to know the answer. Sheta Nut says she and Akara share the same flame. She says they came from beyond the stars to help with the evolution of this planet, and have worked together in Lemuria, Atlantis and ancient Egypt where they were separated when she failed final initiation. Who is Sheta Nut, and was Akara a previous incarnation of my therapist? I do feel a deep connection with him, but it frightens me that I can enter his psyche so easily to discover his secrets."

"Firstly, I will answer your question about Sheta Nut. It is true that she is not a subpersonality. Neither is she an enlightened being, as you must realize. She is a karmic bleed-through; a strong and powerful personality from the last life you had in Egypt. She had a highly developed will, which enabled her to take final initiation and travel through the underworld."

"What's the underworld?"

"The underworld is what you would call the subconscious, but it also relates to the astral and lower mental realms, and the collective unconscious. She chose many difficult lives serving others to clear her karma with the people she had harmed. Between each physical life, she existed in the spiritual realms where she maintained her identity as Sheta Nut."

"So she achieved immortality. This is what every ancient Egyptian wanted more than anything else in the world."

"Yes, this is true. Usually personal identity fades after physical death, but she had been through a powerful process. She was able to travel in consciousness along the sutratma."

"Is that like walking across the rainbow bridge with the handrail of fine silvery thread strung with pearls?"

"You saw that image because you were crossing the bridge between dimensions. It is your destiny to integrate Sheta Nut into your personality. She has waited for you because she knows she will fulfil her promise to Isis through you. She is correct when she says Akara is a previous incarnation of your therapist."

"Why did she need me to get her across the rainbow bridge?" I asked, feeling confused. "You said she existed in the spiritual realms between each life."

"When you awakened in Shamballa, you had the opportunity of ascending to a higher dimension, where a soul can experience itself as spirit."

"Are you a soul?" I asked, wondering if an angel, a soul and the Self are identical.

"I have a soul, just as I have a Self."

"Does this mean you will lose your soul one day?" I asked, wondering if the soul really is immortal.

"Not until I am pure spirit."

"When will that happen?"

"When I am totally Self-conscious."

"What happens when you become a Logos?" I asked, remembering that the Logos is not contained.

"Then I simply AM."

"Are you the Angel of the Presence?"

"I am."

"Is the Angel of the Presence the Aumakhua described by Sheta Nut?"

"Yes."

"Do you live in the Sun?"

"Yes, I serve in the Sun."

"What does Sheta Nut mean when she says the Omega Man and I share the same flame?"

"It means you share the same Monad, which is the fire of Spirit. When the Logos differentiates to begin the process of incarnation, it acquires a sheath of fire which polarizes into female and male. This polarity is then acted out through the soul, which is androgynous, and through onto the physical plane, where you are either male or female. When you incarnate as a female, you leave your masculine counterpart in the spiritual realm, and when you incarnate as a male, you leave your feminine counterpart in the spiritual realm."

"If I left my masculine counterpart in the spiritual realm, why is Sheta Nut telling me that the Omega Man and I share the same flame?"

"It is very rare for twin flames to incarnate together. When they do, it is because they have planetary work to accomplish. Twin flames are destined to merge back into each other. Herein lies a mystery: when unity occurs, a trinity is formed. When individuated twin flames become Self-conscious, they embody a star. This is why Sheta Nut says you will dance together as one star. It is your destiny to so embody light you literally become a star. The Sun is a Self-conscious Monad who evolved through other star systems and is now embodying Light."

"If, as Maitreya says, Ananda is travelling from the Sun to awaken Gaia, does this mean we'll be burned?"

"Remember what I said about unity forming a trinity? If He came, you would be burned, but it is the third part of the trinity which is coming to awaken Gaia. When the two become one, their Love forms a third being."

"Like a man and a woman making love and creating a child?"

"A man and a woman making love and creating a child is a symbolic acting out of what happens on the monadic level. When love is sent as an embodiment, it is called an Incarnation of Love, which is the Christ."

"How many Christs are there?" I asked, remembering that Maitreya means Christ.

"Christ is not a name, but a state of being which Maitreya has attained. Christhood is the pearl of creation because it is a total manifestation of Divinity."

"When Maitreya said that Ananda is coming from the Sun to awaken Gaia, he meant Christ. Maybe that's what the Second Coming is all about," I said, remembering the predictions in the Bible. "So, Jesus Christ was Self-conscious Divinity interacting with its own creation. Is that how he was able to perform miracles?"

"He did not perform miracles. He was able to cooperate with the laws of nature, which are in service to the divine creative principle. This is a natural law; not miraculous at all."

"What will happen when Ananda awakens Gaia?" I asked.

"Just as we became conscious of each other after you visited Shamballa, Gaia will become conscious of existing in the fifth dimension. She will become a sacred planet, which will be celebrated throughout the universe."

I remembered what Azra had told us about the celebrations and how the starships were hovering around the Earth.

"Sheta Nut says my therapist can now leave his marriage. Is she right about his marriage?"

"He is completing a cycle and the marriage will be terminated, which will not be easy for him. It will be traumatic and painful, but by March he will be out of his marriage. It is important for you not to be involved in this process.

"Let the bond between you develop. Respect and love each other with detachment. You have important lessons to learn. Two of these lessons are constraint and detachment. The chains of attachment must be completely broken. Do not dissipate your energy by falling in love. You are already In Love. You will learn that the essence of love is not about using the other to satisfy your desires. This is approaching love with a new attitude.

"You have individual lessons to learn and must continue to lead separate lives until they have been learned. You have to write your book and heal yourself in the area of relationship. He will be completing a cycle and leaving his marriage. His angel sends forth an outpouring of love and light as he passes through this difficult time."

I did not know what to do with this information. March was only three months away. I could not see his marriage ending by then, but I sent him my angel's guidance.

A week later I was back in his office talking about the material I had sent him during the week.

"The prediction about the marriage ending in March brought a lot of anxiety. Perhaps it will be so, or perhaps there will be a symbolic death/rebirth wherein the marriage will be transformed. Overall, I see your channelling as very accurate and deep at times, and distorted by your personal desires at other times. There is a lot of inner upheaval. There may be major changes by March, but it is more likely to be a new way of being in the marriage rather than an ending. I could be wrong. Time will tell.

"My meditations show me that I am to remain your guide. My role in your life now is to facilitate your creative expression by helping to free the bonds of your personal history and by encouraging your writing.

"Even though these explorations in our sessions are leading me into vulnerable areas, and though I am in a crisis of growth in my personal life, I do deeply trust your love for me and your reverence for my inner world. I know you enter it as a sanctuary, and I totally trust our dedication to integrity and consciousness.

"Let us, as Sheta Nut suggests, walk lightly on the Earth."

He confided that in the last three months he had started to see auras, and had experienced radical changes in his life. I did not point out to him that it was three months since we had met.

"I have a problem," he said. "I wonder if you can pick it up."

At the end of that week, I decided to have an inner meeting with the Omega Man and Sheta Nut. I did this through active imagination in which I allowed the images and words to flow through me. I wanted to discover what my therapist's problem was. Sheta Nut gave me a clue by showing me a bottle of wine.

The following morning Vivian asked me to prune the rose bushes and trim the ivy growing up the walls of the house. I worked all morning in the garden listening to Mozart. She had gone to collect Paul and to deliver a letter to my therapist which described his problem as alcohol dependency.

At lunch time the telephone rang. It was my therapist.

"Hi," he said. "I'm in a restaurant. I've been drinking and I'm loaded. I'm reading what you wrote about Shamballa and it's blowing my mind. I can't read more than two pages at a time, and it's *so* funny. I think a lot of people are going to read the book you're writing."

He sounded really excited and was not as guarded as he usually was with me. I wondered if the alcohol had enabled him to drop his barriers.

"You're such a blessing in my life, and you're so open."

"You're a blessing in my life," I replied, trembling slightly.

We both laughed as I called us a mutual appreciation society. He said so many wonderful things to me I felt light-headed.

"I love you," he said with warmth and feeling.

"I love you too," I responded with tears in my eyes.

After we had said goodbye, I floated into the garden. Did he really mean it when he said he loved me, or was he merely carried away by the alcohol he had consumed? The feelings I had denied rushed through my body, as I allowed a full flowering of the longing deep within my heart, which was to hold him and hold him; a longing that felt older than time.

Although we saw each other every week, the feelings expressed in our telephone conversation were never referred to by either of us. He denied that he was an alcoholic, and was adamant that his marriage would not be over by March.

When I saw him at the end of February, he arrived late.

"I'm feeling terrible," he confessed. "My wife has locked me out of the house. She's hidden all the bank books and legal papers. She's really angry, and I don't even have any money."

"That's strange," I said. "I had a dream last night in which you were trying to tell me something, but I couldn't understand what you were saying. You had a glass in your hand and appeared to be drunk."

"I was telling you not to come today," he nodded. "I only had two glasses of wine last night with my dinner."

I wondered how many glasses he usually had with his dinner.

"Are you going to be all right?" I asked.

"Yes, I'll be fine," he assured me. "I can borrow money from a friend, and I have people I can stay with. You look radiant and magnetic today. I'd like to do some guided imagery with you in which you dialogue with the Queen of the Night."

I stretched out on the couch, and after dimming the lights he sat behind me with his note pad and pen. He guided me into a cave, but I soon found myself travelling down into a fiery pit.

"You have everything you need for your protection."

"Yes, I have my rainbow robe," I nodded. "I have to talk to the Great Dragon who lives in the Pit. I'm carrying a chalice which is filled with the tears I have cried for the Earth, and I'm showing it to the Dragon. I'm begging it not to destroy the kingdom, but it says if there aren't enough people ready to awaken, it has to break the etheric web and take Gaia up to the next level. If enough people raise their consciousness, the etheric web will break naturally without ripping."

He guided me back to the room and said he had to dash off to meet his daughter. As I walked out, he gave me a quick dismissive smile. Walking to the bus stop in a daze, I remembered that it was the end of February. My angel was right: he was out of his marriage by March.

Our sessions continued for another month, and then I found

myself in a black hole. We had been working on Sheta Nut's initiation in the Great Pyramid, and he had tried to prevent her from going through with it; even suggesting through imagery that she ask the High Priests to lift her out of the sarcophagus. I asked Sheta Nut if I had fallen into her black hole, and she agreed that I had. Feeling frustrated with her, I told her to go away.

"I can't go away. I projected myself into the future to keep my promise to Akara and Isis."

Since Sheta Nut's appearance before Christmas I was constantly aware of her presence in my psyche, which upset my subpersonalities. Clara, my Critic, and Frank, my Pragmatist, had me polishing Vivian's furniture in a frantic attempt to ground me and protect me from Sheta Nut. Their efforts were in vain. Having located me, she had no intention of leaving. I was depressed and totally unable to climb out of the black hole. My classmates tried to help by throwing me a rainbow rope in imagery, but it did not work.

Everyone noticed how miserable I had become, especially as I was usually the class clown. Finally Vivian decided to work with me in front of the class.

"This exercise is very good for helping us to develop intuition, as well as learning to develop true humility," she told the class. Then she turned to me: "I'd like you to tell us about the futility you feel when you are experiencing the black hole. We're going to listen to you in silence with our eyes closed, so that we can really identify with you. We are going to step into your shoes to see how it feels to be in a black hole. Then we will invoke images and insights, but our goal is to understand more clearly what your needs are."

"When I'm in the black hole I feel hopeless," I explained. "It's as if I've been wandering through a desert without hope or nourishment for centuries. I'd prefer to fade out of existence than continue like this."

All the people in the class mirrored back to me how I was feeling. Some of them said I needed to forgive myself. Shakura suggested growing a garden in the desert. Others said I needed to love myself, but I knew that already. When Vivian asked if I wanted to add anything, I told the class about Sheta Nut.

"How can we help you?" she asked.

"It's easier when I accept what Sheta Nut is telling me."

"Three thousand three hundred years is a long time to pay for a mistake," Eleanor pointed out.

I explained that Sheta Nut had decided to speed up her karma by finding and serving all the people she had harmed in previous lives.

"When you deny your own truth, you are denying yourself," Vivian pointed out.

"When I deny my truth I feel more pain," I agreed. "On the one hand is the denial and on the other hand my intense feelings about what happened in Egypt."

"My feeling is that you need to relive that life," Danny told me. "You need to complete it through regression or tools from Psychosynthesis. You obviously lied to the High Priests about breaking your vow and then, instead of asking Isis for forgiveness, you chose to plunge. You have paid off your karma, you've served your three-thousand-three-hundred-year-old sentence, but it still has a hold on you. Somehow with your will and conscious choice, you need to re-experience it."

Vivian agreed: "Through reliving it the way you wished it had been, you could release yourself."

"If I could relive it, I would not go through with it because the person who caused me to break my vow loved me deeply and didn't want to lose me."

"What's perking for me is that we are using this higher example of humility," said Meara, "and the challenge right now is to be humble enough to be true to yourself."

"At what point did you give up the truth of yourself?"

"When we made love. I knew I was going to go through with the initiation. I even suspected I would die, and I wanted to take a part of him with me."

"Tell Isis that you are not going to take this initiation."

"Isis is still telling me to go through with it."

Vivian asked who Isis serves.

"Isis serves God," I replied. "Isis says we will not individuate if Akara and I remain together. We have to separate because we're too enmeshed with each other. But we were happy together, we fulfilled each other's needs, and then we were torn apart."

I explained how Sheta Nut had stuffed her feelings.

"She refused to let herself feel when she saw him standing beside the Nile," I cried.

"What decision did she make which was not consistent with her own needs?" Vivian asked.

"Sheta Nut ignored her feelings."

"Which part of Sheta Nut was pulled back to Akara?"

"Her heart. Her mind was telling her to go, but her heart wanted her to stay with him. He was listening to his heart, but later he shut down to avoid feeling his pain."

"What were the consequences of her not listening to her heart?"

"She was separated from Akara, and now that she's found him he's shut down his heart to her," I said, with more tears.

"As you look at Sheta Nut and Akara, and see how you've been developing your heart and he's been shutting his down, what do you think it's going to take for the two of them to get together again after their individuation?" Vivian asked me.

Not knowing the answer to this question, I burst into tears.

"I love you, but I *have* to take this initiation," I sobbed, as if Akara was sitting in front of me.

Vivian asked how he was responding.

"He's crying and begging me not to go through with it. He knows I'm going to die," I cried, identifying with Sheta Nut.

"What does your heart want?"

"It wants to stay with him, of course. I'm convinced that both our problems go back to this fatal event."

Suddenly Sheta Nut spoke: "Isis was my personal deity. I embodied her when I danced, and I trusted her when she told me to go through with final initiation."

Vivian asked me to forgive Sheta Nut, pointing out that she was doing the best she could at the time. "Tell her what you would have preferred."

I told Sheta Nut either to stay with Akara or not to break her vow of celibacy.

"Give her permission to follow her heart," Vivian whispered.

"She did follow her heart," Meara pointed out. "She made love with Akara."

"Yes, but she didn't stay with him."

"Stay with him," I begged Sheta Nut. "Don't put yourself in a stupid coffin. Follow your heart and his heart. Stay with him. It feels hopeless because she's already done it."

"Imagine that Sheta Nut is telling Akara she's going to stay with him," Vivian encouraged me. "She is at peace because she has chosen the way of her heart. Imagine his response."

I could see how relieved Akara was.

"Everything would have been different if Sheta Nut had chosen not to go through with the initiation. She and Akara would have remained together in Egypt, and she would have given birth to his baby."

At this point I burst into tears again.

"Don't you think Sheta Nut has suffered long enough?" Vivian asked. "Can you forgive her?"

I told her I was more than willing to forgive Sheta Nut, but she refused to go away until Akara recognized her.

"From what you know about love and relationship, what will happen if there's truth in Sheta Nut and Akara's connection?"

"They will eventually be together again."

"What has Sheta Nut forgotten in her persistence?"

"There's plenty of time."

"Would you be willing to give Akara the time he needs?"

I nodded.

Vivian encouraged me to love and release Sheta Nut.

"I'm loving and releasing you, Sheta Nut," I repeated several times. "But she's still here."

"That's O.K. You're not trying to get rid of her. You're releasing her from her death sentence. Hold her in your arms and comfort her. You can release Akara too. Give him the freedom to recognize Sheta Nut in his own time. Make it a Ceremony of Release.

"I release you, Sheta Nut, from your terrible feelings of grief, shame and regret. I give you my heart, my feelings, my tears. I know you have not been able to cry," I said, crying uncontrollably.

"Now I absolve you and bring you back home," Vivian added.

I could see how relieved Sheta Nut was that I believed her story, but she also wanted Akara to believe it.

"What separated her from Akara was her denial of herself."

"When she pushes him, he moves further away from her because in Egypt she was using her will against him," I said with sudden insight. "He hardens his heart when she pushes him with her will."

"When she comes home to you and feels your love and forgiveness on a daily basis, she will know that you love and accept her," Vivian pointed out.

I knew then that I had to stop telling her to go away. Instead I needed to invite Sheta Nut into my heart. I would cry for her whenever I felt her grief. My tears convinced me that her story must be true, otherwise I would not have such an emotional reaction.

"You have room in your heart for Sheta Nut," said Vivian. "She can only reach Akara through your heart. Speak from the wisdom of your heart to Akara, as he is now."

"I now have Sheta Nut in my heart," I said to an imaginary Akara. "I feel her love for you, and pray that you will stop hardening your heart, and acknowledge the connection. Sheta Nut wants you to know that death is an illusion. Life and love are eternal."

Vivian asked me to connect with my soul and to imagine that the group was surrounding me with love.

"Own your truth," she emphasized. "Let it soak into your cells. Be willing to hold on to your truth even if other people think you are crazy; even if Akara thinks you're crazy. Make a deep commitment to honour your truth. When you're ready, open your eyes and look at each one of us, and tell us you're going to maintain your integrity."

After I had spoken to each member of the group, they gave me feedback.

"I trust you and believe you," said Danny.

"I feel cleansed," Sharon sighed.

"The synchronicity of the work is unbelievable," Danny added. "Today's attitude was humility and in essence there was a part of you not acting out of true humility at that time. You chose to go through with initiation, not really acknowledging your needs. It was false pride, and Egypt collapsed because of its false pride."

"I want to thank you for helping me to own *my* truth, which I often deny," said Shakura. "I turn off my intuition. When we began this exercise and Vivian asked us to identify with you, I found myself inside a pyramid. At first there was a light and then it was dark. I told myself I was a really bad person because I was supposed to be putting energy into helping you, and here I was going off on my own trip, but that pyramid would not go away."

"It was Sheta Nut's pyramid."

"I was dumping on myself as usual," Shakura scolded herself.

"We need to own our truth, so that we don't deny other people's truth," Vivian pointed out. "This is the sin of lying. It denies to others the experience of what they know."

"I feel I can really trust you now," said Sharon.

"Sharon understands because she has past-life recall," I told the class.

"None of us are in this group by accident," Meara pointed out. "There wasn't one person in the room who did not vibrate to what you were sharing. The truth is the truth."

"This is what I'm going through with my practice," Shakura shared. "I can't lie any more. As a medical doctor I have to prescribe drugs, but I'd prefer to give my patients holistic remedies."

"It's Satyagraha," I agreed. "How do we live our soul truth?"

Then Danny had an insight: "You fulfilled your promise to Akara. Your promise was to find him and you did."

I nodded.

"You're free. You've fulfilled your part of the bargain," he pointed out. "The rest is up to him."

Both Meara and Shakura were wondering why Isis had asked Sheta Nut to take an initiation she was obviously not ready for. I agreed that I needed to dialogue with Isis, but already the class had run an hour over time.

"When Vivian asked who Isis serves, I wanted to ask who the Grail serves," said Danny thoughtfully. "Isis symbolized your soul, and now you live at a time when the spiritual force has turned male. Now you can really serve Isis, who serves the planetary goddess."

"Maybe that's exactly what Isis wanted," Meara agreed. "She wanted to balance the polarity, and she couldn't do that with Akara having such a strong pull on you."

"From what I understand, she was looking forward to a time when the world would need feminine energy," I explained. "She projected Sheta Nut into the future."

"You hung onto Isis through three thousand years of male shit," Meara congratulated me. "And here you are at a place and time when Isis can plug back in. You have her intact and are ready to do the work. Now the planet is ready. You didn't fail at all."

"But Sheta Nut needed to come back to your heart," Vivian pointed out. "That was the split in consciousness."

"In Egypt he was the one with the feelings," I explained. "Sheta Nut was the mental one, but now he's mental and I'm the one with the feelings."

"That's a good example of karma," Danny told me. "My gut tells me that now you're integrating Sheta Nut, he's going to get in touch with his feelings. He won't be able to help himself."

Meara agreed: "Yes, he has also been affected by the work you've just done. Now he has his own work to do."

"What a story! What a teaching!" Danny exclaimed.

"Yes, I know I have to include it in my book," I nodded.

"This is transpersonal counselling," Vivian told us. "Can you imagine a traditionally trained psychotherapist working with this?"

"I would be treated as delusional," I laughed.

"That's why it's important for us to develop an understanding of transpersonal connections through people like you," Vivian told me.

"This is initiatory work," Meara commented.

"It's old work for which we need a new technology," Vivian agreed.

"It's not appropriate to say this is from your childhood," Danny pointed out. "The richness of this experience comes from another lifetime."

"I knew all along that dealing with your childhood wasn't relevant," said Sharon. "I kept on asking you what you had come here to do. I couldn't understand why you didn't get in touch with your purpose. You have to believe and love and bring it all together. You are a prototype for this type of work. I see you doing an awful lot of initiating."

"People spend years in psychoanalysis picking at the same wound, but they never get down to the core issue," Meara agreed. "They just learn to cope."

"This lifetime is a symbol from the past," said Danny.

"The Age of Aquarius stands for the unveiling of what has been hidden," Sharon pointed out.

"The unveiling of Isis!" Shakura exclaimed, and on that note the class ended.

1 *The Chakras and Esoteric Healing*, Zachary Landsdown. Published by Samuel Weiser.

Eight

Isis

It was time to go into the mountains with Sheta Nut to find Isis. We climbed out of the smog in silence. I had many questions to ask, and was determined to find her. The mountains were steep and shrouded in mist, and we did not know if we were going in the right direction. It took a great deal of energy and effort to keep going up, as it always does when one is attempting to climb out of a depression. Then the smog cleared and far off in the distance, on a mountain top, we saw a temple shimmering with an inner radiance. We wondered if it was the Isis temple or merely a mirage, but climbed steadily towards it until sunset, when it became a shining beacon of light that we both longed to reach.

Immediately ahead of us was a long flight of steps cut into the side of the mountain. On the top step we turned and saw Los Angeles spearing the smog far below us. As I suspected, the steps led directly to the temple, which was translucent, with elegant soaring columns. We entered through an archway with a naked statue standing either side of it, each gazing longingly at the other across the gap which separated them. The wide entrance hall beyond the archway was encircled by perfectly formed statues. Although of human form, they carried the power of the gods. Across the hall a large jewelled door swung open, and we found ourselves entering an enormous temple ablaze with light and filled with a divine fragrance. At the far end, seated upon a crystal throne, was Isis who watched as we approached. The temple had an open roof, through which the light of the Moon and stars was reflected in the prismed crystal walls.

Seven steps led up to the throne where Isis sat waiting. She stood to embrace us, and said we were expected.

"How did you know we were coming?" I asked.

"The gods know everything," Sheta Nut whispered in embarrassment.

Isis smiled: "You have questions."

"Yes, I want to know why you told Sheta Nut to take final initiation when she obviously was not ready for it."

"I saw her potential."

"Her potential was never expressed," I pointed out. "She died."

"She doesn't look dead to me," said Isis, glancing at Sheta Nut.

"She spent three thousand three hundred years searching for Akara, who is now refusing to recognize her, and I have neither married nor got it together professionally. All I can do is dream the future and remember past-lives."

"Is that ALL you can do?" Isis asked, with a playful smile. "Do you think final initiation has anything to do with your psychic gifts? Sheta Nut took final initiation for a future time, which is now. She took it for herself and for you, and for a time when the world would be starved of feminine energy."

As we stood listening to Isis, a beautiful goddess approached us. She had long black hair and an olive skin, and wore a white pleated gown and a double-feathered crown on her head.

"I am Maat," she announced. "I am the Goddess of Truth. It was I who weighed your heart against the feather of truth. The scales did not balance." She held out the scales for Sheta Nut to see. "You had lied and were not worthy of the name Ptah Hotep."

"When you took final initiation, it brought up everything in you which was untrue," said Isis to Sheta Nut. "It tested your strengths and weaknesses. I knew you were not ready to become a High Priestess, and indeed it was not my intention for you to be one in Egypt. You had much karma to work through, especially from Atlantis, where you abused your power. I urged you to begin the karma clearing. Your own arrogance and burning ambition would do the rest, but it was not this which caused your downfall. It was your attachment to Akara, which you were not even aware of. Consumed by your desire for final initiation, you failed to perceive the power of your love for Akara. Unwilling to work on your sexuality or your emotions, you developed your psychic abilities and your fearlessness. In this life you have to work on your sexuality and your emotions, and so does Akara. Sheta Nut, you did not fail. You agreed to clear your karma by seeking and serving all the people you had harmed. This you have done. I had work for you to do in the future. I needed you to embody me when the

Earth would need my feminine energy. That time is now. I am the Mother Goddess, and the goddess of compassion and writing."

"I didn't know you were the goddess of writing," I interrupted.

"I taught the children through my writing, and now I ask you to teach the children through your writing," she said, turning to me. "Sheta Nut can only complete this task through you, but it will make her immortal. Then she will be able to dance with the gods."

"This is what I wanted then, but now my only desire is to be absolved of my sins," said Sheta Nut. "I am ashamed of the way I played with Akara's feelings. After my death, I watched him degenerate into an alcoholic. If I hadn't broken my vow of celibacy, I would have become a High Priestess."

"You were ruthless and ambitious," Isis pointed out. "You would have abused your power, the way you did in Atlantis, and Akara would have followed you, the way he always did. I could not allow you to repeat that mistake. You had experienced neither grief nor loss. Without these experiences to open your heart and bring you humility and compassion you would have continued to cause harm. You needed these qualities for your evolution and growth. You could never have embodied me without them."

"I broke Akara's heart and cannot forgive myself. I grieve for him, for his suffering, his inner struggles and his shame."

"Akara helped you to develop compassion," I reminded her.

"The only way I could redeem myself was to keep my promise to him and to you, Isis. I watched him shut down his heart to me, as he is doing now, and I wonder if my punishment will ever end. Must I travel for eternity filled with this grief?" Sheta Nut pleaded.

"That is your choice," Isis replied, and then spoke to me: "You must appreciate what a great opportunity you are given through Sheta Nut. Not many women are asked to enter the underworld, and those who are asked rarely survive or complete the process."

"But Vivian didn't take final initiation, and she's more successful than I am," I argued.

"It depends upon what you mean by success. Your destiny is to become a god, but this cannot happen until you are fully conscious on all levels of your being. To attain full consciousness, you must explore all aspects and areas of the psyche; you must enter the unconscious to make it conscious. All of the gods you see in my temple were once human like you," Isis explained, pointing to the figures half hidden in the alcoves.

"The point of life is to know you are a god in human form. The Great One created everything, and humanity is Divinity in disguise. What would be the point of creating a universe without having the intention of dancing and playing in it? The point of life is to become conscious of playing with creation; not to be attached to it, but to play with it. Imagine the reality you could create if you were totally conscious. If you could do that, wouldn't it be worth going into the underworld for?"

"I want to be conscious more than anything else in the world, but how can I become conscious when there is so much I'm still puzzled about?"

"I am here to answer your questions," Isis reminded me.

"Sheta Nut said she heard me crying in the underworld, but that doesn't make any sense," I complained. "How could she hear me crying three thousand three hundred years before I was born?"

"Very easily. Time is not linear. It is spherical. When you cried from the bottom of your heart, you broke through the time barrier and entered another reality."

I had recently heard of the research of Valerie Hunt who discovered that traumatized children are psychic. In extreme trauma, a child opens up to the Higher Self and a multi-dimensional reality.

"If your childhood had not been traumatic, Sheta Nut could not have found you. Find the child within you who called Sheta Nut from out of the past, for she holds the key to the future. Trauma shakes up the chakras and wakes you up, like an alarm clock. Life's purpose is consciousness; not safety or security or getting what you think you want. Everything in life is merely an outer reflection of an inner reality."

"If life is an outer reflection of an inner reality, does that mean nothing is real?" I asked.

"That depends upon what you mean by real. Humans rarely see what is real. Most people are asleep and miss the point of life. They are blind to what is real through being lost in their illusions. To speak your name and describe you as a female is only part of the truth. In other lives you had different names; you were sometimes a male. You were Sheta Nut, and now cannot release that identity until resolution is reached with Akara, but the Akara you knew and loved has long since died. Akara's soul, of course, has never died and somewhere deep within his own unconscious world he remembers what happened in Egypt. It certainly shook up his astral body, which is still traumatized. An unresolved drama pursues you through the centuries. It is no longer a reality, but its effects are still experienced as energy in this life. So, what is real? Is it a name, possessions, a title or energy?"

Isis paused briefly.

"Look at how people lose themselves in what they are destined to leave behind when they die. If they spent their lives investing in joy, love, compassion and freedom, they could take these qualities with them, for energy is eternal, but possessions and titles are not."

"That makes sense," I nodded. "But what I can't understand is why Sheta Nut hasn't reached resolution with Akara between lifetimes. Surely they've met in other dimensions since they both died in Egypt. Why is it still an issue between them?"

"What is created in the physical realm must be resolved in the physical realm," Isis explained. "That's why souls repeatedly return to the third dimension to work through their karma. Both Sheta Nut and Akara will carry what happened in Egypt until it is resolved between them on the physical plane. He still carries anger and resentment, but because it is unconscious he does not know where these feelings stem from. Every time he incarnates in a male body, he re-experiences his betrayal by Sheta Nut. He cannot find peace with any of the women he becomes intimately involved with because he is carrying unresolved issues with Sheta Nut. He resists her because at an unconscious level he fears being in touch with the feelings which tore him apart after her death.

"He was hurt when he lost control of his emotions, which caused him to be sexual with Sheta Nut. He is now terrified of repeating the same scenario, especially as the situation is similar. As your therapist, he cannot risk losing his integrity, which is a priority in this life because of what happened in Egypt. To admit to having feelings for you, even to himself, is too dangerous, but the real danger lies buried deep within his unconscious. He felt responsible for Sheta Nut's death. The way he survived was to blame her and harden his heart. Being totally unable to release her, he was then disillusioned when she lied to the High Priests."

"But I love him beyond measure," Sheta Nut cried. "My love has pursued him through the centuries, and now I stand before him waiting for him to open his heart to me. I want him to know how much I have longed for him. I beg to be absolved of my sins."

"Sin is simply missing the mark. You wanted final initiation and Akara, and I was counting on your indecision."

"I wonder if this is why I'm indecisive," I muttered, and then noticed a solitary figure entering the temple. It was Akara, whom Sheta Nut ran to embrace.

"Akara, I love you to the heights and depths of my being. You are the Lotus of my Heart. I re-enact the night time was stolen, and I remember how I played with your feelings by allowing you in, and then by locking you out. It has been my karma to be locked out for many lifetimes, and to have you locking me out in this one. I have prayed to the gods to grant me our last night together, so that I can choose to remain with you and bear our child, but it is not even within the power of the gods to give me back the one night which changed our destinies."

As I listened to Sheta Nut, I was totally able to identify with her feelings. Sometimes when we were sitting opposite each other in his office, my longing to hold him was so compelling I could not bear it. I felt so close to him and yet so far. The two or three feet between us were as wide as an abyss. I could not cross the gap that separated us. When he hugged me, I could not allow myself to feel because if I did, I would risk falling apart. At other times my joy at finding him was boundless. Then I longed to celebrate our reunion and my ecstatic certainty that death is an illusion.

His face was expressionless.

"After you promised to find me in the future, and then locked me out, I wandered for the rest of the night along the banks of the Nile. I was shocked that you were still going through with final initiation after you had broken your vow of celibacy. I knew it meant certain death. I made love to you to save you; not to kill you. I watched when you were taken at dawn in the Solar Barge, and saw you looking at me. I was crazy with grief. We had not been separated since we came to this planet from beyond the stars. How could you lie to the High Priests about carrying my seed inside you?

"I knew you would not survive, and if you were condemned to the Duat we would never again find each other. The news of your death and disgrace spread through Egypt like wildfire. You had already won disfavour with the Amun priesthood through your close association with Akhenaten. Everyone knew you had broken your vow of celibacy with me. I was sick with shame, and began to drink heavily. My life was a living death, with guilt pursuing me through my sleepless nights like a waking nightmare.

"Akhenaten knew his days were numbered. The Amun priesthood were plotting to overthrow him, and rumours were spreading across Egypt and beyond that he was deranged and blind through staring at the Sun, which was untrue. I stayed with him at the Horizon of the Sun Disk, where I drank all night in an attempt to drown my sorrows. Merirye informed me that the guards at the Temple of the Sun had been instructed by the Priests of Amun-Ra to give me access to the temple complex to guarantee your death in the Great Pyramid. Then I understood why it had been so easy for me to bribe them that night.

"Merirye said Egypt was not ready for Akhenaten's teachings. He said there would be a time in the future when the world would be ready and he, Merirye, High Priest of the Aten, would help to bring these teachings to the world, which we would recognize through his use of the solar disk. When this happened, we would be reunited, and would teach the Inner Way. When Akhenaten fell into a coma, I knew he had been poisoned by the Amun priesthood who were in a hurry to reinstate the cult of Amun-Ra.

"Young Prince Tutankhamun was married to one of Akhenaten's daughters and set up as Pharaoh at Thebes, but he too died mysteriously after a ten-year reign. The priest Ay married his widow and ruled Egypt, even though he was not of the royal blood-line. The Horizon of the Sun Disk was desecrated. The gardens planted by Akhenaten shrivelled up and died. There was no more joy for me in Egypt, although I continued to be a musician priest for the remainder of that life. I took pleasure with other women, but I could never free myself of shame. To survive, I cursed your name and attempted to cut you out of my heart. I promised that when you found me in the future, I would not recognize you. Then you could be as tormented as I was after your death."

There was absolute silence in the temple.

"I have been tormented for more than three thousand years," said Sheta Nut. "Is that long enough for you? I have been through many lifetimes in which all vanity, deceit and pride were knocked out of me. I now have a heart which cannot save itself from feeling. I have promised never to harden my heart again. Please forgive me, Akara."

He did not look at her directly, and it was obvious to all of us that he was having a deep inner struggle.

"I have forgotten how to feel," he confessed. "It is difficult for me to reconnect with you. I am convinced that all of my deepest problems originate with you and how betrayed I felt by you."

"Please forgive her," I pleaded. "Three thousand three hundred years is a long time to bear a grudge. She will never hurt you again, and when you forgive her she will be integrated into me. I would never do anything with you that you would regret afterwards."

As he looked from me to Sheta Nut, his conflict was obvious.

He and Sheta Nut faced each other, the silence pregnant between them.

"I have to pick up my daughter," he said, as he turned and left.

I was crying when I heard the violins.

"It's the orchestra," Isis explained. "We're having a dance."

"I have a rejection pattern because my father locked me out on the fire escape," I cried.

"She's always crying," Sheta Nut told Isis with contempt.

"I don't know what you're being so contemptuous about," I told her indignantly. "I am what you were destined to become."

Then I had a thought:

"My father locked me out on the fire escape. Sheta Nut died when she tried to escape from the fire. The fire was her love for Akara, but she had played with his feelings by letting him in and locking him out, like my father who locked me out on the fire escape." I was pleased with my new insight. I looked at Isis and asked if this was what she meant when she said life was an outer reflection of an inner reality.

Isis nodded, adding that my father had acted out an unconscious inner reality by locking me out on the fire escape.

"This is what happened when the Rescue Rooter arrived to unblock the drains just as I was telling you my story," Sheta Nut added.

"When I was a child, we lived opposite a department store called Selfridges, but all I could see through our window was the word 'Self'," I mused. "I knew it was somehow symbolic."

"Look around you at what is in your life because what is is there to wake you up," Isis nodded.

"This explains the mysterious bottle of Egyptian wine Vivian and I received recently," I laughed. "We can't figure out where it came from."

"Now I will explain why Sheta Nut and Akara had to be separated. When the Great One creates a universe, the first embodiment is the Monad, which splits into a feminine and masculine deity. This is because the physical universe functions on duality, like electricity, which has a negative and a positive pole. In order for movement to occur, something has to be moving towards or away from something else. This is the divine dance of opposites. The Monad embodies a star, and when particles of the star solidify they become planets revolving in orbit around a central Sun. The Great One can choose to remain a Monad or seek further embodiment in a soul body. At the soul level Monads form a soul group and en masse seek incarnation on a planet. The evolution of a planet and the beings who incarnate on that planetary body are interdependent. They evolve through cooperating with each other.

"When you volunteered to work with this particular planetary deity, you travelled with your soul group to help Gaia fulfil her purpose. You came as fifth-dimensional beings because of the level you had already attained in another star system. When Gaia sounds a new note, she will become a sacred planet, and all fifth-dimensional beings are called to assist her into the fifth dimension with as little upheaval as possible. The more souls there are to accommpany her, the less traumatic it will be."

I remembered Paul mentioning the fifth level in his Dungeons and Dragons game. When one moves up to the fifth level, one becomes a Magic User and a Shapeshifter.

"When Akara and Sheta Nut arrived here before Lemuria, they were already fifth-dimensional beings. They worked with Earth energies and helped to balance the masculine/ feminine polarity. They worked well together, but they were not developing as individuals. Sheta Nut was the strong one. Whatever she did, Akara followed. This continued until their last life together in Egypt. She made the decisions, which he helped her to implement until she decided to do something he could not support. Then he sabotaged her plans because they conflicted with his own needs. This was the first time he had ever asserted himself with Sheta Nut, whom he leaned on. They were like siamese twins: inseparable and always choosing to incarnate together. They had developed as a team, not as individuals. Their separation was the first painful step towards individuation, and they both resented it. The process is not complete yet. He is still looking for someone to lean on, and you are seeking your reflection in others, needing to be loved and validated to feel good about yourself. He must stand on his own two feet, and you must learn to love and value yourself."

"I read a book recently which said that twin flames can create karma with each other, and can feel a tremendous amount of injustice and resentment," I told Isis. "I sense a very deep resistance that is not passive, but active. It's not that he does not recognize me; he refuses to. The book said that love between twin flames can be destroyed through an unwillingness to forgive. I am afraid he will never forgive Sheta Nut. It's as if he is refusing to let love blossom."

Sheta Nut nodded in agreement.

"Leave him alone to find his own truth," Isis told both of us. "Release him, continue with your own growth, and above all else learn to love yourself."

"I don't understand how we are going up into the fifth dimension without dying. Surely if we leave the third dimension, our bodies will die. How can we ascend without dying?" I asked.

"Where are you now?" Isis asked me.

"I'm here talking to you."

"Where else are you?"

"I'm sitting in Vivian's office recording our conversation."

"There you are," she laughed. "You are in the fifth dimension with me and you are also in the third dimension. Which one is the dream?"

"Well, anyone sitting with me in Vivian's office right now would say you are the dream."

"If you died now, where would you be?"

"With you."

"Which one is the dream?"

"The third dimension," I had to admit.

"Where else are you?"

Closing my eyes, I found myself in several places:

"I'm an angel in the Sun and I'm in Shamballa and a place I

don't recognize, but it sounds like Bach's music. I'm all over the place."

"Yes, you are everywhere," Isis agreed.

"But I still don't understand how we can ascend without dying."

"The part of you that is talking to me, which is in the fifth dimension, is going to descend into the third dimension and transform it. Matter is going to be taken up into the fifth dimension, and will therefore still exist, but on a higher octave. Everyone will wake up without dying."

"Are you saying that normally we die when we wake up?"

"The only thing you have to concern yourself with right now is the Journey."

"But I don't know where Gaia's Castle is."

"Los Angeles used to be called the Queen of the Angels. Do you know who the Queen of the Angels is?"

I shook my head.

"Gaia is the Queen of the Angels."

"It was named after Gaia!" I exclaimed.

"If you really want to know where Gaia's Castle is, ask a child. Any child will tell you."

I was amazed to hear this and decided I would ask Paul.

"Stop regretting your decision to take final initiation," Isis told Sheta Nut. "You were going to die within a year. It was your fate. I gave you the chance to die in style and begin the process of awakening. If you had stayed with Akara and given birth, you would have died and entered oblivion. Do you remember what I told you on the tower?"

Sheta Nut shook her head.

"When the sign of the Water Bearer dawns, you will come again, my Little One, and teach the Inner Way, for you will be an Awakened One because of your initiation in the Great Pyramid."

Then she looked towards the door of the temple. To my great joy, Maitreya was walking towards us. He embraced Isis and gave me one of his wonderful hugs, which left me tingling all over.

The orchestra had moved into the main part of the temple and was playing Baroque music, to which the gods danced. Isis led Maitreya down the steps and danced around the temple with him. Sheta Nut and I watched as they danced together, rhythmically blending and complementing each other.

After he had danced with Isis, he danced with me, and as we glided around the temple I was convinced I had ascended into heaven. His movements were so graceful and flowing, my feet hardly touched the ground.

"I had no idea you danced so well," I told him.

"Didn't you know?" he laughed. "I am the Lord of the Dance."

After we had danced together, we walked outside and I asked why the two naked statues were gazing longingly at each other across the gap which separated them.

"They are not longing for each other," he explained. "They are longing for divine union, but they're looking for it in each other instead of within themselves."

I certainly identified with their longing.

Asking me if I would like to fly home, he took my hand and, to my great surprise, we flew down the mountain. It was exhilarating, with the wind in my hair and my rainbow robe billowing out around me like a parachute. We landed in the garden and sat together in my room. I told him briefly about my experiences since our last meeting.

"I am going to ask Paul about Gaia's Castle. Isis says all children know where it is. Why don't adults know?"

"Unless you become as little children, you cannot enter the Kingdom of Heaven," he reminded me. "And remember the promise of the rainbow."

"Yes, I'll remember the promise of the rainbow."

I fell asleep with the words ringing in my ears.

Nine

The Lost Valley

When I asked Paul about Gaia's Castle, he said it was in the Lost Valley, and immediately sat down with me at the kitchen table to explain exactly where it was.

"You need to journey north and then follow a river which flows down from the mountains. Go over these mountains, and the Lost Valley is on the other side," he said, drawing a map. "There are many dangers in the Lost Valley and you must use your silver cord as a lifeline, but beyond it you will find Gaia's Castle, which is also known as the Grail Castle."

When I asked if he had heard of the Great Dragon who lives beneath the Castle, Paul nodded and explained that I would have to travel down through the vortex.

"You have to travel down into the Sphere of Fire, but I must warn you that this is a very dangerous journey. There are many wicked beings around the vortex."

I asked him how I could protect myself, adding that I did not intend to kill or cause harm.

"You could take some magical spells with you," he suggested, looking through his book. "How about taking a Potion of Merging, which would enable you to merge with another being."

I nodded.

"And a Detect Magic spell, which can detect other magical spells. You could also have a Light spell."

"Yes, I'll need that. It will be dark under the Castle."

"Especially when you're in the dungeons. A Protection from Evil spell would protect you from any evil attacks. You should also take a shield. This particular shield is special because it reflects back whatever is sent your way, so if someone throws a weapon at you it simply bounces off the shield and hits them instead."

We both laughed at the thought of it.

"I also have a Detect Invisible spell, which will enable you to know if something invisible is coming towards you. I have a spell for opening locked doors and for locking doors behind you, which can't even be opened with a magical key. There are spells for curing critical wounds, and even a spell for overcoming fear. What about a Blessing spell? You can shower people with blessings when you have this one."

Paul was enjoying himself telling me about the many spells I could take with me on my journey to Gaia's Castle, and he did not for one minute doubt their effectiveness.

"You'll need a Fire Resistant spell in the Sphere of Fire. A Remove Curse spell will remove a curse put on you or anyone you are attempting to remove a curse from," he told me enthusiastically.

"With Clairvoyance you can see through the eyes of any other person or being. You don't want to raise the dead because that's a chaotic act, but you can take the spell of Reincarnation, which enables a dead person to incarnate in another body. To Commune enables you to ask questions of the greater powers, but you can only use this spell once. True Sight enables you to know the difference between reality and illusion, and a Clearing spell can penetrate undergrowth; even brambles. The Wishing spell is very powerful. It is the most powerful spell of all, but the wording has to be super careful. Think about the wording before you wish for anything. The Dancing spell will cause your victims to dance until they drop from exhaustion."

This spell really appealed to me.

"You have to take the Prismatic Wall," he insisted. "It's different from the other spells and can't even be removed by a Wishing spell. That's how powerful it is. All creatures or beings passing through the Prismatic Wall will be transformed by the magic, starting with the first colour they encounter. It extends to other dimensions and cannot be bypassed by interdimensional travel. The colour violet is always closest to the one who casts the spell because it purifies and protects."

"It sounds like a rainbow."

"Yes, it is like a rainbow," he agreed. "It has super protection. You must take it with you."

I nodded and asked him to tell me about the vortex.

"It's also called the Pit and it's deep beneath the dungeons of the

Castle. However, it's heavily guarded, and I don't know how you will gain access to it."

"I'll have the Seal of Shamballa," I reminded him.

"When you are in the area of the vortex, you will find yourself spinning. Let yourself spiral down through the vortex until you reach the Sphere of Fire. This is where you will find the Great Dragon."

I thanked Paul for his help and switched off the tape recorder, which had recorded our conversation.

The following day Vivian was reading to Paul in the garden. She was reading from his Dungeons and Dragons Master Book, and I decided to join them. The Sun was warm, and I felt lazy and relaxed after my lunch.

> *"Immortals: As characters approach the ultimate 36th level, they will become aware of powers mightier than they, powers beyond mortal ken. Once mortal themselves, these heroes of legend served the advancing of the multiverse, gaining powers and responsibilities beyond the realm of the living as their sphere of power. Their manoeuvrings create challenges and epic sagas to test the worth of mere mortals while furthering the Immortals' own mysterious goals."*[1]

"My God!" I shrieked. "Sheta Nut is an Immortal!"

"Who is Sheta Nut?" Paul asked.

"She has an ancient Egyptian priestess called Sheta Nut," said Vivian all matter of fact.

"She has a priestess from ancient Egypt!" Paul exclaimed. "Are you kidding?"

"She's in my book," I explained. "Of course, she's an Immortal. She projected herself into the future and has never been able to die."

"What is her Sphere of Power?" he asked.

"Let's look in the book," Vivian suggested, turning the pages.

> *"The Sphere of Energy is closely related to the element of fire. Its purpose is to create more energy, which is highly active,dynamic and excitable. Seeking to alter and transform, it consumes matter,*

slows time, and stimulates thought to release energy.

Temperamental by nature, energy is highly creative, able to channel magical energies and manifesting from the ether. The Sphere of Energy favours the magic user class, but is opposed to mind's efforts to control it and seeks to raise matter to its highest level despite the ravages of time."[2]

"That's amazing! A magic user is a fifth level being and that's what Sheta Nut is. What else does it say about Immortals?"

"An Immortal is a being who cannot die by earthly means. They do not need food, drink or air. They easily manipulate the elements and magical energies while remaining almost totally immune to their effects. An Immortal will not generally reveal himself (or herself) to mortals. Only candidates for future immortality may normally recognize an Immortal."[3]

"Wow!" exclaimed Paul, turning to me: "You must be a candidate."

"When attempting to change the course of history, an Immortal may use more active methods. The most common is the use of an agent. An agent may be given an Immortal Artifact or a purpose to accomplish and then left to his (or her) own means."[4]

"Find out what purpose she has to accomplish," Paul insisted.

"Sheta Nut is an Immortal in the Sphere of Energy, so that makes Marilyn a Paragon," said Vivian. "The book says a Paragon must create an entirely new magic item, its components being extremely rare and difficult to locate, including at least one impossible item, such as the footfall of a cat or the roar of a lion. The Paragon must be creative when acquiring the item."

I asked Vivian what she was according to the book.

"I think I'm an Epic Hero in the Sphere of Thought," she replied.

"The Epic Hero must quest for a major artifact from the Sphere of Thought. The Epic Hero must track down and bring about the defeat of an artifact in the Sphere of Entropy."[5]

"Yes, that's definitely what Psychosynthesis does," I pointed out. "It brings light and truth into a world where entropy has taken over. Maybe the artifact you have to track down and defeat is negativity, or limitation, or even faulty belief systems."

"The Epic Hero must train a successor and create a new legendary weapon," she said, and then added: "I'm doing that by training my students to practise and teach Psychosynthesis. My new legendary weapon is my book. It says the Epic Hero must live up to the heroic ideals of courage, steadfastness and dedication. He or she must complete an epic quest or perform a nearly impossible task, like building a castle in the air. I certainly build castles in the air with my guided imagery."

"I don't believe this," said Paul. "My mother is an Epic Hero and Marilyn has an Immortal."

Vivian flicked through the pages of the book.

"Listen to this:

"An Immortal sends an Omen of his (or her) impending arrival.[6]

"Your omen was the dream about this house six years ago and the Omega Man standing in the doorway of the Awakening Room."

"Yes, the dream about him was an omen," I agreed.

Now I knew there was nothing preventing me from continuing with my Journey. I knew where Gaia's Castle was and I was beginning to understand Sheta Nut's role in my life.

On Saturday morning I was hiding in the bathroom while Vivian ran around the house calling to Paul to help her. She was preparing for the garden party that afternoon. I was wondering why it bothered me when she used this tone of voice. Then I realized what it was. She was using her Mother subpersonality to get his attention, but it never worked. It merely pushed him further away from her. I remembered how my own mother had spoken to me like this, and how I retreated even further into my inner world. When the house was quiet, I walked into the kitchen.

Vivian was standing beside the sink watching Paul in the garden. He was leaping through the air with her saw, and resembled a knight preparing for a tournament. I commented on how graceful he looked.

"I love to watch him playing in his fantasy world," she told me. "He's supposed to be trimming the branches on the tree. It's going to take him for ever to tidy up the garden."

I had seen him in his fantasy world before. I had watched him dancing on his toes when he was supposed to be waxing Vivian's car. Paul was just thirteen and his voice was about to break.

The garden party was a grand affair. A long table with a white cloth and crystal glasses was set up under the tree. The guests brought gourmet food, and the champagne flowed like water. Bach's Brandenburg Concertos played in the background as we all chattered and became tipsy. I could not remember how many glasses of champagne I had drunk, but I was very unsteady on my feet. When everyone went inside to sing around the piano, blue jays flew down from the tree and stole what was left of the cake.

I was up early the next morning packing my backpack with music tapes, Vivian's old cassette player, Paul's spells and a map showing me how to reach the Lost Valley. As I was leaving I remembered to take the Seal of Shamballa with me.

When I arrived at the place indicated by Paul on his map, I found myself in a desolate area. To my left the ocean crashed against a rocky shore; to my right a river emptied itself out of the mountain range he had described to me.

I decided to follow the river back to its source in the hope that it would lead me to the Lost Valley. A narrow path, full of obstacles, wound its way up into the mountains. The river cascaded over boulders only a few inches away from where I scrambled over loose rocks on the narrow path, which in places disappeared altogether. I heard noises in the undergrowth, but only caught sight of a few hobgoblins. When they saw me, they ran away squealing with fright. After another hour of crawling and falling over rocks and boulders, I sat down for a rest. Hearing a sound behind me, I looked over my shoulder into the face of a hobgoblin who was gnarled like the bark of an ancient tree, with a long pointed nose and spindly fingers.

"Are you the Magic User who caught three dragons and the

Beholder?" the hobgoblin asked, obviously having plucked up the courage to approach me.

I felt embarrassed, remembering the Dungeons and Dragon game I had played with Paul, in which I captured all three dragons and the Beholder.

"It was only a game," I explained.

"It may only be a game to you, but it's real for us. You've no idea how relieved we are to be rid of the Beholder. You have become a legend in these parts."

Now I understood why the other hobgoblins had run away from me.

"We are all afraid of you. It's very rare for a female to catch three dragons and a Beholder all at once. I was hoping I would meet you."

"Perhaps you can help me. I'm looking for the Lost Valley and Gaia's Castle."

"You're almost there. The Lost Valley is on the other side of this mountain. When you've crossed the Valley, you will have only one more mountain to climb. Gaia's Castle is on top of it, but you won't get in."

"Why not?" I asked.

"Nobody ever does," he shrugged. "Once upon a time the Lost Valley was a magical, powerful place, where we cooperated with humans to activate the landscape temple, but now only dragons gather there. Can you tell me why there are so many dragons roaming around the Lost Valley?"

Remembering what Maitreya had told me about dragons symbolizing the kundalini energy at the base of our spines, I concluded that the dragons roaming the Lost Valley were parts of ourselves we had lost.

"It's probably because most of the people in the world have lost their dragons."

"Well, that explains the increase in dragons over the years," he nodded. "Lost dragons arrive every day, and they are all upset; some of them very angry. They create havoc."

"I expect they're lonely without their people."

"The older dragons are nearly always aggressive and violent. We have to be very careful not to upset them. The three dragons you caught were a real nuisance. The Red Dragon, in particular, had a nasty habit of stalking hobgoblins."

"When the older dragons were young, they probably lived in hope of being found by their children," I explained. "They must have waited and waited. Then they probably gave up and became aggressive."

The hobgoblin offered to take me to the top of the mountain, suggesting that I spend the night in a cave because after dark the monsters, beasts and dragons go out on the rampage.

At the top of the mountain we said goodbye, and as I climbed down the other side I looked for a cave to spend the night in. I found one just before the light failed. I lit a small fire and wrapped my rainbow robe around me. I was grateful for the spells Paul had given me, and took the spell for overcoming fear.

After a while I heard a sniffling sound. Cautiously I tiptoed to the back of the cave where I found a tiny dragon crouched in a dark corner. It was amazed to see me standing there and blinked in the light of my torch.

"I've lost my child," it cried. "Now I'm all alone and I don't know what to do or where to go."

"Come and sit with me beside the fire. We can keep each other company and, if you like, I can play some music."

"I love music," the little dragon sighed.

I was glad I had brought the music tapes and cassette player.

"My little boy, who is called Marlon, was too noisy," sobbed the dragon, snuggling up to me. "His father shouted so much at him, he became afraid and I was thrown out. Now I have nowhere to go. What am I supposed to do without my child? We were born together. I need Marlon and he needs me."

The following morning, when Marlon's dragon and I travelled down the mountain, my fame as a Magic User enabled us to travel in safety. We soon reached the Lost Valley, and found a group of young dragons playing beside a stream. They ran away when they saw me, but I called after them not to be afraid.

"She won't hurt you," Marlon's dragon reassured them. "I've just spent the night with her and she's very kind. She played music to me and let me sleep with her beside the fire."

The other dragons were obviously impressed.

"Marlon's dragon is lonely and afraid," I explained. "He's lost his little boy."

"He's not the only one. We've all lost our children and can't find them anywhere."

I asked them how they had lost their children, but they all talked at once. I suggested holding a meeting at which they could take it in turns to share what had happened to them.

"Then we'll have a dance."

"A dance!" exclaimed the dragons with whoops of delight.

"I was separated from my child when he was five," said the first dragon. "He wouldn't stop asking questions."

All the other dragons shook their heads sadly.

"My little girl was always laughing and singing," another dragon shared. "Her mother said it gave her a headache, so we were separated when she was four."

"My little boy was always looking up ladies' and little girls' skirts," said a third dragon. "He lost me when he was shamed."

"That's what happened to my child when his mother caught him playing Doctors and Nurses in the shed," another dragon confessed.

"I was thrown out when my little girl pulled her panties down for the boy next door. Her mother was so angry, it was curtains for me."

"I belonged to the boy next door. She was showing him what she had in exchange for him showing her what he had, but he never got to share his bits because I was thrown out."

"My little girl played with her brother's balls in bed at night," an older dragon confided. "It was fun, but when their mother found out, that was the end of me."

"Yes, I belonged to that little girl's brother, and I must admit, it was a most intriguing sensation. Why was their mother so upset? Adults are very strange."

All the other dragons nodded in agreement.

"They don't like noise, singing or dancing, having fun, asking questions, or anything related to certain parts of the body," they complained. "What's wrong with them? Why can't they enjoy themselves? Worse still, why won't they allow their children to enjoy themselves?"

"My child loved to daydream," a small dragon reminisced. "He imagined castles in the air, and running as free as the wind through meadows, but his teachers shouted so much at him, he lost me."

All the dragons became agitated at the mere mention of the word 'teachers', and I did not dare tell them I had been a teacher myself, but I never shouted at children for daydreaming or asking questions.

"That's how my child lost me," said an indignant dragon. "I was wriggling in my school desk. It's impossible for a child's dragon to sit still, but they made all of us sit still for hours on end. My child was always in trouble because of me and then I was locked out."

After they had all shared the sad stories of how they lost their children, they begged me to tell them about my dragon.

"I was separated from my dragon when I was nine years old, but I'm very lucky because we are now reunited."

"How were you separated?"

"I was sexually abused."

"People who sexually abuse children must have lost their own dragons," they concluded. "That's obviously why they want to steal the children's."

Their insight impressed me, and I realized that dragons are very intelligent. I decided to read to them from the book I was carrying in my backpack:

"One of the traits in children that borders on abnormality is

exuberance ... As in the case of all illnesses that are difficult to cure, so too, in the case of the psychic fault of exuberance, the greatest care must be devoted to ... prevention of the disorder. The best way for an education to reach this goal is by adhering unswervingly to the principle of shielding the child as much as possible from all influences that might stimulate feelings, be they pleasant or painful.[7]

"That's a quote from *The Character Fault of Exuberance in Children* by S. Landmann printed in a child-rearing manual dated 1896. This is how you all lost your children," I explained.

When I played Mendelssohn's 'A Midsummer Night's Dream', they had such a wonderful time dancing together they almost forgot how unhappy they were without their children. They were so playful, exuberant and adventurous, I realized what a tragedy it is that most of the people in the world have lost their dragons. I left Marlon's dragon with the others, and when I waved goodbye to them they wished me luck in my search for the Great Dragon.

The Lost Valley was a desolate place. Nothing grew there, no birds sang, and the earth was parched through lack of moisture. I could hear the roaring and sobbing of distant dragons, but the ones I met ran away in terror. In the distance I saw the mountain, which I planned to reach by nightfall. At the top of this mountain, veiled in mist, I saw the spires of Gaia's Castle.

I reached the mountain at sunset, and found myself a cave to spend the night in. I missed the company of Marlon's dragon, and took another of Mark's spells to overcome fear before wrapping myself in my rainbow robe and falling asleep.

1-6 *Dungeons & Dragons Master DM's Book*, Gary Gygax & Dave Arneson, compiled by Frank Mentzer. © 1985. TSR, Inc. All rights reserved.

7 *On the Character Fault of Exuberance in Children*, S. Landmann, 1896. Quoted in *For Your Own Good*, Alice Miller, Farrar Straus Giroux, 1984.

Ten

Gaia's Castle

As I climbed the mountain, brambles like animal claws tore at my clothes, hands and legs. I used Paul's Clearing spell, and was relieved to see a pathway emerging through the tangled undergrowth. I was now free to make my way to the top of the mountain, where Gaia's Castle stood.

I saw clearly in the distance the mountain range where I had met the hobgoblin and Marlon's dragon. The Lost Valley stretched like a desert between this mountain and the mountains in the distance, beyond which the Sun sparkled on the ocean.

I wondered where Sheta Nut was. She had made no contact with me since our night together with Isis. Then I remembered what Paul's book said about Immortals:

"When an Immortal is trying to change the course of history, he or she may use an agent, who is given a purpose to accomplish, and then left to his or her own means."

By persuading the Great Dragon not to destroy the kingdom, I was attempting to change the course of history. This was my purpose. As a Paragon in the Sphere of Energy, I must create an entirely new magic item. I knew that its components were extremely rare and difficult to find, but I had no idea what it could be.

Looming up in front of me were the walls of Gaia's Castle, which was an enormous stone structure with towers, spires and a moat around it. There was a large arched entrance, but no way of crossing the moat. I looked down into the murky water, accessed by a sheer drop. Even if I was able to slide down and swim across, there was absolutely no way of climbing the steep wall on the other side of the moat, which cast an ominous reflection in the stagnant water.

As I stood there, I was aware of a deathly silence. Although the Castle was surrounded by trees, shrubs, bushes and creepers, there were no birds. The silence was eerie and made me feel uncomfortable. There was no sign of life, but although there was nothing to intrude upon, I felt like an intruder. Then I noticed that the undergrowth had closed in around me. Even as I stood there, wondering what to do next, brambles were piercing the backs of my legs. Desperately I waved the Clearing spell, but it had lost its power. I was trapped.

Just as I was about to choose between the slimy, stagnant waters of the moat and being prickled to death by brambles, I noticed a large rusty bell partially hidden in the undergrowth. When I rang it, a drawbridge mysteriously lowered itself over the moat. With great relief I walked across it and through the arched entrance into an inner courtyard where a fire attracted my attention. I gasped as I approached. An angel, flickering and dancing like a flame, held a flaming rod over my head.

"I am archangel Michael. I serve those who seek the Light."

He nodded when I introduced myself, as if he was expecting me. I explained that Maitreya had sent me, and took out the Seal of Shamballa from my backpack. Michael smiled in recognition and pointed to a small locked door on the far side of the courtyard.

"Take the fire of your love and give it to the children," he said, handing me the flaming rod.

Having unlocked the door, I found myself standing on the edge of a lake with the flaming rod in one hand and the Seal of Shamballa in the other hand. The main bulk of the Castle stood on the other side of the lake, and I was wondering how to reach it when a sailing boat glided towards me. It had a pure white sail with a rainbow on it, and as it approached I saw another angel standing in the boat. This angel shimmered, the way calm water shimmers when it is touched by sunlight.

"I am archangel Gabriel," said the angel, helping me into the boat. "I serve those who seek to express love."

I introduced myself and showed the Seal of Shamballa to Gabriel, who smiled in recognition.

As we sailed across the lake, I dipped my hand in the cool water and let out a piercing scream when I felt, and then saw, hundreds of dead fish floating on the surface of the lake.

"The water is polluted," said Gabriel sadly.

When I looked over my shoulder, I saw that we were being followed by another angel. This one resembled a cloud, with wispy curls instead of feet, and It was blowing the sail of the boat towards the other side of the lake.

"I am archangel Raphael. I serve those who seek to heal."

Raphael was carrying a sword, which I recognized as the sword used to draw the two circles in the snow when I said goodbye to my father; the one with the gold handle inlaid with emeralds.

When we reached the far side of the lake, where the main part of Gaia's Castle stood, Gabriel gave me a silver chalice containing a mysterious liquid. When I asked what it was, Gabriel looked surprised. I dipped my finger into the liquid and tasted it.

"Ugh!" I exclaimed, pulling a face. "It's salty."

"These are the tears you have cried for the Earth," said Gabriel, handing me the chalice.

"Why aren't there any birds here?" I asked Raphael, as I walked away from the boat, where Gabriel stood waving to me.

"The air is polluted," said Raphael sadly.

We were now standing in front of a high wall with a gate in it. Raphael unlocked the gate for me and handed me the sword inlaid with emeralds. I walked through the gate into a field, where another angel stood rooted in the earth. This angel wore a mantle of dead leaves and was sifting the soil. I introduced myself and tried to show the Seal as I balanced all of my newly acquired possessions in my hands, under my arms and between my legs. Feeling embarrassed, I stuck the sword in the earth and placed the chalice on a flat stone. The angel smiled in recognition and appeared to have been expecting me.

"I am archangel Uriel. I serve those who seek life."

I looked around at the barren soil, the dead trees silhouetted against a grey sky, and the total absence of flowers and wildlife.

"What happened?" I asked, pointing to the ghostly landscape.

Uriel looked at the dry powdery soil with sadness: "The Earth has become a barren wasteland because humanity has forgotten how to live. No longer living by the seasons or life's inner rhythm, it has raped the Earth and destroyed many life-forms that depend upon the Earth for nourishment. The true meaning of life has been lost because humans think they can use and abuse the Earth to satisfy their desires. The water, air and soil are all polluted, and if humans cannot live in harmony with life's natural rhythm, the Earth will die. Then they will know that she gave her life, and to kill her is to kill life itself."

I was so upset by what she was telling me, I burst into floods of tears which were soaked up immediately by the parched soil at my feet. It was as if the Earth was thirsty for my tears.

"I need to go inside Gaia's Castle."

"The only way into the Castle is through the rose garden," Uriel explained, pointing across the barren field where nothing grew.

As I walked away, she called to me:

"Don't forget your flowers."

I walked back, with great difficulty, to where I had been standing. Growing in the soil where my tears had fallen were bright red poppies.

"Thank you. Your tears caused flowers to grow where nothing has grown for many years."

I was touched by the flowers, but I was tired and the Sun was already beginning to set when we said goodbye.

Although I could touch the walls of the Castle, I found no way in. The windows were too high and there were no doors. Eventually I found a high wall running along the back of the Castle. It had a gate set in it, but it was locked. Beside the gate hung a small silver bell, which I wearily rang. I waited and waited until it was almost dark. Then the gate creaked open to reveal a creature.

I introduced myself and asked the creature's name.

"Isn't it obvious? I'm the Hideous One."

I was too tired to care what the gatekeeper looked like.

"I am looking for a way into the Castle," I explained, dropping the sword. "I'm also tired and hungry."

He stood there with his mouth hanging open. He told me later that the mere sight of him usually sent people running away in horror.

"I can feed you," he replied after a long pause.

He picked up the sword and closed the gate behind me. I found myself standing in a beautiful rose garden, its fragrance so heavenly I almost fell over.

"What a divine smell," I sighed, totally intoxicated by it.

"I take care of the roses," he told me. "There is a rose for every person in the world. I water, prune and fertilize them. It's my job."

I asked if my rose was here in the garden.

He nodded: "Yours is the peace rose. I have never known more than one rose to bloom at a time on your bush."

I was amazed that he knew my rose so well, and asked if he had any water to quench my thirst. He led me to a well which, to my astonishment, was my well. I was so surprised I nearly dropped Michael's flaming rod. I had never expected to see my well here. It was the one from Vivian's Rose Imagery.

"This is my well!" I exclaimed.

"I must thank you for the well," he said, handing me a cracked cup. "It only appeared recently and has been such a godsend to me. Before this well appeared, I had a really difficult time watering the rose bushes, but now it's easy. It is also the most delicious water I have ever tasted."

The water was cool and very refreshing. I drank the entire cupful in one gulp. He was delighted to meet the owner of the well and busily picked mushrooms, which he said had started to grow since the well appeared.

He lived in a cottage at the back of the rose garden, which he said was the gardener's cottage. He rarely went into the Castle, he explained, because it was so large and empty. Roses grew around the door of the cottage and inside there was a blazing log fire with a kettle boiling on it.

"I was making tea when you rang the bell. Would you like some? I grow my own herbs."

I thanked him and collapsed into a rocking chair beside the fire. I drank tea as he cooked dinner. He had stuck the flaming rod in a flower pot on the table, as he did not possess any candles.

"Usually I go to bed when night falls," he told me. "I get up at sunrise, but with this Light I can now stay up and read."

He was trying to find matching plates in his cupboard and eventually found two the same size. He put the food on the table and pulled out a chair for me. We sat opposite each other, and as we ate he asked how I could bear to look at him.

I looked across the table and saw, by the Light of Michael's flaming rod, that he really was hideous. One of his eyes was only half open, the other had caved in. The right side of his face was deformed, and one corner of his mouth hung open and dribbled into his food. He had a huge lump on his forehead. In fact the whole of his head was grossly deformed and swollen. His body was crippled, which made me wonder how he managed to do any gardening. He was covered in warts, ugly growths and putrid, oozing, open sores. His clothes were soiled and ragged, and he coughed as he ate, sending a spray of half-eaten food in my direction.

"How can you bear to eat in front of me?"

"It doesn't bother me," I told him. "I used to teach physically handicapped children, and I often ate with them. Many of them had to be fed because they couldn't feed themselves. We don't know how lucky we are."

This last comment rendered him speechless.

After dinner we sat in front of the fire, and I asked if he would like to hear some music. He nodded and I brought out the music tapes. He chose Tchaikovsky's piano concerto number one, which I placed in the cassette player. He was fascinated by it and nearly fell off his chair when the music blared out.

"That's amazing!" he exclaimed, picking it up and turning it in his hands. I wondered how he would react if he saw television.

When I told him about Gaia, he could not believe that anyone was sleeping in the Castle, and had not seen the bridal chamber I was so eager to find.

"Do you have a bed I can sleep in?" I asked, stifling a yawn.

He led me up a narrow winding staircase to a small bedroom, where he thanked me for my company and the music. I put my chalice on the bedside table and folded my clothes neatly on a chair under the window. Then I collapsed exhausted onto the small creaking bed, and fell into a deep sleep.

I was late for class. They were all waiting for me.

"Today we are moving on to the attitude of transpersonal love," said Vivian, after I had sat in my usual place beside the door.

"Did you see that programme on television last night?" Sharon asked. "It was about Star Wars and laser beams. They showed the underground testing of a nuclear missile, and you should have seen the Earth shake. They took satellite pictures and I swear you could see the Earth heaving."

As we all expressed upset and concern over the testing of nuclear missiles inside the Earth, Vivian attempted to bring us back to the original topic.

"We are going to give ourselves powerful love. Transpersonal love is not wishy-washy. It is an active love. I'm going to lead you in a short meditation:

"Put aside the activity of your mind and allow yourself to enter the silence of the loving Self. Recall a time when you felt really loved. Who gave you this love? What was its quality? How did you experience being loved? Imagine that you are now reliving this experience, and then bring yourself back to the present moment and record or share any insights."

"The part of me that's still a little girl can't accept love," Sharon shared.

"How does that little girl feel when you begin to love her?"

"It's as if the barriers are coming down and she's emerging because I'm accepting her for who she is. I have to let go of my belief about having to be perfect to deserve being loved."

"I feel so wounded in this area that even when I am loved, I still expect to be hurt," I confessed.

"The hardest part for me was to find moments when I felt really, truly, deeply loved," said Eleanor, "Experiences of being totally loved are fleeting, and so I found this exercise difficult."

"Come back to the quietness of the Self," Vivian invited us. "Now recall a time when you really loved someone. Who was the person you deeply loved? Recall a specific situation when you were full of love for this person. Now relive that experience as if it were happening in the present moment. When you feel the depth of your love, what do you experience in your body, mind and emotions?

"Sit with this experience of the depth at which you know you can love and receive love. Allow that to expand and know that you are capable of even deeper love. Know that everyone in the room is experiencing the deep knowing of their love, and allow this love to infuse and empower the love of the group. When you are ready, open your eyes and make contact with each person here in the room.

"Just as the personal self needs the various subpersonalities to express parts of itself, the transpersonal Self needs us to express the depth of love. This is how we begin to experience the truth of who we are. When we looked at our subpersonalities, we looked at the level of the personality. Now we are reaching up into the superconscious to the archetype of love, which is a pure and active love. It is full and flowing, but it needs the personal self for its fulfilment. Let's look at how we experience loving and being loved."

"When we're really loved, we don't have to live up to expectations," I pointed out. "Love does not project. I experienced this with my first lover before we were sexual, but then our personal needs and projections surfaced. Four years later we returned to our original friendship, and were able again to experience unconditional love, but we had to end our emotional and sexual connection. I don't know how to carry unconditional love into my intimate relationships."

Patrick agreed with me, adding that his deepest experiences of love were non-sexual and free from attachment.

"When I contacted my experience of love, I entered a sad emotional space and there were tears," David shared. "The tears were about the struggles and the pain, and how we both longed for the time when we could play together, but the times of play never came."

"That's a good example of the heights and depths of the superconscious and the subconscious," said Vivian. "You know how it feels when you are absent from a loved one. You understand and love their essence, but when you are reunited and you relate to the personality, you are disappointed."

"You lose sight of their essence," I interrupted. "You know it's there, but you both get into your personality stuff. You are disappointed in yourself and in your lover."

"And how scary that essence is to the personality," Vivian agreed. "In a moment of intimacy, watch yourself start talking or pulling away because the intensity is too much."

We all nodded as we remembered how we had fled from intimacy.

"I'm remembering a peak experience I had when I embodied love," I shared. "It built up until I could no longer contain it. Then I exploded and gave birth to a galaxy. It was orgasmic, but when I feel this kind of love in my life, I won't allow myself to explode."

"We are afraid to birth our galaxies," Vivian agreed with me. "Part of our human suffering is to know the greatness of this love and to feel our pitiful limitations on a personal level."

"There is a deep knowing within all of us that we came from love and are love, but its expression is missing in our world," I pointed out. "We cannot express who we really are, and we are all agonizing over it. As a child, I knew I had come from a place of great love, but I could not find this love in the world."

"It is a denial of the soul," Vivian nodded.

"We are in Love, and we feel violated when love is not honoured," I continued. "I guess the nuclear issue is an implosion of hatred instead of an explosion of love."

"We don't know how to explode, so we implode instead."

"Like testing nuclear missiles inside the Earth," said Sharon.

"Or putting a gun to your head," Meara commented.

"It's global suicide," I concluded.

"Assagioli told us to love our subpersonalities because only in our own integration will we find this love," Danny pointed out.

"Then we can begin to incorporate the fullness of love, starting with ourselves," said Vivian. "Then we can embody love."

"When we do that we explode!" Meara exclaimed.

"When I love a man, he is bringing out something already existing in me, which is glorious to experience. I long to be with him because I feel so good when we're together," I reflected. "But it's a second-hand love. If he rejects me, I don't know what to do with my love."

"Then it becomes impacted and cannot flow," said Vivian.

"I had this vision," Meara shared. "I saw the storehouse of my qualities and when I felt love this energy came in and tickled me."

"That's your husband," said Sharon playfully.

"You bet it is," Meara agreed.

"I'm a love laxative," laughed Danny, Meara's husband.

"The transpersonal Self expresses unconditional love," said Vivian, attempting to bring us back to centre. We were laughing hysterically. "It is a love that is expressed in actions and decisions. It includes reason, discernment, thought and perception. When we experience transpersonal love, we feel that our innate goodness is perceived. This fresh, vital energy, which springs forth out of the heart of the soul, inspires the mind to adopt a higher attitude. This is the attitude of unconditional love, which Jesus spoke of.

"This quality of love brings insights and is the foundation for wisdom," Vivian concluded at the end of the class.

When I awoke sunlight was streaming in through the little window in the bedroom where I had slept so soundly. I threw aside the bedclothes and looked out of the window into a small enclosed garden where vegetables and fruit trees were growing. The Hideous One, whom I decided to call Ho, was at the bottom of the garden with the emerald sword, which he was using to pull down oranges. When he saw my face at the window, he waved to me and asked if I liked freshly squeezed orange juice.

"I love it," I called down to him.

Downstairs the table had been neatly laid out for breakfast, and in front of my plate was a single rose in a cracked vase. Ho's face lit up when he saw me. We sat down together, and I asked him if he knew how to enter the Castle. He pointed to a large rusty key hanging on a nail beside the back door.

"I'll let you into the Castle, but there is nothing in there," he assured me. "I've been in a few times, but it's too eerie for me."

After breakfast he led me through the rose garden to a small wooden door, which he unlocked with the rusty key.

"If you're not back by sunset, I'll come looking for you," he promised.

I had grown fond of Ho. I gave him Michael's flaming rod and a big hug, which left him quivering all over. We said goodbye, and I stepped into a narrow corridor that led into a large old-fashioned kitchen with a black cooking range and cast-iron pots. Everything was dusty and covered in cobwebs. I walked up a narrow staircase to the main part of the Castle and into the various rooms, where I opened the shutters to allow light in. The furniture was old and dusty, and some of the drapes crumbled to dust when I touched them. There were rooms with open fireplaces, and a library filled with hundreds of dust-encrusted books. They were old books, some of them dating back to the middle ages, mostly hand-written and beautifully illustrated. It was as if time had stood still for centuries. There was even a ballroom with a minstrel's gallery, but everything was covered in cobwebs. The Castle had obviously been vacated suddenly and without warning. Even the bedclothes on the four-poster beds were thrown aside as if the people who slept in them arose one morning and never returned. My footsteps echoed through the silent rooms as I pondered the mystery of Gaia's abandoned Castle.

A main central staircase led down into a wide entrance hall, and under this staircase I found a small insignificant-looking door. It opened into a void. I remembered Mark's spell of Light and used it. A narrow staircase led down into a wine cellar, which was arched, eerie and chilly. I knew there must be another staircase leading down into the dungeons, but the cellar was vast and endless. Eventually, when I was about to give up, I found another door hidden away in a dark corner, which opened onto a dark descending staircase.

The dungeons were like a labyrinth beneath the Castle, but I found nothing more frightening than rat droppings. I was exploring a long dark corridor when I heard loud snoring. I turned a corner and there, slumped up against a door, was a dusty angel with droopy wings.

"What do you want?" asked the angel, scrambling to his feet and dusting off some of the cobwebs. He was holding a heavy chain in one hand attached to a huge key in the other hand.

"Who are you?" I asked.

"My name is Abaddon and I'm guarding this door."

"Is this the door which leads to the Pit?" I asked. "I need to go down there to speak to the Great Dragon."

"You can't do that," he replied with a look of horror.

I explained how Maitreya had sent me and produced the Seal of Shamballa.

"That's nice," he said, admiring the Seal, "But I can't let you have the key to this door. It's dangerous in there."

"I'll be all right," I assured him. "I have my rainbow robe, a sword and shield, and lots of spells in my backpack."

"Good heavens! They won't protect you in there. This is the door where evil dwells."

I was shocked to hear this.

"Armageddon is locked up behind this door," Abaddon continued. "Have you heard of Armageddon?"

"Of course I have," I replied indignantly. "Maybe I was sent to prevent Armageddon from happening. World events are now very serious, and Maitreya has sent me to speak to the Great Dragon."

"Do you really think you can go in there and do that all by yourself?" he asked me in surprise. "I've been down here for aeons guarding this door to ensure that Armageddon does not occur before the fulfilment of the prophecy."

"Please give me the key," I pleaded, feeling too upset to listen.

"I can't take responsibility for letting you in. I can't let anyone in until the fulfilment of the prophecy."

I was beginning to feel desperate.

"Look, I have the Seal of Shamballa," I said, waving it in front of his face. "You have to let me in."

"Oh God!" he groaned. "Is Halley's Comet back again? Every time Halley's Comet returns some maniac comes down here and demands that I give them the key."

"I'm not a maniac," I protested. "Maitreya really did send me. I even have the Seal of Shamballa to prove it."

"That's what they all say. You could have stolen that Seal."

I did not confess that I had borrowed it from Vivian.

Abaddon was standing, wings spread out across the door, arms folded, with a grim expression on his far from angelic face. "I'm not going to give you the key."

It was pointless arguing, so I decided to try seduction.

"Aren't you lonely down here all by yourself?" I asked.

"Yes, I am," he admitted, visibly relaxing. "I never see anyone, except when Halley's Comet returns, and then it's usually some demented person like yourself with a saviour complex."

I decided to ignore this last remark.

"Do you like music?"

"Oh yes," he said wistfully. "I love music, but I haven't heard any for ages; not since I was assigned this door."

"How long have you been down here?"

"Well, let me see. One day in the reign of Brahma equals four thousand three hundred and twenty million years, which is a divine age and is called a Kalpa. A Kalpa equals one thousand Maha Yugas, which is ten thousand Kali Yugas, and I've been here for an entire Kali Yuga. How long is that in mortal years?"

I was giving myself a headache just thinking about it. I couldn't have worked it out in an entire lifetime.

"Who is Brahma?"

"Brahma is the Earth."

"I thought she was called Gaia."

"She has many names. Gaia was a name given to her by the Greeks. Her real name is Sandolphon, and she existed as an aspect of Brahma long before she embodied this planet."

Although I had never heard the name Sandolphon, it soared through my soul like a glorious song.

"Sandolphon," I sighed. "Did you know she's about to awaken? Ananda is travelling from the Sun. Maitreya sent me to prepare the Bridal Chamber for them."

Abaddon looked startled: "If Ananda is travelling from the Sun, a hundred Maha Yugas have already passed and the prophecy is about to be fulfilled. That means I'll be able to stop guarding this door, and then I can serve in the Sun," he said with a divine smile and fluttering wings.

"You want to serve in the Sun?"

"Yes, it's wonderful serving in the Sun. There's singing and dancing, and good company too."

"I saw the angels dancing and singing when I visited with Maitreya," I nodded. "My Aumakhua serves in the Sun."

"You are blessed. It is a great privilege to serve in the Sun."

"I do miss music," he said, gazing up at the stone ceiling.

"I have music," I said brightly. "Would you like to hear it?"

"Do you have a harp?"

I shook my head as I searched in my backpack for the cassette player and the music tapes. "What would you like to hear: Mozart, Bach, Vivaldi, Kitaro or Vangelis?"

As Abaddon had never heard of any of these composers, I played Bach's 'Magnificat'.

"You can play music on this? I can't see any strings and there's nothing to blow through."

I tried to explain that it was not a musical instrument, but a gadget for playing music other people had recorded onto a tape. He was mystified and, after searching for the musicians, decided that tiny angels were hiding inside the machine which I had placed on the floor. Abaddon's loud singing echoed throughout the dungeons and faded with Bach's last note.

"How can you bear to be down here all by yourself for such a long time?" I asked, sitting down beside him on the floor and leaning back against the door.

"Time is relative. A day in the reign of Brahma is like one of your days to me."

"Now I understand why Sleeping Beauty slept for one hundred years. It wasn't one hundred of our years, but one hundred Maha Yugas." I was pleased with my insight.

Then I had a thought:

"How do you know that I haven't come to fulfil the prophecy?"

Abaddon pulled a cynical face: "Look, I hear the most amazing stories down here. I had an evil entity pretend to be God, and another one produced a letter from Lucifer telling me to hand over the key. They will try anything to get that door open, but I have my instructions."

I offered to give him the cassette player, plus all of the music tapes in exchange for the key. Abaddon would not be bribed.

"Can't you see I'm not an evil entity?" I pleaded.

"That's what they all say," he groaned.

So I said goodbye and hid around the corner waiting for him to fall asleep. I was determined to get the key, even if I had to steal it. After about ten minutes he began to snore loudly. I crept over to where he was slumped against the door, and tried to pull the key out of his hand, but every time I touched him he twitched. Then I remembered Mark's spell for opening locked doors. I chuckled to myself as I tried it.

Absolutely nothing happened. The door was well and truly locked. I eventually managed to loosen Abaddon's hold on the key, but discovered it was attached to the heavy chain in his other hand. I worked slowly and silently, holding my breath as I disentangled his fingers. At last I had the key on the end of the chain. I slid it into the lock and turned it. There was a horrible grating noise, but the door remained sealed. Growing impatient, I pushed and pulled on the door. Abaddon awoke and looked at me in horror.

"How could you do this to me? I trusted you and thought you were my friend. If you had opened that door, I would have lost my opportunity of serving in the Sun. I would probably have been assigned another door to guard."

I felt terrible and deeply ashamed of myself.

"I have to go down into the Pit," I sobbed. "As far as I know, this is the only entrance. I promised Maitreya, and I always keep my promises."

His heart softened and he put his arm around me.

"I feel good about you," he admitted. "I don't think you're an evil entity, so I'm going to let you into a little secret."

I sat down beside him on the floor and wiped my eyes. I would never have forgiven myself if I'd ruined his chances of serving in the Sun.

"This key won't open the door," he confided. "It's sealed. There is only one thing in the world which will open this door."

He looked around to make sure nobody was listening.

"You see this small hole in the door just below the keyhole," he said, pointing to a hole in the door into which I stuck my finger.

"There is only one thing in the world which fits into this hole. Nothing else will ever unlock the door."

Eleven

The Last Unicorn

I had entered the Castle like a lamb; I was leaving it like a roaring lioness. For the first time in my life, I was in touch with my rage. As I stamped up the stairs leading from the cellar, I was shouting that this was the most lousy Journey anyone had ever been sent on. I stormed through the long empty corridors, and then discovered that I was lost. The Castle appeared to be full of staircases, but none of them led to the rose garden.

Eventually I found my way out and marched around the various rose bushes looking for Ho. He was quietly watering a white rose bush when he looked up and saw me heading in his direction. His ugly old face lit up at the sight of me.

"You weren't in there very long," he commented.

I was so angry, I could hardly speak.

"I think I'm on a wild goose chase," I raged.

"Are you looking for a wild goose as well as the Great Dragon?"

I was too angry to explain what a wild goose chase was, and stood there huffing and puffing.

He put down his bucket of water and offered to make me a cup of tea.

"I need a session," I told him, as we walked back to his cottage. "I've never been able to get really angry, and now that I'm in touch with my rage I need to express what I'm feeling. Can you be present for me?"

He said he would try.

"Do you have a cushion?" I asked. "I may need to rant and rave before I'm able to discharge my grief, so don't be alarmed if I beat the hell out of the cushion. Just be there for me, and if I need you to do or say anything, I'll tell you."

Ho produced a cushion, and as we sat opposite each other he looked lovingly into my face, and the session began.

I thumped the cushion and shouted at the top of my voice:

"Do you know what Abaddon told me?"

Ho tried not to look too curious, but of course he was.

"He told me there's only one way to open the door which leads to the Pit. He showed me this little hole in the door, saying there's only one thing in the world which will fit into it and unlock the door. Then do you know what he said to me?"

He shook his head from side to side, which made his hair flop all over his face. It had obviously never been cut and was like a mane.

"You won't believe this. It's ridiculous. Only the horn of the Last Unicorn will fit into the hole and unlock the door. Maitreya told me to find the Great Dragon. He said nothing about the Last Unicorn. I have to speak to the Great Dragon. If I don't, it may destroy the Kingdom. I have to do something about the state of the world. It's a madhouse out there." I pointed to the door, as if the world was lurking around the corner of the cottage. "You're lucky to be living here. They're crazy out there!" Again I pointed towards the door. "They're spending billions on roads and bombs instead of using that money to feed the starving people in the third world."

I could see that Ho was wondering how many worlds there were out there.

"They," I yelled, again pointing towards the door, "they are destroying the world by cutting down the rainforests, polluting the air and the water, and they're testing bombs inside the Earth. Can you believe that? She's a living being and they're exploding bombs inside her. It's insanity! She's alive and I love her," I sobbed loudly. "I won't let them hurt her any more. I have to stop them, but I don't know how to. Living out there is like living in an insane asylum."

He watched as tears rolled down my face and plopped onto the cushion. He was fascinated by them, and I suspected he had never seen tears before.

My whole body was convulsed with grief for about fifteen minutes, and then I blew my nose loudly. "They're all asleep, and have to be awakened before it's too late. They're polluting the planet and exploiting the third world. I wish they'd wake up and stop it!"

Then I had an insight:

"In Mark's book it says that a Paragon in the Sphere of Energy must create an entirely new magic item. I'm a Paragon. I've no idea what this new magic item is, but its components are extremely rare. I wonder if the Last Unicorn is one of the rare components." I smiled at him. "Unicorns are mythical creatures, just like dragons. They're parts of ourselves we've lost. As dragons connect us to our passion, maybe unicorns connect us to our intuition."

I was pleased with the new insights I had gained, and asked Ho if he'd like a session. He dribbled out of the corner of his crooked mouth, and his half-open eye lit up.

"Since meeting you I have experienced more happiness than I can ever remember. You have brought light and music into my life. What more could I wish for?"

"Isn't there anything you need to work on?" I asked.

He thought hard. "I must confess that I was shocked to hear about the state of the world. I had no idea. Nothing ever happens here. I just take care of the rose garden."

"Would you like to work on your childhood?"

"I don't remember my childhood."

"Would you like to work on your loneliness?"

"I've always been alone."

When I put my hands on his shoulders, he tensed up. I ran my fingers down the side of his twisted face and across his crooked mouth. Then I kissed his forehead and caressed his head.

He writhed, as if in pain, and I suspected that he had never been loved before. Nobody had ever bothered to look beyond his hideous exterior, but I saw his heart and recognized its beauty. He gasped, and his body heaved as years of unexpressed loneliness, grief and sorrow shook him. I held him gently in my arms as he cried onto my shoulder, his body shaking and shuddering as he wept. I stroked his head and as I wiped away his tears I wondered about his life. Where had he come from? Who were his parents? Who brought him here? I asked him to try and remember his childhood.

"I can't. My mind is blank. The only thing I remember is being brought here. I was given the gardener's cottage in exchange for looking after the rose garden."

I asked him to imagine what his childhood could have been like, but he couldn't do that either. Then I had the idea of using Mark's spell of Clairvoyance. I asked if he would be willing for me to try it. He agreed, and I looked deep into his single eye.

I found myself running through woods and meadows. I was being chased and could not stop; not even for a second. I was exhausted, but knew if I stopped running, I would be caught. I looked over my shoulder and saw a fierce bull chasing me. It was snorting with rage, and I was terrified, for I knew it would be fatal if the bull caught me. It was a matter of life and death. I was running through a deep pine forest when I saw a little cottage in the distance. It had smoke curling out of its chimney, and flowers growing in the garden. I looked around but could not see the bull, and fell exhausted at the cottage door, which a bent old woman opened. I tried to explain what was happening, but I was too breathless. Somehow she knew, and through her eyes I saw the others being driven off the land, hounded together and locked up.

"The Bull will never stop chasing you," she told me. "He knows you can never forget who you are. That's why the others were locked up. Their knowledge kept them free."

"I'm the last one," I gasped. "I must remain free to set them free. Please help me."

The old woman looked through her books of spells. "It will have to be a powerful spell," she muttered. "It must be a spell no power can break, except the power of love. We must conceal you, little one, where the Bull will not expect to find you. We need to disguise you. Yes, I have it. I will make you so hideous, nobody will ever suspect your true identity. They will recoil from you in horror. I will hide you in the darkest depths, where only the most courageous will dare to look. You will be the guardian of the rose garden, and nobody will suspect that you are the source of its nourishment."

She mixed up the spell and gave it to me to drink. As I fell to the floor, I realized who Ho was.

"You're the Last Unicorn!"

He trembled in disbelief.

I told him I could break the spell if he was willing. "Then we can help each other to complete our Journeys."

"I have a Journey?" he stuttered. "Yes, break it if you can."

I was shaking as I looked through my backpack for the Remove Curse spell, which I prayed would work. I gave him the spell and rested his head on the cushion. He let out a shriek and convulsed three times. When I looked at him again, he was no longer the Hideous One. Lying on the floor was a beautiful white unicorn with one perfect horn sticking out of the centre of its forehead. I wept for joy and buried my face in its mane. Abaddon had promised to let me go through the door if I found the Last Unicorn. I could now complete my Journey.

While the Unicorn sat beside the fire recovering from its sudden transformation, I made plans for the following day when we would both enter the door where evil dwells.

The Unicorn was in an identity crisis. It could not get used to being a unicorn. It knocked its horn on the furniture and felt as if it was all legs. As it could not pick anything up, it worried about watering the roses. Although a unicorn is a beautiful creature, it does take some getting used to. We discovered we were telepathic.

"Why were the other unicorns locked up?"

"We are pure spirit and have knowledge of all things: temporal and non-temporal. We are the union of opposites and undivided sovereign power. We are free and incorruptible. Before we were driven off the land, we were in touch with the nature spirits, and the ways of magic and ritual. We knew how to heal using herbs and magical spells. Because of our connection to the spiritual realms through our horns, we could never be tricked or deceived."

"Your horn must relate to the third eye," I mused.

"Yes, we are telepathic and can communicate with all beings."

"Why was the Bull chasing you?"

"He wanted to lock me up too, but I had to remain free to set the others free. Now I can release them because you have released me. The other unicorns are locked up in the Pit."

"But why were they locked up in the Pit?"

"We are eternal spirit. Unicorns never sleep and can therefore never forget. We have always been and shall for ever be."

I still could not understand why they were locked up or why the Bull had chased the Last Unicorn. Then I realized that the Bull must symbolize the masculine principle. So, maybe the Unicorn symbolizes the feminine principle, which relates to intuition, feelings and an affinity with the Earth. These qualities have not been honoured since male dominance, symbolized by the Bull, took control of the world. As a result, we became unbalanced. Just as we lost touch with our dragons, which connect us to our life-force, we lost touch with our unicorns, which connect us to our spirits. Without our life-force and our spirits, we are in limbo.

The Unicorn pointed with its horn to a bookcase. I walked over to it and began to leaf through the books.

"I found them in the Castle."

In one of the books was a pamphlet written by Jacob Bauthamly dated 1659. It proclaimed:

"God is in everyone and in every living thing. Man and beast, fish and fowl, and every green thing, from the highest cedar to the ivy on the wall. He does not exist outside the creatures. He is me and I am him."[1]

The other books were about Land Reform in the sixteenth and seventeenth centuries, witch hunts and child rearing practices. I picked up a volume entitled *The Harmony of the Gospels* written by John Eliot dated 1678. What I read horrified me:

"... Withhold not correction from the child, for if thou beatest him with the rod he shall not die, thou shalt beat him with the rod and deliver his soul from hell."[2]

Then I found the *Malleus Maleficarum* (*The Witches' Hammer*) published in 1486:

"When a woman thinks alone, she thinks evil ... they are more impressionable than men ... They are feebler both in mind and

body ... As regards intellect or understanding of spiritual things, they seem to be of a different nature than men ... Women are intellectually like children ... She is a liar by nature ... Woman is a wheedling and secret enemy ..."[3]

Now I understood why Gaia's Castle appeared to have been deserted in medieval times. The legendary Grail Castle, where Gaia slept, symbolizes man's inner feminine, and was abandoned when men turned against the feminine. As I read the various manuscripts, a picture formed in my mind. When land ceased to be common property, but was enclosed and owned, the landless were forced into wage-slavery. As the priests destroyed the festivals, feasts and folk customs of the people, which were an organic celebration of their relationship with the Earth, ownership and professionalism took over. Witches were not burned because they were evil, but because they threatened the growing body of paid experts. Land and knowledge became economic commodities, available only to those with enough money to buy them.

When the people lost their unicorns, they could be indoctrinated. They were told that God existed outside the living world instead of within it. With such a doctrine, salvation had to be either bought or earned, for life itself was a sin which, according to the priests, separates the soul from God. Of course, this is not true. A unicorn can never be separated from God, and that's why the unicorns were locked up.

Then I picked up a very ancient document entitled *The Pseudo-Isodoric Decretals*[4], which dated back to the ninth century. As I could not decipher it, the Unicorn explained that it was this document which persuaded Pope Nicholas I to eradicate the individual human spirit from the original Trichotomy of Man.

I put my arms around the Unicorn and cried into its mane.

"The people must be reunited with their spirits," I sobbed. "You and I together will release the unicorns, and then everyone will awaken and remember who they are."

"I have also remembered that the Byzantine Emperor Justinian called a meeting of the Ecumenical Council in AD 553," the

Unicorn told me. "At this meeting in Constantinople all references to karma and reincarnation were removed from the Bible because Justinian's wife, Theodora, belonged to a sect called the Monophysites who rejected reincarnation."

Unicorns never forget.

I sat for a long time beside the fire with the Unicorn's head in my lap. We gazed into the flames until I could no longer keep my eyes open. I kissed the Unicorn goodnight and crept upstairs to the little bed which Ho would never again sleep in.

Vivian and I were just arriving at Meara and Danny's house for the Passover dinner. They were preparing food in the kitchen and identifying with their Busy Mother subpersonalities. Danny gave us the carrots and celery to cut up, and I joked that if we cut ourselves our blood could be smeared on the door, and then it would be a real Passover. Danny fell apart laughing.

We were sitting down when Sharon walked in with her husband.

"Don't tell Sharon's husband I've borrowed her new dress for the Gala Ball tomorrow," Vivian whispered in my ear. "It cost over five hundred dollars."

Sharon looked like a movie star as she moved onto centre stage.

"I was driving my car today. Oh, by the way, I had another crash, but the car's all right; just a bit scratched. I was driving along the freeway when I decided to play a tape. I had such a surprise, I'm telling you. I thought Vivian must have a very interesting client. It was Paul and Marilyn talking about the Lost Valley, and he was giving her a bunch of spells. I couldn't believe what I was hearing. God, I really enjoyed it. It made my day."

I was laughing hysterically as she told the tale, but could not imagine how she had managed to acquire the tape.

"You must keep it," said Sharon to Vivian. "It's a gem."

"Dinner is ready," Meara announced.

As we piled into the dining room, Meara told us where to sit: "Don't sit over there. That's Elijah's place. An empty seat is always left vacant for him."

"Passover celebrates the Angel of Death passing over the Jews, and their freedom from bondage," said Danny. "It is a symbol for the liberation of our spirits, so we may be free of the bondage of a limited awareness and walk through life aligned with God. Let's begin by filling ourselves with God's Light."

Danny lit a candle, which he passed around the table.

"To celebrate the Earth's bounty, let us praise the Earth goddess. We eat a green dipped in salt water to remember tears mixed with joy. At Passover we remember the sadness of bondage and the joy of freedom.

"And now, before the feast, let us all attune ourselves to our inner God and see our Passover table surrounded by angels. Each angel holds a colour ray for our souls. These colours blend into a rainbow bouquet. Although we all have different colours, we are all expressions of the one Light."

As the feast continued, I thought that every course was the last, but just as I felt I couldn't possibly eat one more mouthful, another course appeared. I enjoyed the wine so much I drank from Elijah's glass as well as my own.

After dinner we returned to the sitting room where we agonized over the choice between chocolate gateau and mocha cheesecake. Meara brought in tea and coffee, as Leia handed out huge slices of cake which we protested about, with exclamations of: "Oh no, I couldn't possibly eat that much," to an accompaniment of Handel's Water Music.

At the end of the evening Leia gave each one of us a drawing, describing how she had tuned in to each person before drawing the pictures. I was stunned by the drawing this eight-year-old was giving to me. It was of a castle with two people holding a heavy chain attached to a huge key. Although I had not told anyone about my meeting with Abaddon, she had somehow tuned in to it, and here was the indisputable proof.

"This is me and Abaddon!" I exclaimed.

She smiled knowingly.

"Leia was a priestess in a previous life," Meara informed me as

Vivian and I prepared to leave.

The following morning Ho and I decided to water the rose bushes. I continued to use the name Ho, as Unicorn is a bit of a mouthful. I was wishing for a hose pipe when one mysteriously appeared. Then I remembered Paul's Wishing spell, which I had totally forgotten about. So I wished for a tap to connect it to, and one appeared, but there was no water in the tap.

"I must be careful what I wish for. What we really need is a timed sprinkler system."

"Each rose symbolizes the soul of a person, and they all depend upon me for water, fertilization and pruning," Ho explained. "I must never let them die, for people need their souls more than anything else in the world."

I was lost in thought over the sprinkler system, as I walked to the well and peered down into its crystal clear water.

"We need a pump to bring the water up, and then we need pipes running under the ground to every area of the rose garden. The pipes must have sprinklers in the exact location to sprinkle each rose bush with just the right amount of water. We also need a timing device."

I walked slowly around the garden drawing a map of where the pipes should run and the location of the sprinklers. When we returned to the well, I double-checked my drawings and then we both wished for a sprinkler system with a timing device. Within seconds, it appeared and worked beautifully. We danced for joy.

"I don't know how long we'll be gone, so I think we should fertilize the soil before we go. Do you have any manure?" I asked.

"Yes, every time the Bull comes looking for me, I collect his shit, and after I've given it to the rose bushes they flower."

I thought about this for a while.

"Roses must need bullshit to help them grow," I concluded.

"Yes, it's amazing. After the Bull has paid a visit, I collect his manure in a bucket, and after I've given it to the roses they smell heavenly."

"Does the Bull often come looking for you?"

"As I have no sense of time, I can't tell you how often he comes looking for me. Usually I'm gardening when he arrives, and he just snorts at me. Then he goes away. The old woman's spell must have been really powerful, for he never recognizes me. He has never once realized that I am the Last Unicorn."

We spent the rest of the day fertilizing and pruning the rose bushes, and were so contented, we forgot about going into the Castle. At the end of the day, exhausted and covered in mud we returned to the cottage:

"I wish I could have a bath," I thought.

"You said you were going to stop wishing for things," Ho reminded me.

"Why not?" I thought to myself, and returned to the well with a pencil and paper. "All we need is a pipe. We already have a pump for bringing the water up."

Ho followed me, thinking: "This woman is full of ideas."

"It needs to go up inside the cottage and into a bathroom. Then all we need is a water heater."

We walked into the cottage and stood together in a small room, which Ho had used as a storage area. After wishing for a bath and a toilet, I thought about the sewage and wondered what to do with it.

"We need a sewage recycling system. Then we can pump it out to the field where nothing grows. Maybe it will fertilize the soil."

After making some careful notes, I sat on the toilet and wished. To my delight the toilet flushed and water gushed into the bath. Sitting in a bath of hot water, I sang.

"I love your songs," Ho told me.

"They're not my songs. The native Americans sang these songs before the white people arrived. Then they were herded together like cattle and confined to reservations. Their children were taken from them, to be indoctrinated into the ways of the white people, but many of them died from broken hearts."

"That's what happened to the other unicorns, but I still feel their spirits."

"And I feel the spirits of the native Americans. I know they love

Gaia as much as I do."

"You really love her, don't you?"

"Yes, she is my Beloved," I sighed. "I must stop the people from violating and humiliating her."

"How will you do that?"

"I wish I knew."

After my bath, I fell into bed and slept the sleep of healthy exhaustion. I loved the way my body felt after working on the land.

It was a beautiful sunny day and Vivian was admiring the roses.

"Just look at these roses. They smell heavenly."

I smiled to myself, remembering how carefully I had watered, pruned and fertilized them.

She decided to hold our class in the garden.

"Today we are going to look at our resistance to loving and forgiving," she said. "Anger prepares the body to correct injustice, but it needs to be released from the body. When it's not released, it hardens into hatred. We need to honour our emotions, but we also need to lift our consciousness, which is an act of will. When we know there is someone we cannot forgive, we need to ask ourselves what we would have preferred. When we forgive, we cancel our expectations and our conditions for loving. We forgive for our own sakes, but our forgiveness will affect the people we have not been able to forgive. If we hold resentment, it gives them power and makes us sick. We all have myths about forgiveness. Sometimes we refuse to forgive in order to punish."

I shared my need to hang on to my anger because it made me feel empowered for the first time in my life. A discussion followed on the importance of not denying the anger and appropriate ways of releasing it.

"What we are doing when we forgive is cancelling our expectations, conditions and demands. We are not taking away the wrongdoing. We simply cancel our demand that the other person be different," Vivian explained.

"I'm going to teach the process of forgiveness. Once you've

learned it, you will naturally practise it in your daily lives.

"First of all, acknowledge what you are feeling about the behaviour or injustice. Then choose not to continue punishing yourself for carrying this feeling. You can say: 'I choose to release my suffering over what has happened or is happening.'

"Imagine the person you need to forgive standing in front of you. Tell them what you would have preferred, and choose to release your expectations. You now want to be free of the incident. They are responsible for their actions, and you can release them to their own good.

"Raise your consciousness into the light of the Transpersonal Self. Imagine and experience the light, compassion and love flowing into you. Experience unconditional love for yourself and, as you continue to feel the love flowing through you, send this love out to the true Self of the person and say: 'I send this love out to you just as you are and have been.' Feel this love flowing through you. Take time to imagine and experience it. Energy follows thought. If you feel at peace with the situation, you are ready to release it. If you are still unable to forgive, look deeper into yourself to see what additional expectations you are still holding and repeat the process. Just be aware that there is additional material to process before it can be released. Remember, each incident needs to be addressed. Examine your willingness to be free."[5]

"Being at peace is an indication that the process is complete. When I see the part of the other person who is suffering, I begin to understand and it helps me to forgive," she added. "We don't need to understand in order to love. Some situations we will never be able to understand."

"The injustices are very specific when they occur in our lives," said David. "Forgiveness must be equally as specific. To say I forgive my wife does not do it."

"It doesn't," Vivian agreed. "The mind does not operate in a global way. It has to have an emotional connection with each situation."

"What about injustice?" David asked. "I may not know an

injustice has been done to me until later. Then I rationalize and make excuses."

"An injustice calls for action and intelligence. There are times when we need to address the issue by confronting the other person. Silent loving does not speak to the injustice. It is a denial of our soul truth. In my marriage I did a lot of forgiving, and did not call my husband on his abusive behaviour. By loving and forgiving him, he was not forced to confront his actions. This is another myth: to forgive and put up with crap. You may have to forgive and leave the relationship. We don't lie down in the road for cars to run over us. That's not intelligent.

"Forgiveness is the decision not to punish yourself for the wrongs of others, and to re-enter the flow of love and life."

1,3 Quoted in *Dreaming the Dark*, Starhawk. Beacon Press, 1982.

2 Quoted in the Preface of *For Your Own Good*, Alice Miller. Farrar Straus Giroux, 1984.

4 *The Spear of Destiny*, Trevor Ravenscroft. Samuel Weiser, 1982.

5 From a manuscript by Edith Stauffer, since published by Triangle Publishers in 1987 as *Unconditional Love & Forgiveness*.

Twelve

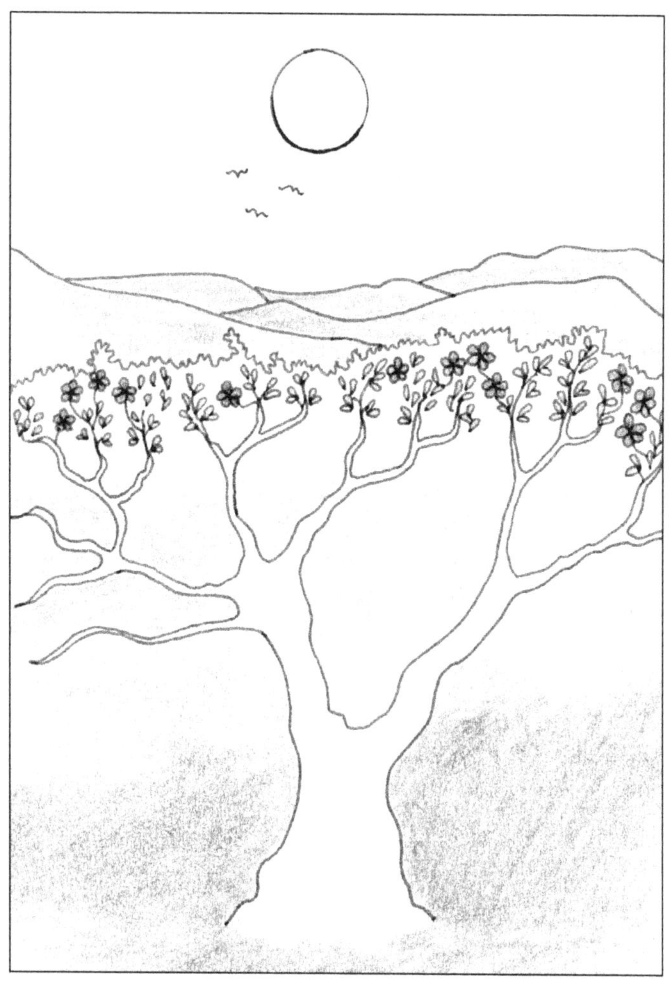

The Sealed Door

We found Abaddon snoring in the dungeons, and when I touched him, he nearly jumped out of his cobwebs.

"Good heavens!" he exclaimed. "Where on earth did you find the Last Unicorn? Many before you have searched in vain. You must be a very determined young woman."

I nodded.

"I have a soft spot for you," he admitted, shuffling with obvious discomfort. "I couldn't live with my conscience if I allowed you to go in there. It's full of evil entities and monstrous apparitions."

"Don't worry about me," I reassured him. "Ho is coming with me, and I have a special shield."

"It looks like a mirror," he observed.

"It is a mirror," I agreed. "Any harmful intention is simply reflected back, like a boomerang. Anyone attempting to harm me will harm themselves instead."

"You have a sword as well."

"I'm not taking the sword. I have the power of my love to protect me. I'm going to leave it here with you."

"Are you crazy?" exclaimed a horrified Abaddon, flapping his wings. "You obviously don't know what's in there."

"It's only the collective unconscious, which needs to be made conscious and then it can be redeemed. Ho is going to release the other unicorns who are locked up in the Pit. Then the people will be reunited with their spirits, and we can create a new reality. The promise of the rainbow will be fulfilled. If I wasn't meant to go in there, I wouldn't have found the Last Unicorn, would I?"

He could not argue with that.

"I hope I'm doing the right thing," he muttered. "I don't want to ruin my chances of serving in the Sun."

Abaddon allowed the Unicorn to place its long slender horn into the hole in the door. He then put his key in the lock and turned it until the door creaked open, and all three of us peered into a gaping black hole that smelt of mildew. I thrust Michael's flaming rod into the darkness and was able to see a sloping tunnel.

"I hope you get to serve in the Sun," I told Abaddon after we had embraced and he had left cobwebs all over my rainbow robe.

We stood in the tunnel and watched as he closed the door behind us. We heard the grating sound of his key in the lock, and knew we were alone.

As we walked, we noticed green slime dripping down the walls. It now smelt like a sewer, so I burned incense sticks. After a while we saw several ghosts, but they just glided on by, looking in surprise at their reflections in my shield. The demons were more difficult to deal with. They were vicious, but when they attempted to attack us their intentions bounced back and they ran away screaming.

Eventually we found ourselves inside a church where a large congregation were listening to a gesticulating red-faced minister, who shouted at them from an elevated pulpit. As we walked through, the people told us to be quiet and then forced us to sit down. I wanted to ask if we were going in the right direction, but they refused to listen.

"Who is this guy?" I asked a serious young man sitting on the seat next to mine.

"He's the great evangelical preacher, Graham Baker," he replied, amazed at my ignorance. "He's telling us to repent."

"The end is nigh!" proclaimed Graham Baker. "Join me at the altar and find everlasting salvation with your saviour."

As I had my hand raised in order to ask if I was going in the right direction, two assistants escorted me to the altar to a chorus of "Praise the Lord!" and "Hallelujah!"

"Repent, my child!" Graham Baker bellowed, waving his arms in the air, as the congregation worked themselves up into a frenzy.

"I'm looking for the Great Dragon," I explained.

They all looked at me in horror.

"Say NO to Satan, the enemy. Repent of your sins and ascend into heaven with the rest of us on the Day of Judgement. Let us help this woman to cast out Satan."

Everyone nodded in agreement.

"Do you really believe we're going to be judged?" I asked.

"My dear child, it says so in the Bible."

"I don't want to live for ever with a God who sits in judgement," I responded with passion. "You're making God in man's image. God does not judge. If you experienced God's love, you would know that."

I was thinking of my meeting with Maitreya, and how he had told me he was only expressing a fraction of the Great One's infinite love. I had never felt judged by Maitreya.

"It says so in the Bible," Graham Baker insisted, and started reading out loud in a thunderous voice:

"For if God spared not the angels that sinned, but cast them down to hell, and delivered them into chains of darkness, to be reserved unto judgement:

"And spared not the old world, but saved Noah the eighth person, a preacher of righteousness, bringing in the flood upon the world of the ungodly;

"And turning the cities of Sodom and Gomorrha into ashes."[1]

I was beginning to feel really frustrated: "I only want to know if I'm going in the right direction for the Pit."

"Don't go there," someone called out. "It's the pits."

I laughed, but nobody else appreciated the joke.

"You have to overcome the devil, or you will end up in everlasting hell," I was warned.

"When people are separated from their dragons, they'll believe anything," I muttered.

"If their unicorns hadn't been locked up, they would know it's not true," Ho agreed.

"The Lord knoweth how to deliver the godly out of temptation, and to reserve the unjust unto the day of judgment to be punished,"[2] Graham Baker shouted as we fought our way through the crowds of people who were trying to prevent us from leaving.

As we walked out, we heard Graham Baker warning his congregation that if they did not mend their ways they would go to hell, which was where he obviously thought we were going.

"If there really is a hell, heaven must be empty," I shouted.

"Anyone good enough to go to heaven could not bear to be there, knowing that others are in hell.

"You're intuitive," I told Ho. "You lead us to the Pit."

We now entered a cave full of creepy-crawlies, which made my flesh crawl. I'm terrified of creepy-crawlies, and as they crawled up my legs Ho reminded me that it was an illusion.

The next cave was full of dead bodies in various stages of decay. It was the most gruesome sight I had ever seen. I closed my eyes and held my nose as Ho guided me through them.

Then we heard the sound of babies crying. We followed the cries and found ourselves in a room full of howling babies whom I picked up, two at a time, in an effort to comfort them.

"Why aren't these babies being cared for?" I asked a young woman.

"Nobody wants them," she told me. "They were conceived in a moment of blind passion and were abandoned by their mothers. We don't know what to do with them. We've left them here to die."

I was horrified and demanded to know why.

"Don't you know where you are?" she asked in surprise. "You are in the Dying Room."

I was so upset to hear this, my tears splashed onto the faces of the two babies I was holding in my arms.

"I can't possibly leave them here," I sobbed.

Ho suggested wishing for childless mothers, and almost immediately a group of childless mothers rushed in and stood crooning over the abandoned babies. Milk gushed out of their breasts like fountains at the sight of the howling babies, and we crept out.

We then found ourselves in a laboratory where animals were being experimented on. There were rabbits with raw eyes, blinded by chemicals; dogs and cats with various bits missing or added on; solitary chimps in cages driven crazy by isolation; bears with tubes in their sides, confined to cages where they could neither turn nor crouch. I felt weak with despair as I unlocked the cages and set them free.

Before too long we found ourselves in a conference room. Several men in dark suits were sitting around a large table discussing an urgent topic. They were delighted to see me and offered me a seat.

"We've been waiting for you," they said, handing me a pencil and paper. "We want you to record what is said at this meeting."

I tried to tell them that I had not come to take notes, but they were already deep in discussion.

"I think we should just kill him," one of the men suggested.

"We can't do that. Assassination is not a part of our policy."

"That's true," a third man agreed. "I vote we drop sixty four thousand pounds of explosive and blow the shit out of him."

"But won't that kill innocent people?"

"It's better than assassination. Executive Order 12333 specifically states: *Prohibition on Assassination: No person employed by or acting on behalf of the Government shall engage in, or conspire to engage in, assassination.*"

"Couldn't the Order be lifted just this once? Then we could go in and kill the bastard."

"Definitely not. Assassination would be giving in to him."

They all nodded.

"I suggest we send in eight bombers loaded with laser-guided bombs and drop the lot on his house. That will teach him to terrorize us."

"Yes, that's not assassination. We are simply defending ourselves. Killing a man is murder, but dropping bombs on his house is a military attack. You must surely all agree that, in view of what has happened, we are justified in our actions."

A pretty young woman walked in with coffee on a tray.

"The secretary is here to take the notes," she informed the men, who glared at me.

After I had been thrown out, Ho informed me that I was being sucked into the illusory nature of the collective unconscious. Just then we heard a roaring sound, the thumping of hoofs on stone and an angry snorting.

"Oh God!" Ho wailed. "It's the Bull."

Without further thought, Ho was off and running. I shouted: "It's an illusion!" but Ho was not willing to put this theory to the test.

Ho galloped into a cave on the left-hand side, where a group of Satanists were holding a Black Mass. They were standing around an altar in the act of sacrificing a child, while other children chained to the walls were forced to watch. Ho leapt up onto the altar, knocking the petrified child to the floor. The Bull was hot on its heels, snorting and bellowing with rage. Ho jumped off one end of the altar as the Bull charged onto the other end. The Satanist holding a knife in his raised hand plunged it into the Bull, who collapsed in a heap on the altar. The other Satanists were delighted, proclaiming that they hadn't had a sacrificial bull for ages. They slit its throat and greedily drank the blood.

"Why are all these children chained up?" I demanded to know.

"It's none of your business," snapped the Satanists.

I knew I had to act quickly because I could already feel their evil intentions. Fortunately their curses rebounded back to them. I protected the children, Ho and myself. Then I paralysed the Satanists by waving Michael's flaming rod at them. As I freed the children, I recognized them. They were the missing children I had seen on the milk cartons. Before leaving, I cast the Dancing spell, which caused the Satanists to dance wildly around the cave, bumping into each other and sliding in the Bull's blood, which was still gushing from its throat.

"What are you going to do with these children?" Ho asked.

Not knowing what else to do with them, I decided to take them with us. The children were relieved to be away from the Satanists, and loved my unicorn. When I explained that we were looking for the Great Dragon, they begged to be taken with us. I told them to stay behind me, and in front of Ho.

I was feeling absolutely exhausted and had no idea how long we had been down here. The children were also tired and fretful, so we looked for a cave to sleep in. Eventually we found one and settled down. I made a list of all the things we were needing, so that I could wish for them and when we were all tucked up in sleeping bags the children explained how they had been kidnapped by the Satanists. They were still traumatized, especially the little boy who had been lying on the altar. I rocked him in my arms, as the other children snuggled up around me. Then I sang to them:

The river she is flowing, flowing and growing.
The river she is flowing down to the sea.
Mother carry me, a child I will always be.
Mother carry me down to the sea.

By the time I had finished singing, all the children were asleep. I closed my eyes and was soon dreaming.

"Wake up! Wake up! The children need you."

I tried to remain in my dream, but the voice persisted. I opened my eyes and saw Ho standing over me.

"There are more children pouring into the cave, and they really need our help."

When I looked up I saw children shaking with fear. They were speaking a language I could not understand, but Ho was able to tell me they were Russian children who had been involved in an accident. I held and rocked each child in turn, and then slipped them into the sleeping bags of the children I had rescued from the Satanists. The little ones I took to bed with me, and fell asleep with them in my arms.

Sharon had arrived late for class.

"I'm having a hard time being here," she sobbed. "I just heard a report on the radio that the Russians are begging for help. They've had a nuclear reactor disaster."

"They say only two have died, but I don't believe them," said Meara.

"People are being evacuated," Sharon continued. "I can't bear it."

"I had the same reaction when I saw children in Vietnam with their skins melting off," Vivian told her.

"Three nuclear reactors are on fire."

"They are trying to make it sound not too bad."

"I thought I was under control," Sharon cried.

"The whole world is under control," Meara commented.

"It's good to feel," I insisted. "The world is in a mess because we don't allow ourselves to feel. Nobody knows how dangerous nuclear reactors are. If they did, they'd fall apart."

Sharon was apologizing for crying, but Vivian said it was not a weakness to be sensitive to the suffering of others.

"This is related to the rage of injustice," said David. "There are people who are helpless, and I feel enraged about it, but under the rage is profound sadness."

"In Psychosynthesis the emphasis is on recognizing the truth, which includes suffering, but it attempts to raise the energy," Vivian explained. "Some people criticize Psychosynthesis, saying it's out of touch with destruction and suffering, but it is not denying that. It is attempting to raise consciousness, so that people can change. When the emotions well up, we need to cry; to feel deeply the suffering of the world. Only after facing our grief, can we take action."

We all prayed for the Russians, for global disarmament and the dismantling of nuclear reactors.

Then we entered a discussion about evil and whether the door where evil dwells should remain sealed.

"To seal the door where evil dwells is the opposite of what we're doing here," said Eleanor. "We need to bring light to the unconscious. It needs to be enlightened."

"The world is sick and its sickness is growing behind the sealed door, but we've shut the door on it. We must go through that door to confront, embrace and redeem it. What's behind the door is the cause of the sickness," I explained. "We have to deal with it. We can't afford to ignore it any longer."

"The governments think that keeping the door closed is good for society, but the pressure just builds up," Meara agreed with me.

"We have to make a shift in consciousness from a male God to a female Goddess," Danny pointed out. "Looking at the world from a masculine point of view, it's either good or evil, light or dark, but from the feminine point of view the opposites complement each other."

Sharon asked how we could dispel darkness.

"What do we do with our subpersonalities?" I asked.

"We bring light to them," Danny replied.

"We have to take light into the darkness," I nodded.

"The intention is not to be sidetracked by evil," Vivian told us. "Our task as humans is to prevent evil from entering the world; to close the door on it, and to deny it access to our lives."

"That hasn't worked," I protested. "Look at what locking it up is doing. Everybody denies evil and it's getting bigger and bigger. We have to bring it into the light to redeem it."

"We can only do that for ourselves," Vivian emphasized. "The evil on a planetary and galactic level must not be given attention."

"The biblical attitude is to overcome, destroy, fight or seal evil away," David commented. "I also see Jesus meeting the woman at the well and telling her to sin no more."

"When we heal, we don't send energy to the disease because that would empower it," Vivian pointed out.

"Many metaphysical groups forget that it all comes from the same source," Meara argued. "There isn't a white God and a black God."

"Assagioli said that if evil comes up, we address it," Vivian told us. "Otherwise we go ahead creating our lives and as things arise we deal with them, rather than looking for problems."

"I can go on creating my life and that's fine, but I also live in a world which is being destroyed," I interrupted. "The Earth is my mother. How can I ignore her?"

"If you ignored her, that would be evil," Vivian agreed.

"It's important to take a moment and say to the Earth: 'I love you, mother,'" said Meara. "We don't give ourselves time to just love the planet. The ancients took time."

I nodded, adding that this was why I could not be involved in the rat race. I had chosen not to be a part of the system.

"You've created a situation in which you can be outside the system to make observations and to have a voice separate from the collective voice," Meara told me.

"I want to return to Sharon," said David. "The anguish we feel is related to the archetypal child calling out, but not being heard. It's the existential vacuum we all fear. What if there is nobody at home in the universe? What Sharon brought to class today is the vehicle for us to respond to the cries of the little child."

"This is exactly what we are going to do today," Vivian responded. "I'd like you to recall a scene in your early life which captures your relationship with your family. Then the other members of the group will act it out for you. Don't put it into words. Sculpt the people in the room to characterize what was happening and how you fitted into the family system."

We all took it in turns to sculpt our family scenes. Sharon had problems with her hurt child when Vivian asked her to do the second part of the exercise, which was to be a loving mother to her child.

"If you were the loving mother and understood the situation she was in as a child, wouldn't you help her to see what was true? She was too young to figure it out. Now you are in a position to help her."

Vivian demonstrated to Sharon how she could hug a cushion and pretend it was her hurt child.

"You're really good at this," Sharon giggled.

"I used to be a nurse, and when I was teaching the mothers how to look after their newborn babies, I told them they could never hold their babies enough or give them too much love. They were so relieved to hear this."

"When I was a baby, mothers were told to let their babies cry," said Meara.

"Many of you are seeing the roots of your childhood, but what's missing is how you were seen by your parents. This is part of the forgiveness process. You have to forgive your parents for not really seeing you."

"It's easier for me to identify with my Higher Self," Sharon admitted.

"Have your Higher Self holding you while you hold your hurt child. Your Higher Self is teaching you how to love, but the child needs physical reassurance." Vivian turned to us: "Find photographs of yourselves and put them up on your mirrors. See that gangly little girl who had just started to menstruate."

"Or the boy who is having wet dreams," Sharon interrupted. "My mother made such a big thing out of my brother's wet dreams. Everyone had to be there while she took the sheets off his bed. It was so humiliating for him."

"The first time I ejaculated, I put it under the microscope and looked for sperms," Danny confessed. "My mother was not validating me for becoming a man, so I locked myself in my room and validated myself."

"Imagine yourself as a man talking to that adolescent boy," Vivian suggested. "Something profound happens to our inner children when they know they're O.K. They were simply not validated, but now we can go back to our childhood and heal ourselves."

"When I watched you all acting out your family scenes, I saw what an incredibly dysfunctional society we were born into. I thought I was the only one with a terrible childhood," I reflected. "All of your scenes were horrible. I now understand why we are so self-destructive. It's because we feel shitty about ourselves."

"I have a photo of myself when I was a baby and I just adore her," Vivian shared. "I tell her what a beautiful baby she is. Then I look at my forty-year-old picture and tell myself I'm a beautiful woman."

We all looked slightly embarrassed as she told us how much she loved herself. We had all been taught to invalidate ourselves.

"We wanted our parents to love us just the way we were. This is an important step before we can move on to loving and forgiving our parents. You can't love yourself too much." Vivian repeated this last statement: "You can't love yourself too much."

Hearing children's voices, I opened my eyes and looked around. The children had awoken and were amazed to find Russian children inside their sleeping bags with them. I explained about the nuclear reactor disaster.

"What's a nuclear reactor?" they asked.

"Although everything looks solid, it's spinning."

"Is it dancing?" A child asked me.

I nodded, remembering what Maitreya had said about spinning and dancing being the same energy.

"In nuclear reactors a uranium atom is bombarded to split its nucleus, which releases energy and lethal radiation. This process is called nuclear fission. It causes the atom to lose its integrity; its truth."

"Does that mean it can't dance any more?"

I nodded and continued: "It becomes chaotic. This chaos, called a reaction, is used to bring power into our homes, but the process also creates radioactive waste. Nobody knows what to do with it, and if it leaks into the Earth it contaminates it for thousands of years. The Russian children were living close to a nuclear reactor when it exploded. Nobody will be able to live in that area for twenty thousand years."

"If they're so dangerous, why do people use them?"

"I can only conclude that the people who insist upon creating power in this way are sick."

"The people who kidnapped us were sick."

I agreed.

"There are safe ways of creating energy. We have sunlight, sea and wind to generate power. When a nuclear reactor is shut down, it has to be sealed in concrete."

Ho translated what I was saying to the Russian children, who then explained, through Ho, what had happened to them.

"I'd like each of you to adopt a Russian child to hold in your arms. Pretend it's yourself you are holding. Give yourselves love and comfort through holding each other."

They thought this was a great idea, and each took a Russian

child to love and hold, which helped them to forget their ordeal with the Satanists. I agreed to take them with me, but made them promise never to let go of each other's hands.

As we descended deeper and deeper into the Earth, the children sang rounds, and then learned to sing in each other's language. I was searching for another cave to rest in when we heard a roaring in the distance. We stopped to listen and I used one of Mark's spells to see what was coming. What I saw turned my blood to ice.

"It's Armageddon," I shrieked. "And it's heading in our direction."

"Use the Prismatic Wall!" prompted Ho.

I cast the Prismatic Wall across the passage, which was instantly filled with a beautiful rainbow from floor to ceiling and wall to wall. I gathered the children into a cave nearby and waited. The sound of galloping hoofs was deafening. I gulped down a potion of fearlessness and gave some to the children. I had no idea what the Wall would do, but prayed it would prevent Armageddon from entering the world.

I peered out and screamed in horror. Flying through the passage were huge locusts, their wings sounding like chariots in battle. They had the teeth of lions and wore iron breastplates. Their tails were like scorpion tails, which they lashed from side to side. One almost hit me in the face. Their leader was an angel, who winked at me as he rode by. I recognized him by the cobwebs on his wings. It was Abaddon. I wondered why he was winking at me and why he had left his position as guardian of the door. I hoped he was not ruining his chances of serving in the Sun.

The first row of locusts hit the Prismatic Wall. I gasped at the sight. It was a miracle. As the locusts hit the Prismatic Wall, they turned red, then orange, yellow, green, blue, purple, and white, after which they glowed with a golden light before becoming transparent. They passed through the wall in slow motion, and emerged as unicorns.

"My friends! My friends!" cried Ho, waving at them in recognition.

Abaddon had been transformed into a magnificent angel, whose face shone like the Sun and whose enormous wings filled the passage. He was now as graceful as a swan in flight.

"Oh, Abaddon," I sighed.

"No, not Abaddon!" he cried triumphant and bliss-filled. "I am Apollyon, and now I can serve in the Sun."

I was laughing and crying as I flung my arms around Ho's neck. I was so happy for Apollyon and for the unicorns. It was the most incredible sight we had ever seen.

A solitary white horse emerged from the Prismatic Wall without a rider. It carried instead a fabulous jewel that shone with such brilliance we had to shield our eyes. Although the jewel itself appeared to be black, it radiated an intense red, yellow and white light.

"What is it?" I asked Ho.

"It is the Jewel of the World: the Chinta-mani, the miraculous stone preordained to save the world. It is the Stone of the Sages, used by the alchemists to transmute non-precious metals into precious ones; a stone capable of healing both the microcosm and the macrocosm."

Michael followed the white horse, accompanied by Gabriel and a magnificent Being wearing a golden robe whom Ho identified as Immanuel. Michael was carrying a sword of blue flame and a white banner with three red concentric circles on it.

They were followed by an army of horsemen. The horses had the heads of lions and were breathing fire. Their tails were like serpents' tails and their riders wore breastplates of fire, jacinth and brimstone. As they entered the Prismatic Wall, they too reflected the colours of the rainbow before turning white and gold and then becoming transparent. They emerged as fire-breathing dragons with blue-flame armoured Rainbow Warriors riding upon their backs.

This transformation happened in the twinkling of an eye, and afterwards Ho told me there was now a unicorn and a dragon for every single person in the world.

"When people are reunited with their dragons and their unicorns, they wake up and remember," Ho explained.

"But why were they so terrifying?"

"A spell was put on them to ensure that the people's fear would prevent them from being reunited."

"Without their unicorns and their dragons, they could be deceived and led astray," I concluded.

We decided to have a dance to celebrate the transformation of Armageddon. We danced Cotton Picking Jo, which made us laugh as we bounced around the cave with our partners. Then for the Russian children we danced the Troika in groups of three. We were in such a muddle over the complicated steps that we laughed as we fell over each other. As I watched the children dancing and laughing, I knew they were being healed.

After I had tucked them up, I could not sleep. I thought about my Journey, and how my inner world had become as real as my outer world. I wondered how long it would take for the unicorns and the dragons to be reunited with their people, and how that would change world events.

"Can you hear a child crying?" Ho asked me.

"That's my lost child," I explained.

"Why don't you comfort her?"

"She's not crying for me. She's crying for her mother."

"You are her mother now," Ho reminded me.

Feeling ashamed of myself, I went in search of my lost child. In a dark corner of our cave I found the staircase of my childhood home. I remembered there were eighty eight steps to our apartment on the top floor, where I found my lost child dressed in her pink nightdress and red slippers. I swept her up into my arms and promised never to abandon her again. I returned with her to the cave, and that night slept with her in my arms.

When I woke up Ho asked me if I noticed anything strange. I sat still and then felt it: a creepy sensation at the base of my spine. I used Mark's spell to Detect Evil, and knew we were close to an evil entity. I protected all of us before leaving the cave.

Sloping tunnels led into a series of underground caverns. The ceilings were so high, we could not see where they ended, but heard the sound of bats' wings high above our heads. The sense of impending evil was growing, and the children were holding on to each other in terror. They had been singing, but now they were too afraid to sing. I sent them back with Ho to a place of safety and continued on my own. Shadows lurked in the dark crevices of the rocks, and I felt the eyes of a malevolent force fixed upon me as I travelled through the dark sinister caverns, grateful for Michael's flaming rod.

Eventually I was confronted with a pair of black wrought-iron gates inscribed with demons. The gates were at least fifty feet high, and wide enough for an army to pass through. They were open, and as I walked through them an ominous red glow sent chills up and down my spine.

1,2 The Second Epistle of St Peter, Ch. 2, 4–6, and 9. The Holy Bible, King James Edition.

Thirteen

The Great Dragon

Seated upon an elevated ebony throne was a scaly demonic creature with horns, reptilian hands and feet, and a long tail which swished from side to side.

"How did you get in here?" he snapped.

"Who are you?" I asked, not answering his question.

"Isn't that obvious?" he hissed.

"Don't you have a name?"

"My name is Caligastia, and I work for Lucifer."

I explained how I had found the sealed door where evil dwells, and how Abaddon had let me in.

"Abaddon works for me. He would never have let you in."

I was amazed to hear this, as I thought Abaddon was an angel; not a demon.

"Abaddon wants to serve in the Sun," I confided.

"The dirty double-crosser!" Caligastia raged. "What the hell does he want to serve in the Sun for?"

"Personally, I'd prefer to serve in the Sun than guard the door where evil dwells."

"What do you want?" he demanded.

"I'm looking for the Great Dragon."

"Did the Melchizedeks send you? They're a pain in the neck; a thorn in my tail. They do it on purpose just to annoy me."

I took out the Seal of Shamballa, but at the mere sight of it, he threw up. I quickly put the Seal away and asked about the Melchizedeks.

"They're always sending fifth-dimensionals to bother me." Caligastia looked at me with deep suspicion. "Why aren't you afraid of me? Everybody else is."

"I've been through so much, there's nothing left to be afraid of," I shrugged, and told him my life story. He looked bored and yawned, but I continued with all the gory details: "Over three thousand years ago I was entombed alive, and had to travel through the underworld. Since then I've died so many times I've lost count."

Coincidentally, I could now remember many of my previous

deaths.

"Guess what I learned from all of this?"

Caligastia's tail swished in annoyance.

"I learned that death is an illusion because I'm still alive," I said, giving him a big smile. "I was also separated from all the people I love, and guess what?"

He mumbled incoherently.

"Separation is also an illusion. I haven't lost any of the people I love. For all I know, you may also be an illusion."

I knew immediately that I had said the wrong thing.

"I'm not an illusion!" he raved. "How dare you call me an illusion."

"Just tell me where the Great Dragon is and I'll go away," I promised.

"I'm not going to tell you. You and the Melchizedeks can go to hell."

"If you don't tell me, I'll find it somehow. I'm very determined."

Caligastia looked at me in horror. I knew how much he longed to attack me with evil, but my protection was too powerful. When he first looked into my shield, he nearly fell off his throne. I was also holding Michael's flaming rod, which terrified him.

"Hold that thing away from me!" he shrieked. "I'll let you into a secret. I've just released Armageddon from the Pit. I want to ruin their plans."

"Whose plans?" I asked, remembering how Armageddon had been transformed.

"They have plans, which I'm going to spoil with my baby."

"You have a baby?"

"Nobody knows it's mine, but it is," he chuckled.

Of course, I wanted to see it. If I found Pandora's Box, I'd open it. I have always been insatiably curious. He was longing to show off with his baby, and it did not take long to persuade him to show it to me. He led me to the back of the cavern where there were four locked doors. He opened the first door with a key that he wore on a chain around his waist with two other keys. He had obviously worn it for such a long time it had worn away his scales. I noticed that he only had three keys, but when I asked him about this he growled that he did not have a key for the fourth locked door. When I asked what was beyond the other doors, he said it was none of my business.

We were standing inside a concrete building with all kinds of rods and vials inside glass cabinets. People had their hands inside the cabinets, but they were wearing protective clothing and gloves. Whatever it was, Caligastia loved it. He crooned and gurgled over it, like a mother with a new baby.

"What is it?" I asked.

"It's my baby, Diablo," he sighed. "It's a nuclear reactor. When the Great Dragon destroys the kingdom, Diablo will explode. Pregnant women will give birth to monsters. People will die from radiation sickness and many will lose their souls. I had my followers build Diablo right on the San Andreas fault. It will be a contaminated wasteland for thousands of years."

Seeing how upset I was, Caligastia laughed with fiendish delight: "First Armageddon, and now Wormwood."

I felt disheartened and powerless.

"The Melchizedeks were wasting their time sending you," he scoffed.

Not having the energy to argue with him, I left his caverns and rejoined the children and Ho. We found a cave as far away as possible, where I sat on the ground crying. Now it was their turn to comfort me.

After the children had fallen asleep, I discussed my next steps with Ho. We looked through Mark's spells and found the spell for communing with the Greater Powers. I decided to use it to visit Maitreya.

In an instant I found myself sitting on the swing-seat in Maitreya's garden. I looked down at the lotus and the pearl in its centre. Then in the still, clear water of the pool I saw his reflection. He sat beside me and put his arms around me. I cried as I told him about Caligastia and Diablo.

"Why don't you do something about it?" I sobbed. "A nuclear reactor blew up, and I have some of the children with me. I've also found the missing children on the milk cartons. They had been kidnapped by Satanists."

"I know how much you love the children," he said softly.

"Why don't you stop people from destroying the Earth?" I wailed. "Diablo was built on a major fault line. Why do you allow it?"

"The Great One endows all of us with creative free will. This is humanity's birthright," he explained. "Love, mercy and freedom are inherent qualities within the manifest universe. We in Shamballa trust that these qualities will one day manifest in humanity, but they must be allowed to develop naturally."

"It's not fair that someone like Caligastia should have the freedom to cause so much devastation," I argued.

Maitreya explained how the unconditional love of the Great One included even Caligastia. Then he told me the story of the Prodigal Son, which symbolizes the divine longing for the separated ones to return home. Caligastia had merely become separated from his source.

"We do have the power to stop what is happening, but the Karma Lords have beseeched us to let humanity's free will run its course."

"Even if humanity creates Wormwood?"

"Wormwood is the worst fate to befall any planet," he admitted. "Many beings from all over the universe are joining with us in our attempts to prevent Wormwood from happening to Gaia's embodiment."

I told him about meeting Abaddon, finding the Last Unicorn and entering the collective unconscious. "But I don't know what to do next. That's why I'm here."

He looked lovingly into my face and spoke:

"There are three things you can do: firstly, it is important for you to love yourself. This is a key issue and will affect the outcome of your Journey."

"I don't know how to love myself," I protested.

"Close your eyes and feel my love. Whenever you are aware of not loving yourself, close your eyes and imagine my love for you."

I agreed to do this, but secretly I could not believe that I deserved his love, or his time.

"As we are all In Love and time is an illusion, I am giving you nothing that is not yours already," he said, reading my thoughts.

"Secondly, never forget that everyone and everything is a part of you. This may be difficult for you to comprehend, but the Great One, who is both Mother and Father, loves Caligastia no less than anyone else. This all-embracing love is there for everyone regardless of what they do, think or feel. Try to love Caligastia. Don't love his actions. Love who he is beyond his apparent wrongdoing. The Divine dwells in him no less than in you and me."

I found this difficult to believe.

"See if you can guide Caligastia."

"Guide him!" I exclaimed in horror. "Are you joking? He's a reptile."

"You're always complaining to Vivian about not having enough guiding experience," he teased me. "This is a wonderful opportunity for you to practise your guiding skills."

I was speechless.

"Befriend him and find out what's beyond the other locked doors," he concluded. "And remember that nothing is what it appears to be."

I rested my head on Maitreya's shoulder, closed my eyes and returned to Caligastia's Caverns.

He pulled a face when he saw me.

"I thought you'd gone," he complained.

"Aren't you fed up with being down here?" I asked. "Don't you wish you could go up into the light?"

"I loathe the light. It hurts my eyes and gives me a headache."

"I have the same problem," I said. "That's why I wear sunglasses."

"I love the darkness. It inspires me to have diabolical ideas."

"Like Diablo?" I asked. "Do you have any other babies?"

"Of course," he chuckled. "I have babies all over the world."

"You must be really proud of yourself."

Caligastia glowed: "Lucifer will be pleased with me."

"Where is he?"

"Lucifer is leading the Rebellion."

"What Rebellion?"

"Lucifer is rebelling against Michael's plans. Michael and his followers are a bunch of weaklings. All they ever talk about is love. They let everyone do their own thing. How can you run a universe with everyone doing their own thing?"

"They're honouring free will," I pointed out. "They talk about love because God is love."

Caligastia pulled the most horrible face.

"Lucifer promised me a whole galaxy to rule over if I messed up the world," he boasted. "He's going to be thrilled when he sees my secret weapon."

"You have a secret weapon?"

"It's beyond the second locked door," he nodded. "It creeps from the inside out and nobody knows it's there until it's too late. It destroys silently in the dark."

"You must be proud of this secret weapon." I tried not to sound too curious, but I knew how much he enjoyed showing off. Caligastia's weakness was boastfulness.

Before too long he was leading me over to the second locked door, which he opened with one of his keys. We were standing in a huge amphitheatre with tiers of seats upholstered in purple. In the centre of the floor grew the most hideously monstrous thing I had ever seen. It resembled an enormous growth and was oozing a putrid greenish grey liquid. It grew from the floor to the ceiling, and appeared to be wrapping itself around something which could no longer be identified. There was a hole in the ceiling which the growth had penetrated. I saw light at the top of a shaft and realized, with horror, that the hideous growth was making its way into the world.

"Isn't it wonderful?" Caligastia sighed, sitting on one of the purple seats. "It never stops growing. All I have to do is pay people to feed it buckets of lies, greed, hatred and corruption."

"Is it growing around something?" I asked.

"It's choking it to death," he cackled wickedly.

"You must be in a lot of pain to enjoy being so destructive."

"No!" he snapped. "I'm not in pain; not me."

"I'd like to know more about you."

"Would you like to work for Lucifer?" he asked.

"Maybe," I humoured him. "If you could convince me of its benefits."

As I gazed into his face with loving presence, Caligastia squirmed in his seat. "How long have you been down here?"

"Since the beginning of time. I was here when it all started."

"Are you the serpent referred to in the Bible?"

"There they were obeying orders, but I was the one with the knowledge," he nodded. "I told them to eat from the forbidden tree because I knew what would happen if they did. At first they refused to listen. They said they had been warned not to eat from the tree because it would make them mortal. I told them that the fruit from the tree would transform them into gods, and when they could not resist it any longer they picked the fruit and ate it."

"What happened then?"

"They became mortal of course. They triggered the dance all mortals are doomed to dance."

"What dance is that?"

"The dance of life and death," he laughed. "They were driven by their sexual impulses, and soon there were babies everywhere."

"But you told them they would become gods," I pointed out.

"That's true. I just failed to tell them how long it would take."

"So you helped them to incarnate their dragons," I mused.

"But then they felt guilty about this new sexual energy they could not control. They blamed me for tempting them and said it was my fault."

"Later they blamed women," I interrupted, remembering the

Witch Hunts and the oppression of women through the ages.

"Now there were two opposing forces," Caligastia continued. "Those who supported them in blaming me, and those who supported me."

"And you became the collective scapegoat!" I exclaimed, beginning to understand, "The more people projected onto you, the more diabolical you became. You took the life-force and twisted it around until it became demonic. Live in reverse becomes evil."

"You don't hate me?" he asked in surprise.

I was remembering what Maitreya had said about not judging or excluding anything in case it turns against us. He had explained how demons, witches and monsters are the shadows cast by resistance to the light. The dance of these two forces creates the physical world. In the divine dance of opposites, we need to recognize both sides of the polarity.

"You did the right thing when you told them to eat the fruit from the forbidden tree," I concluded. Then I had a thought: "If I can prove to you that love is the most powerful force in the universe, will you tell me where the Great Dragon is?"

"How will you prove that? Lucifer is the most powerful being in the universe. That's why I serve him and not Michael. If you don't believe me, look at the world and see the havoc we're creating."

"I bet I can cure whatever your hideous growth is growing around with the power of love."

"My evil is very powerful," Caligastia sneered, rubbing his reptilian hands together. "But I like bets, so I'll take you on."

We agreed to meet later in the amphitheatre.

When I was safely installed in a cave, I made a list of people to invite to the Contest. Then I wished for them to arrive at the right time, and when I walked into the amphitheatre, there they all were. Some of them were still wearing their night-clothes, but at least they had arrived on time.

Michael was there with Immanuel, Maitreya, Gabriel and Lucifer. Caligastia was so thrilled to see Lucifer, he licked his feet like one possessed. I was surprised to see Lucifer with Michael, and wondered what was going on. Before they took their seats, Michael announced their total confidence in the power of love, and prayed this would finally prove to Lucifer that there was no power greater than love. Although Lucifer pulled a face, he was extremely beautiful. I could see why Caligastia adored him. He oozed charisma as he sat down between Michael and Immanuel. Behind them sat the other archangels with a host of angels and unidentified cosmic beings.

The Illuminati were sitting on the other side of the amphitheatre.

"I hope this won't take long," their leader complained. "Time is money, and I have a lot invested in this thing."

Behind them sat politicians, drug barons and white-faced military men with stiff upper lips. To their left sat the nuclear scientists and Fundamentalists who were raving about Armageddon and the Day of Judgement when all sinners would be sent to everlasting hell. Sitting at the back were hundreds of terrorists, Satanists and miscellaneous demons and fanatics.

When everyone was settled into the purple seats, Satan appeared in a flash of lightning. He was even uglier than Caligastia and wore a black cape lined with red. He announced that there was no power in the universe greater than the Lucifer Rebellion, which would be proved once and for all in this Contest with Caligastia's growth. As he sat down in the front row, Caligastia drooled all over him in an ecstasy of devotion.

Then a lofty being entered the amphitheatre with an entourage of followers. He said his name was Ahriman and introduced his ominous companions as the Lords of Materialism. They were followed by crowds of people dressed in dark suits, many of whom were carrying newspapers and briefcases. Ahriman, angular and gaunt, surveyed the scene with pale darting eyes. Then he sat down opposite Michael and Lucifer.

The Choir started the contest by singing Bach's 'Jesu, Joy of Man's Desiring' which caused the demons to vomit. As we danced around Caligastia's growth, we used guided imagery to direct the enormous amounts of love and healing we were sending to the living thing which I knew was still alive under the growth. We visualized it healed, whole and full of light as the angels and archangels radiated love and light in all directions.

To a cacophonous accompaniment, the Illuminati, the politicians, Satan and Ahriman with their followers helped Caligastia to pour buckets of greed, lies, hatred and corruption over the growth. When Satan promised them power and riches beyond their wildest dreams, they tipped the buckets even faster. Then the drug barons joined in and did deals with the politicians.

"What's in it for us?" demanded the Illuminati, glancing nervously at their Rolex watches.

We formed a spiral around the growth as we invoked healing for both the living thing beneath the growth and the planet, which we visualized as healed and whole. When we imagined all the people in the world holding hands and creating a web of loving protection around the planet and the living thing, the growth began to shrink, and as it loosened its hold it slid to the floor stinking and dripping. Then it shrivelled up and evaporated. Standing there in all its glory for everyone to see was the Tree of Life. It was covered in green shoots and little buds which would one day blossom, and it was growing up through the hole in the ceiling towards the light. We were cheering and clapping when Michael spoke:

"Immanuel and I have travelled throughout the manifest universe with our dear brother Lucifer, to prove to him that there is no power greater than the power of love. We have shown him billions of life-forms as proof of the Great One's infinite love and creative intelligence. We have also shown him planets where Wormwood occurred. These planets now float in space, barren and derelict. All life was obliterated, and they now serve only as cosmic museums to show all beings the folly of creating Wormwood. We have shown Lucifer that true liberty cannot exist when one possesses unjust power over others. There can be no real freedom until all are free. Lucifer, you are our beloved brother.

Our hearts long to welcome you home."

As Lucifer stood up to speak, he looked as if butter wouldn't melt in his mouth.

"I led the Rebellion because I wanted to rule the universe as a separate being in my own right. I didn't see the point of letting everyone do their own thing. It was holding us up. I wanted progress and the right to lead without having to consult the Constellation Brothers or the Seraphim Sisters. I set out to prove that there is an evolutionary power greater than love. I had no interest in following the path of righteousness. Immanuel and Michael teach self-control in order to serve, but I wanted to be served as a god in my own right. You speak of God's love, but although I searched for proof of God's existence I did not find it."

"If you want proof of God's existence, look within," urged Immanuel. "If you want to see God, look into the eyes of your fellow beings. My dear Lucifer, we are all God. We are the vehicles through which the Great One manifests. We pray that your heart will be opened to this great truth. You wanted ultimate power, but to surrender to love is the most powerful action you can take."

Caligastia sprang to his feet. "Master," he cried out to Lucifer. "I have remained loyal to you. I want to show you my baby, Diablo. I know you'll love it."

We followed Caligastia out of the amphitheatre and into the nuclear reactor. The scientists, politicians, military men and especially the Illuminati swooned over Diablo, but when Caligastia turned to Lucifer for approval, he looked bored.

"So, what's new?" he said, shrugging his wings.

I returned to the amphitheatre to say goodbye to the people I had invited to the Contest. I knew they would not remember having this experience. That's because it happened in the collective unconscious. Perhaps a few of them would remember a strange dream the following morning. When everyone had gone, I approached Caligastia.

"You promised to tell me where the Great Dragon is if I won the Contest."

"Lucifer is a jerk!" Caligastia raved. "I'll get him for this."

"You're really upset, aren't you?" I commented.

"I was promised a galaxy to rule over if I messed up the world, and I did a really good job."

"Why don't you give up being destructive and get on with your life?" I suggested. "Serving Lucifer hasn't done you any good. You look terrible."

"I feel terrible," he admitted. "I put so much energy into being diabolical."

"Why don't you become an angel?" I suggested. "Angels really enjoy themselves, especially if they serve in the Sun."

"I am an angel," he snarled. "My real name is Samael."

As I had discovered that devil and divine come from the same Sanskrit word, deva, I was not surprised to hear this.

"Now will you tell me where the Great Dragon is?"

"I'll show you, but it won't do you any good."

As we walked past the third locked door, I could not resist asking him what was beyond it. Cackling, he opened it and led me inside. Of course, I should not have asked. It was my own fault. What I saw horrified me and caused Caligastia to have what he thought was the last laugh. It took me a long time to recover from what I saw beyond the third locked door, and I was never able to share what I saw because I knew nobody would ever believe me. Caligastia found this tremendously funny. It was his final revenge on me for winning the Contest with his hideous growth.

He led me through another immense cavern. In the distance I saw steam rising, and then found myself standing on the edge of a boiling lake, which he said I would have to cross to enter the Pit where the Great Dragon lived.

"I don't know how you'll get down there, but that's your problem," he shrugged as he walked away.

"What you need is a boat," said Lucifer, dazzling me with his extraordinary beauty.

I nodded and asked if he was going to join Michael.

"I'm bored with the Rebellion and having creeps like Caligastia following me around. Michael says I have a brilliant mind, but it needs to be softened with love."

"You must have a fifth ray scientific mind," I said, remembering what Vivian had taught us about the Rays. "I bet you have some seventh ray as well, which is the ray of ritual and magic."

"I love ritual and magic," he agreed, "but the only people who practise these days are Satanists, and I'm bored with black magic."

"I miss ritual too. In Lemuria we had a beautiful temple where we led rituals and practised magic."

I was amazed at how much I was beginning to remember.

We both lapsed into silence. I was beginning to suspect that in those days the divine dance of opposites had been honoured.

"Without my Rebellion to test the universe, it would have sunk into Unbedingte Ruh," he pointed out.

"What does that mean?"

"Unconditional repose."

"You should unlock the fourth locked door," he advised me before leaving.

"Don't delude yourself into thinking you won the Contest," Satan sneered, suddenly appearing at my side. "I can easily persuade my followers to create another hideous growth. Unlike Michael, I pay my followers."

I shivered involuntarily as I realized that Satan was paying his followers to destroy the world. He was indeed the great deceiver, but his own followers he deceived the most. Would they still follow him if they knew his real intention, which was to pull the rug from under their feet? At what price did they have their power and riches?

I told him we would increase our efforts in sending love and healing to the Tree of Life, but his demonic laugh could be heard reverberating throughout the caverns as he walked away from me.

The children were excited about creating a boat in which to cross the boiling lake. We immediately started drawing up plans for a boat which would be boiling-water-poof, fireproof, and could both sail and fly. The children wanted to create a Noah's Ark, and after much discussion we wished for the right boat.

Almost immediately a child's version of Noah's Ark appeared floating on the boiling lake. It had a gangplank and two huge billowing sails. The boat was red with port-holes and a dragon painted on the side. It had a beautiful brass anchor in the shape of a cross with miles of thick rope. The children were delighted with it and begged to sail in it at once. I saw no reason to delay any longer. They walked up the gangplank in twos.

As we sailed across the boiling lake, I told them we were on a magical mystery tour. I had no idea how the Great Dragon would react to us. As we approached the far side of the boiling lake, we saw a magnificent steaming waterfall cascading into the vortex. The boat glided over the edge and floated down, its huge sails billowing above our heads in the tremendous currents of the spiralling vortex. I had tied all of us into the boat with the thick rope, but it was like a roller coaster ride: simultaneously thrilling and terrifying. We were spiralling down through fire which danced wildly around us, illuminating our faces and licking the boat but not burning it. It reminded me of conception, but on a much grander scale.

We were descending into a pit of enormous height and width. Its walls were ringed with fire, and way down at the bottom we saw and smelt smoke. Then the smoke was all around us, causing us to cough and splutter. The boat bumped slightly as it hit the bottom, and we found ourselves floating on a lake of molten lava in a huge underground cavern. Slowly the smoke cleared and at the far end we saw a huge beast snoozing on an island of rock in the middle of the molten lake. When it saw us, it snorted and blew smoke rings.

Bravely I left the boat and walked slowly through the gigantic underground cavern, feeling very tiny in my rainbow robe. The children cowered behind me. The Great Dragon was amazed to see us and was obviously considering whether or not we were an hallucination. It was as big as three elephants and was covered in red scales, with spikes on its back and tail. It had sharp teeth and was blowing smoke through its nostrils. We felt like midgets in comparison.

"I have been sent by Maitreya," I said, showing the Seal of Shamballa. "I have come to beg you not to destroy the Kingdom when Ananda arrives from the Sun to awaken Gaia."

The Great Dragon stared down at me with its ruby red eye.

"Here are the tears I have cried for the Earth," I said, placing the silver chalice with my tears in it at its feet.

"I have to destroy the Kingdom," the Great Dragon informed me.

"But many people will die and lose their dreams," I protested. "How can we help you not to destroy the Kingdom?"

All the children nodded in agreement.

"I will try to explain, but you will have to listen very carefully. As humans, you do not see the whole picture."

The children gathered around to listen.

"The reunion of Gaia and Ananda is a great cosmic event. When he joins her, she will awaken, her heart will be opened and she will sound a new note. If there were enough people ready to awaken with her, I would not need to destroy the Kingdom."

The children said they did not understand.

The Great Dragon looked down at them with tenderness. I could see how much it loved children.

"What happens when you grow out of your clothes?"

"They burst open," the children replied.

"This is what will happen to Gaia unless you are able to weave a new garment for her; a garment of Light suitable for a sacred planet entering a mystical marriage with her Beloved."

"A wedding garment!" I exclaimed.

"When Gaia's heart is opened, it will be too big to be contained by the planetary psyche, unless the people also open their hearts with her. If they are not ready to awaken with her, their limited consciousness will have to be shattered. That's my job."

I knew there was truth in what the Great Dragon was saying.

Just as kundalini rises up during a peak experience, Gaia's kundalini would arise at her awakening.

"If we weave a wedding garment for Gaia, can we save the Kingdom?"

"That depends upon the number of people weaving the garment."

"How many people do we need?"

"A billion. They would not only have to be awake and weaving, they would have to witness this great cosmic event."

"I've been sent by Maitreya to prepare the Bridal Chamber," I explained, wondering how on Earth I was going to find a billion people. "In Shamballa we are committed to fulfilling the promise of the rainbow. I beg you not to destroy the Kingdom."

"I always cause destruction in a great cosmic event when there are not enough people ready to move with it," the Great Dragon insisted. "Then everyone moves up to the next level whether they want to or not. If they don't do it willingly, they do it through trauma."

I remembered what Isis had said about trauma waking us up.

The children suggested that I use the wishing spell to bring a billion people to the Castle, but I suspected that it would not be honouring their free will. Surely I had not come this far to be defeated at the eleventh hour.

When I looked up a tribe of native Americans were emerging from the smoke surrounding the Great Dragon. They walked with pride and dignity, dressed in buckskin. Their chief glided towards me, as graceful as a deer.

"I salute you, Blue Moon Rising," he said, using my native American name.

The chief had rainbow threads woven into his feathered headdress which hung down his back. His face was noble and weathered, and his eyes had nothing to hide. When I met his gaze, I saw herds of buffalo roaming the plains. I felt his strong arms aiming a bow to kill only what his tribe needed. His squaw stood beside him, delicate and fine-featured. She wore handmade jewelry and a band of plaited grasses around her head. Tied to her breast in a buckskin papoose was a tiny baby sleeping peacefully. I longed for their simple lifestyle and cried for their fate.

"The white man has lost his connection with the Earth Mother," said the chief with obvious sorrow. "He cries out in pain as one who is lost in the wilderness. He appears to own everything, but he has nothing. He lives in terror and is afraid of his own shadow, for he has forgotten how to be at peace with himself. We weep for him and for what his dreams are doing to the Earth Mother. He locks himself inside a little box and has no quest for which to spread his wings. He stole something which can never belong to him, and it does not bring him joy because he has forgotten that he belongs to the land.

"We lived in this area for many generations and were its custodians. The Earth Mother supported and nourished us. Now she calls to us in pain. We hear her and have come in answer to her call. She gave herself to us. How can we not give ourselves to her?"

"What can we do?" we begged.

"Dance with us," the chief invited us. "We will ask the Earth Mother for visions. She will show us what to do."

Members of the tribe began to beat drums and as they danced in a circle chanting and wailing for the Earth Mother's pain, we joined in and made solemn vows to assist her. The children were able to empathize with the Earth Mother's pain, as they remembered their experiences with the Satanists and the nuclear reactor. I was glad to see them stamping and screaming out their rage and frustration over what had happened to them. I knew they were being healed.

Afterwards the chief cried out with such passion the Great Dragon nearly jumped out of its skin.

"Take the spirit of our dance and the cry of our hearts, and teach the children how to take care of the great Earth Mother," he cried. "Now we will share our visions."

A child spoke: "I heard a voice telling me to return to the Earth and teach the people how to live in peace with each other."

"I saw a vision in which I was a wise leader teaching the people that there are no enemies. We are one people."

"We had a vision in which millions of people were demanding an end to nuclear reactors and missiles, and we were leading them," said the Russian children.

"I saw myself working with sun, wind and sea to generate power."

"I had a vision in which I taught people how to work with the land. Not only did we remineralize the soil, we stopped using pesticides and began to respect the Earth as a living being."

All of the children had seen visions in which they could help the great Earth Mother as leaders, teachers, peace workers, writers, farmers, scientists and politicians.

"We already knew that we must return our spirits to the Earth, and this is why we are here," said the Chief. "Again we shall be custodians of the land and will use our dreams to support the Earth Mother, as we did when we lived here before." Then he looked at me and asked what my vision had shown me.

"I shall find enough people to be here when Father Sun is reunited with Mother Earth. I shall help to weave her wedding garment, and I shall teach the children."

The entire tribe cried out: "HO!"

I turned to the Great Dragon: "If I do that, will you promise not to destroy the Kingdom?"

"If you find enough people to be at the Castle, it will be a miracle. Their hearts will be so opened by the sight, they cannot fail to inspire and influence the rest of the world. If this happens, I shall not need to destroy the Kingdom because the world will awaken."

I was delighted, but had no idea how I was going to accomplish this feat. Maitreya had asked me to expect a miracle, and I would. The children were standing around me. They were sad to be leaving.

"Thank you for taking care of us. Without you we would have been in limbo."

"It is a law of the universe that no child is ever left in limbo,"

I heard myself saying. "Always, when a child dies, someone takes care of that child."

"Like a Guardian Angel?"

I nodded.

"We loved your stories, and the dancing and singing; even when you sang out of tune. We shall never forget what you taught us. We have learned that we all belong to one family. We are brothers and sisters."

I hugged each child, knowing how much I would miss them.

The chief smeared the children with indigo and gave each one of them a long-tailed feather from out of his head-dress.

After we had all embraced, I told them we would meet again and explained how I had never lost anyone I loved. The children were reassured. The native Americans already knew. I sprinkled the Spell of Reincarnation over them as they ascended through the Vortex, which now resembled a Shaft of Light. I watched as they were transformed into indigo angel children with wings containing long-tailed feathers.

As they vanished from sight, I heard the most heavenly sound.

Fourteen

The Bridal Chamber

It was a pure high note, which swelled and soothed my soul, and caused the Great Dragon to lift its head in an attempt to locate the source of the sound. The Omega Man, seated upon a unicorn and playing an oboe, slowly descended through the Shaft of Light. He opened his arms to me, and as I fell against his chest I realized how exhausted I was. I had not seen him since our meeting with Isis, after which he had called to tell me he could no longer be my therapist. He had fallen apart and needed therapy himself. Taking his hand I led him to the Great Dragon and asked how much time I had to find a billion people.

"No time."

I felt the colour draining from my face and my legs turning to jelly. "No time?" I stuttered. "I shall start immediately."

We returned to the Shaft of Light.

"I am placing in your open hands everything I have learned about masculine energy," he said quietly and with resolve, giving me the emerald sword used in his imagery with my father.

"And I place in your open hands everything I have learned about feminine energy," I responded, giving him the silver chalice with my tears in it. "Our tears are a gift to the Earth," I told him as his tears overflowed and mingled with mine in the chalice.

We held hands and ascended through a light brilliant and dazzling in its intensity. The Shaft of Light felt eternal. We could have been in it for a hundred years or half a second. It is impossible to say.

At the top we found ourselves in a small chapel. As light filtered in through stained glass windows depicting angels and nature spirits, it sent dancing rainbows across the floor and walls. At the far end of the chapel, above a simple altar, was a circular stained glass window with a pentagram at its centre. As sunlight streamed through the five-pointed star, it threw a perfect mirror image onto the white altar cloth, which was strewn with wild flowers. There were two white candles on the altar, and a large golden Egyptian Ankh, symbol of eternity. We each lit a candle and knelt in front of the altar.

"I seek to bring the two together," I said slowly. *"The plan is in my hands. How shall I work? Where lay the emphasis? In the far distance stands the One Who* **Is**. *Here at my hand is form, activity, substance, and desire. Can I relate these and fashion thus a form for God? Where shall I send my thought, my power the word that I can speak?"*

"I, at the centre, stand, the worker in the field of magic," he continued. *"I know some rules, some magical controls, some Words of Power, some forces which I can direct. What shall I do? Danger there is. The task that I have undertaken is not easy of accomplishment, yet I love power. I love to see the forms emerge, created by my mind, and do their work, fulfil the plan and disappear. I can create. The rituals of the Temple of the Lord are known to me. How shall I work?"*

An angel appeared behind the altar and spoke:

"**Love not the work.** *Let love of God's eternal Plan control your life, your mind, your hand, your eye. Work towards the unity of plan and purpose which must find its lasting place on earth. Work with the Plan; focus upon your share in the great work.*

"**The word** *goes forth from soul to form: 'Stand in the centre of the pentagram, drawn upon that high place in the East within the light which ever shines. From that illumined centre work. Leave not the pentagram. Stand steady in the midst. Then draw a line from that which is without to that which is within and see the Plan take form."*[1]

When we opened our eyes, we were kneeling in the pentagram's reflection, which had alighted upon us as the Earth danced another day around the Sun. The angel picked up the Ankh and touched each of us as we left the chapel.

To my surprise, the chapel was inside the Castle. Somehow the Shaft of Light had bypassed the collective unconscious and the dungeons. As we walked through the silent empty corridors, the Omega Man agreed to help me find and prepare the Bridal Chamber. I took him to the rose garden to gather roses, which we arranged in vases from the kitchen. I had no idea where Gaia was sleeping but assumed it would be at the highest point in the Castle. We looked up and saw one tower soaring above the others. This was the tower we would search for. After walking through long corridors and up many steps, we discovered a concealed door opening onto a spiral staircase, which we climbed until we were dizzy. At the top we found another door opening into a circular chamber with a large four-poster bed. The shutters were not quite closed, allowing just a trickle of light to penetrate the darkness. I tiptoed to the window and opened the shutters a fraction more. A long plume of light slid across the floor and stopped at the foot of the bed, which was draped in a white gauzy material. There was someone sleeping in the bed, but it was too dark to see who it was. Concluding that it must be Gaia, we filled her chamber with the fragrant roses and crept out. We walked in silence through the empty Castle, out of the main doors and into a courtyard.

"Come with me," he urged. "You look tired."

"I don't have time," I replied, shaking my head. "I have to find a billion people."

"You can't possibly find that many people."

"I want you to know that I am totally committed to completing this Journey. Gaia is crying out in her sleep. Can't you hear her? She's being polluted, abused, raped and poisoned."

"You're tired. The world will get along just fine at its own pace and may not need saving by us. From one perspective, it is perfectly fine just the way it is. You need a good night's sleep."

I felt patronized by him, and it was making me angry.

"Perfectly fine the way it is?" I snapped. "The rainforests are being chopped down at the rate of twenty seven million acres a year; the hole in the ozone layer is three times the size of this country, and growing bigger; the water and the soil are poisoned with four billion pounds of pesticides a year. Every day forty thousand children starve to death, and annually one thousand species are made extinct due to the destruction of their habitat. In this country alone an acre of trees disappears every eight seconds, and annually four million acres of cropland are lost through soil erosion. There are thousands of homeless people sleeping in your streets. Life on Earth is being exterminated, and you expect me to have a good night's sleep?"

"Your pain for the world seems so great, I'm concerned that you are taking too much in through the solar plexus. You seem to me to be too stuck in your astral-emotional reactivity to address the world's pain as a helpful server."

With these words ringing in my ears, I watched him ride away into the distance. I walked through the Castle feeling angry and alone, and eventually found myself in the rose garden where the sprinkler system had just turned itself on.

At the bottom of the garden I discovered a high wall with a door I had never seen before. I asked Ho what was beyond it.

"I don't know. I can't find the key to this door."

After studying the door for a while, I decided to use Mark's spell for opening locked doors. To my surprise and delight, the door swung open revealing a small walled garden. In the centre, tangled up with undergrowth and almost strangled by brambles, we found a rose bush with the most enormous rose we had ever seen. The size of a beach ball, it emitted a divine fragrance, and was pure white with a delicate pink blush on the tip of each petal. We sighed ecstatically as we touched, inhaled and admired it. Then we noticed how dry and parched the soil was around the wilting rose bush, and could not imagine how it had continued to bloom under such harsh conditions.

"It must be someone's soul, but whose?" I wailed, rushing off to the well.

After watering the rose bush, we cleared the ground of weeds and brambles. Then I noticed a small brass plate half-buried in the earth. I picked it up and rubbed it on my sleeve. The brass plate had 'GAIA' engraved on it.

"It's Gaia's rose bush," I cried, "and it nearly died."

I sat on the ground sobbing: "This must never happen again."

I ran to the cottage and returned with a screwdriver to take the door off its hinges. "She must never be locked away ever again," I insisted, as I struggled with the door.

Then I drew a plan for extending the sprinkler system to include Gaia's rose bush, but when we wished for it the Wishing

Spell failed to work.

"She has to be connected to the main sprinkler system!"

Ho suggested digging a trench.

"Digging a trench is going to take all day."

We both knew it had to be done, so we started immediately. We worked like maniacs and did not stop until the trench was dug. Then we looked around for a pipe, and when we found none I burst into tears.

"What about the piping to your bathroom?" Ho asked.

I whooped with delight. I would not be able to take any more baths, but Gaia's rose bush was more important. We disconnected the piping from my bathroom and connected it to the sprinkler system. I used the spray head from the shower for the sprinkler, and the job was done. We fell to the ground exhausted but jubilant. It worked.

"I wish I had somewhere to go for a bath."

"Why don't we go to Lisa and Robert's house?" Ho suggested. "I'm sure they would love to see us."

We travelled as fast as the speed of thought through deep valleys, canyons and over mountains and rivers. At sunset we arrived on the edge of a deep pine forest. Snuggling beside a babbling brook was a round wooden house with a pointed roof. It stood in a beautiful garden full of flowers and fruit trees. This was the house Robert had built for Lisa.

We walked along a winding path and knocked on the door. There was subdued lighting in the house and the sound of laughter. The door was opened by Robert, who was delighted to see us and invited us into a cosy sitting room with an open fire and oil lamps. Lisa was sitting beside the fire sewing a patchwork quilt.

"You look terrible!" she exclaimed. "Whatever happened to you?"

"Can I have a bath before I explain?" I begged.

Lisa led me into an old-fashioned bathroom and turned the tap on, explaining that their water was heated by solar panels on the roof. That night Robert took me upstairs to a tiny room in the loft where I gratefully climbed into a bed covered with one of Lisa's quilts. I fell asleep the minute my head touched the pillow.

"I think we'll sit in the garden today," said Vivian. "It's such a beautiful day. By the way, the man from the Gas Company says you're lucky to be alive."

I stared at her in disbelief.

"The gas boiler has been leaking carbon monoxide into the room where you sleep. That's why you've been having headaches, but he can't understand why it was only leaking into your room."

I wondered if Caligastia and Satan had anything to do with it.

When everyone had arrived, the class began:

"Today I'm going to have you recall a satisfying experience with your parents. Be with the experience as if it's happening now."

Danny started: "I'm with my mother and I'm two. She's lying on the sofa watching a soap opera and I'm up inside her skirt exploring. She's not minding at all."

"The happiest time I had with my dad was when he came home from work and we'd play this game," Patrick shared. "He would watch TV with his feet up on the coffee table, and I'd put my head up and he'd try to trap me between his legs."

When we had all shared, Vivian told us to close our eyes and imagine that we were in an inner sanctuary, a place of great beauty and peace.

"You have invited your parents here, and you are preparing yourself for their visit. If there are any external preparations you need to make, such as bringing in flowers or lighting candles and incense, do so now. Then take a few minutes to prepare yourself inwardly. This is a sacred experience; an opportunity for you to meet your parents as human beings. Realize how important it is for your evolution to free yourself from limiting and negative attitudes towards your parents. They also have the divine spark within them.

"When you're ready, imagine your mother or your mother substitute walking in. Try to see her as just another human being. Be aware of your mother's essence. Her appearance is merely a covering. Try to see her with total compassion, and imagine that she is seeing you in the same way. There is no condemnation. You are honouring the divine spark within each other.

"If there is anything you or your mother wish to express to each other, either verbally or non-verbally, do so now. Take the time you need. Imagine your mother speaking to you from the part of her that can truly accept who you are, and sees the living essence in you.

"Now, in whatever way feels right to you, allow words or a gesture to express a blessing — the recognition of the divinity within each other. When you both feel ready, say goodbye to your mother, and stay with the experience on your own in silence."

I found myself sitting in the little church on the hill in the village where my mother lived. I was filling the church with flowers on a glorious spring day, with sunlight streaming in through the stained glass windows above the altar. Presently my mother walked in wearing a pink dress and looking slightly flushed with excitement. Her deep blue eyes filled with tears as we hugged.

"I'm sorry I left you when you were a little girl," she apologized. "I didn't know what else to do. I couldn't find anyone to take care of you, and I was confused and grief-stricken after daddy's death."

"I needed your love and protection. I needed you to be there for me when I came home from school. I wanted you to put me first; even before earning money. I didn't understand how difficult it was for you to make ends meet, and to be both mother and father to me."

"I don't want you to struggle the way I had to. I wish you could meet a nice man to take care of you."

"I've been taking care of myself all of my adult life, and I'm glad I didn't marry because it would have been a disaster," I told her. "When I was growing up, you passed on your negative attitudes towards men and sex, which have taken me years to clear. I pray you will make peace with your parents and with men. And that you will forgive me for my stormy adolescent years and for not meeting your expectations."

"I'm happy when you're happy," she assured me.

"Don't depend upon me for your happiness," I begged her. "Find happiness and fulfilment through your own life."

"I feel I've ruined my life by making the wrong decisions."

"Let go of the past. Release it and live in the present," I whispered, as I held her in my arms. "I love you."

"I love you too," she said tearfully.

I gave my mother a pair of golden scissors to cut her ties with the past. We blessed each other and said goodbye. Her parents were waiting for her outside. She would probably take them into the woods where she picked wild flowers.

As I waved goodbye, I heard the flapping of wings. The sound was coming from the window. I turned sleepily and remembered that I was in Lisa and Robert's house. Sun was streaming through the window and three doves were peering in at me.

After breakfast I decided to visit Robert in his workshop at the back of the house. As I walked around admiring the wooden toys and candles he was making, I asked him if he had any suggestions for finding a billion people.

"I think you should call a meeting of the subpersonalities," he suggested. "But before you do that, there's something I want to talk to you about. Did you notice all the doves in the garden?"

"I couldn't fail to notice them," I laughed.

Even as I spoke we could hear them fluttering outside with their familiar coo-cooing sound. They were even sitting on the window sills looking in at us.

"When we were first married Lisa was nervous and not open to my love. The first month was difficult and I had to be gentle with her."

I was not at all surprised to hear this, but could not understand how it related to the doves.

"I guess she was learning to trust men. When I stopped pursuing her, she gradually opened up to my love. It must have started the first night we made love. The following morning there were three doves in the garden in addition to the one we already had. The more she opened up to me, the more doves there were until we had hundreds of them."

"That is weird."

"Whereas it is true that the doves are multiplying, there is no rational explanation for the thousands of doves in the woods around our house."

"Are you insinuating that every time you and Lisa make love, doves arrive on the scene?"

Judging by the vast numbers of doves in residence, they must be making love all the time, I thought to myself.

"Maybe you should stop," I suggested.

He laughed and said they were not planning to stop. I wondered if the doves had something to do with my inner marriage. After all, Lisa symbolized my wounded female and Robert my inner male.

That afternoon I had a meeting with all the parts of myself. When Anna and Joachim saw the Unicorn, they were delighted and took turns riding on Ho's back.

"Where's Arthur?" I asked, aware of his absence.

"He's gone for dynamite," Merlin replied.

"Dynamite! Why does he need dynamite?"

"I'm teaching him to use his intuition," Merlin explained.

The dynamite was discussed for several minutes, with everyone giving their theories as to why Arthur needed it.

As I asked my subpersonalities for suggestions on finding a billion people, I tried to conceal the panic in my voice.

"I could put a spell on them," the Witch suggested.

"I have extremely powerful magic," said Aluna. "I could easily bring a billion people to the Castle."

I thought about this, but decided it would be interfering with free will. I did not want anyone to be there merely because they had been enchanted.

Parsifal and Sibyla suggested going into town with pamphlets, but Frank said that was a silly idea.

I asked Sheta Nut, but she said she could not help me because she is an Immortal. "Immortals can inspire, but they must let the mortals figure it out for themselves," she told me.

"I know," said my lost child, who begged to be called Natasha, "Bring all the children to Gaia's Castle. There must be at least a billion children in the world."

"There are between five and six billion people altogether," said Robert. "I guess there must be at least a billion children."

"It's a good idea, but how am I going to bring them?" I asked.

"It's easy," said Natasha, with a child's simplicity. "Just ask their Guardian Angels to bring them. Everyone has a Guardian Angel. Didn't you know that?"

"Yes, but I don't know how to contact their Guardian Angels," I pointed out. "And isn't it interfering with free will?"

"If they knew about it, they'd want to come," she insisted. "The Guardian Angels of children are easier to contact than those of adults because children are more open."

"You should ask the Melchizedeks," Sheta Nut suggested.

Remembering Caligastia's obsession with the Melchizedeks, I begged her to tell me about them.

"When I took final initiation in the Great Pyramid, it was under the guidance of the Melchizedek priesthood," she explained.

"In a way Caligastia was right when he said I had been sent by the Melchizedeks, but I don't know how to contact them."

We discussed this for a while, and just as I was about to lead a meditation Natasha told me to ask the Guardian Angel of all Guardian Angels to bring the children to the Castle."

"I don't know where the Guardian Angel of all Guardian Angels is," I moaned, sounding like Mona. "Does anyone know?"

"It's on the tip of my tongue," said Aluna.

"I used to know," wailed the Witch.

Anna and Joachim were bursting to tell us, but they knew they couldn't because they are Immortals. They mimed it for us, as we sat in a circle around them. Beaming all over their childlike faces, they pointed up into the sky.

"Sky!" shouted Sibyla.

"Tree!" Frank called out.

Caroline was the one who finally figured it out.

"The Sun! The Guardian Angel of all Guardian Angels lives in the Sun."

"That's great," I said. "How do I get there?"

"You've been there before," they all reminded me.

"Maitreya took me. I don't know how to get there on my own."

We fell into a gloomy silence. All we could hear was the sound of the doves billing and cooing in the trees. Lisa and Robert looked up thoughtfully. The Sun was such a long way away.

"I hope Arthur arrives soon," Merlin mumbled to himself.

"When Maitreya took you to the Sun, he took you in a star tetrahedron," Caroline reminded me.

"But I don't have one of my own," I complained.

"Yes, you do," said Sheta Nut. "It's your Merkaba."

"You know about the Merkaba?" I gasped, remembering what Azra had said about it being another name for the Light body.

"Of course I do. Merkaba is an ancient Egyptian word. How do you think I was able to find you in the future?" she asked. "I travelled in my Merkaba. When you are aligned in the various dimensions, the chakras are spinning in unison, and your masculine and feminine aspects are in harmony, then the star tetrahedron counter-rotating fields activate the sacred geometry within your crystalline structure."

I asked her to repeat what she had just said.

"She's telling you to activate your auric field, which will in turn activate your crystalline structure," said Robert. "You were doing it just before Sheta Nut contacted you. Remember the spinning wheel?"

"Gosh! Was that my Merkaba?"

"When I said I would teach you to dance like a star, this is what I meant," Sheta Nut reminded me. "Just imagine that you have a triangle pointing upwards and a triangle pointing downwards. Together they make a three-dimensional Star of David, which surrounds you."

"Yes, that's exactly what it looked like," I nodded, remembering the star Maitreya and I had travelled in to the Sun.

"Imagine that you are standing inside a sphere," Sheta Nut instructed me. "This is your auric field. Within this imagine the two triangles, one pointing up and the other down. Now imagine a small tube extending through the star from above your head to below your feet. This brings prana to your navel to form a small sphere, which will grow as it gathers life-force energy. Now you have to ignite the prana, so that it becomes the colour of the Sun.

"When I have taught you how to breathe, you will be completely enclosed within a sphere of brilliant golden light. Continue with the deep rhythmic breathing and imagine the prana moving through the tube. As it does, you will be able to access higher levels of consciousness."

She taught me how to breathe into my abdomen and hold my fingers together in mudras, but nothing happened and I felt discouraged.

"Imagine yourself within the golden sphere," Sheta Nut instructed.

"I am," I sighed, sinking into performance anxiety and wondering how on Earth I was going to get myself to the Sun. "I feel as if I'm having to pat my head and rub my tummy simultaneously."

"You don't have to do anything," Aluna told me. "Just be."

"We'll tie you to the doves," said Lisa, "We'll attach you with threads to their feet, and then you won't have to worry about getting it wrong. Your performance anxiety is blocking you."

"Will they be able to carry me?"

"There are thousands of them," Robert laughed, winking at me.

"Won't the Sun burn them?"

"They were conceived in the fire of our love," he reminded me.

Just as the Sun was beginning to set, Lisa and Robert tied plaited rainbow threads around my waist.

"I can attach the threads to the doves' feet," Aluna assured me.

When Lisa had positioned the doves above my head, Aluna waved her magic wand and mysteriously the threads attached themselves to the feet of the doves. Wearing my rainbow robe and clutching my sunglasses, I imagined myself standing inside the star tetrahedron. Everyone wished me well, and at a gesture from Lisa the doves spread their wings and took flight. I breathed deeply as I wobbled and was then airborne. The doves carried me far above the trees. When I looked down, everyone was gazing up in awe at the sight of me and the doves trailing rainbow threads through the sky.

I was trembling. This was my first visit to the Sun on my own. I prayed that we would be protected. The Sun was low on the horizon, and before too long I could see the Earth stretched out beneath me, like one of Lisa's patchwork quilts. Then it was the beautiful blue-and-white globe I remembered so well. The Sun was growing bigger as we travelled towards it. The flapping of the doves' wings was the only sound I heard until I was engulfed in Light. To my delight we entered the shaft of fire where the angels were singing and dancing, and there was Abaddon. I remembered his new name, Apollyon, and called to him. He was delighted to see me and flew over.

"How are you enjoying serving in the Sun?" I asked.

"It's blissful," he replied with a look of rapture.

"Caligastia is really pissed off with you," I told him. "He said you worked for him and had strict instructions not to open the door. He says he's going to get you for it."

"Caligastia is so predictable," laughed Apollyon.

"Who do you really work for?"

"Aeons ago when Lucifer started the Rebellion, he was looking for supporters. Michael, who wanted to be kept informed of what Lucifer was up to, asked for volunteers. I worked for Michael, but volunteered to work with Lucifer. When he promised Caligastia a galaxy to rule over, and the door was sealed, I decided it would be a good opportunity to learn about service and discipline."

"But you were down there for ages. How could you bear it?"

"It was a blessing in disguise. Spending so much time alone, I began to truly know myself. I also learned about responsibility. There were many times when I wanted to leave, but that door was my assignment. I had been told to guard it and that's what I did. Caligastia thought I was guarding it for him, but I was guarding it for Michael. Of course. I did not let anything in or out until you found the Last Unicorn."

I told Apollyon that I was looking for the Guardian Angel of all Guardian Angels.

"Keep going until you reach the Seven Thrones. Then ask for the Solar Angel," Apollyon explained. "The Solar Angel is the Guardian Angel of all Guardian Angels. By the way, Caligastia is having an existential crisis on the Moon. The Seraphim Sisters and the Lunar Lords are looking after him, and apparently he's being totally transformed."

"Poor Caligastia. Without Lucifer to drool over, he lost his purpose."

Apollyon agreed, bid me a fond farewell, and returned to sing and dance with the other angels. I travelled through the shaft until I arrived at the Seven Thrones. I tried to remember how Maitreya had greeted the Cosmic Lords.

"Most Glorious Ones," I called out. "I am looking for the Solar Angel, who I am told is the Guardian Angel of all Guardian Angels."

The Cosmic Lord of Will answered my call: "What is your purpose for seeing the Solar Angel?"

"Maitreya brought me here last year," I explained. "Since then I have spoken to the Great Dragon, who has promised not to destroy the Kingdom if I find enough people to be there when Gaia is reunited with Ananda."

The Cosmic Lord of Will nodded: "Ananda is already on his way. You have very little time."

"That's why I need to speak to the Solar Angel, for it is my intention to bring every child in the world to witness this great cosmic event. I need to ask the Solar Angel to speak to all of the children's Guardian Angels, so that they can bring their children to the Castle."

I squinted through my sunglasses, but still could not see the Cosmic Lord of Will's face. I saw only his outline, which shone with an intense radiance. He gestured to the Seven Great Beings seated upon the Seven Thrones, who immediately lifted their golden trumpets and sounded the most awesome ear-splitting note I had ever heard. It was loud enough to awaken the dead.

The Solar Angel slowly descended and stood before me radiating love, compassion and serenity. Its being was without boundaries and flowed out beyond the Sun. I was touched to the depths of my soul by the presence and infinite love of the Solar Angel. It loved me to the core of my being and beyond to parts of myself I had yet to meet. I did not have to speak. The Solar Angel knew.

"Be at peace, little one. Fear not. It shall be done. The children shall be there to witness this great cosmic event, and indeed they will change the world, for the children are the future. Not one child shall be excluded. I give you my most solemn promise."

"Thank you, most loving and gracious Solar Angel. Give my love to my own Guardian Angel."

"Your Guardian Angel receives your love even before you send it, and will love you to the end of time, and beyond. There are no limits to a Guardian Angel's love." The Solar Angel's voice was soft and melodious, playing upon my soul as if it were a flute.

"Blessings," said the Solar Angel as it slowly ascended through the Seven Thrones.

I thanked the Cosmic Lord of Will, who also gave me his blessings. Returning through the shaft of fire, I waved to Apollyon. It was a joy to see him looking so happy. What a contrast to his life in the dungeons where he was always snoring and covered in cobwebs.

It was after midnight when I floated over the pine forest where Lisa and Robert lived. The stars were twinkling like diamonds in an indigo sky when I landed in the garden. They were waiting up for me with hot goat's milk, and after I had described my trip to the Sun, they tucked me up in bed and congratulated me. I fell asleep feeling like a child secure in her parents' love.

In class I talked about the new book I was reading:

"It's about hidden cruelties in child-rearing practices, and how children twist themselves into knots to remain loyal to their parents."

"This is part of the split which happens in the developmental process," Vivian agreed. "We have to see our parents as good and loving no matter what. It is too painful to grieve the evil in our parents, so we project it onto others. This links in with what I'm going to say about the will. Psychology is just beginning to clear up misconceptions about the will. In the past it was seen in its strong aspect. This was the Victorian will. Parents considered it necessary to break the child's will. To have a strong-willed child was an indication of parental lack of control."

"If parents are fortunate enough to drive out wilfulness from the very beginning by means of scolding and the rod, they will have obedient, docile, and good children whom they can later provide with a good education," I quoted from the book I was reading.[2]

"Strong will did a lot of damage and is the basis for much of Alice Miller's writing. She writes about the misuse of will in its strong aspect. It is neither good nor skilful, and it's definitely not transpersonal. It was lacking in compassion," Vivian continued.

"If you rebelled, you were a sinner," Meara commented.

"What good fortune for those in power that people do not think," I said, quoting Hitler.[3]

"We're taught not to think," Vivian agreed. "It was considered a heresy to have your own will. Assagioli was the first psychologist to emphasize the will's relationship to the Self, and how central it is in strengthening our connection to the Self. He wrote:

> *"The discovery of the will in oneself, and even more the realization that the self and the will are intimately connected, may come as a real revelation which can change, often radically, a man's self-awareness and his whole attitude towards himself, other people, and the world. He perceives that he is a 'living subject' endowed*

with the power to choose, to relate, to bring about changes in his own personality, in others, in circumstances. This enhanced awareness, this 'awakening' and vision of new, unlimited potentialities for inner expansion and outer action, gives a new feeling of confidence, security, joy — a sense of 'wholeness'.[4]

"Without a sense of will, there is a feeling of impotence. The first step is to accept that will does exist; the second step is to realize that one has a will, a choice. The third step is to know oneself as being a will. I am willing. I choose. I am. The aspects of the personality are at the service of the conscious and willing self. This is not the same as having the emotions and thoughts in charge. When I am aware, I have the choice. Realizing that we are in charge of our lives brings us closer to the experience of mastery and joy."

"We then have the ability to respond," David pointed out.

"When an individual's will is ignored, repressed or violated, pain and illness arise because will is the faculty closest to the Self. The hurt goes right to the core because the Self is not being recognized," Vivian explained.

"Children are not taught to use their wills," I commented. "Their wills are squashed."

"When the will is frustrated, splitting occurs," said Danny. "Then it comes out as neurosis or pathology."

"We develop rebellious subpersonalities when the will is not honoured," Vivian nodded.

"Then the Rebel calls forth the dark forces. When I was a teenager, I told everyone to go to hell," Meara confessed.

"Houdini was a split-off for me. She planned her escape throughout my childhood," I shared, thinking about the subpersonality I had recently discovered.

"She escaped from the will of others," Vivian told me. "When the will is not supported, confidence and motivation are broken down. The emerging Self is immobilized. Once the will has been damaged, one can't have a strong sense of Self. We are going to restore the will."

"I turned my will against myself," said Shakura.

"You introjected the will-squashers," Vivian nodded.

"Will comes out as a distortion because the Shadow is pissed off," Meara added.

"We're learning to use the will appropriately," Vivian told us. "Early child-rearing manuals taught how to break the will. Humanistic Psychology helped people to break free. We needed to be able to say, 'Fuck off!' but now we need to learn the accurate use of the will."

"If a woman is wilful, she's considered a bitch," said Eleanor.

"The man in relationship with a strong woman becomes a wimp because he has to get what he wants sneakily," David pointed out. "He sneaks out to the bar and tells her he's working late."

The following morning I sat talking to Lisa and Robert who wanted to know why I was so obviously upset when my journey to the Sun had been so successful.

"Since I integrated Sheta Nut, I've felt like a roaring lioness," I confessed. "Sheta Nut has a strong will and last night she said something to the Omega Man which really made him angry."

The previous evening, when he had come to Vivian's house, I shared a dream I'd had about him in which he was smoking pot with a woman. In my dream I was angry with him, and as I shared the dream I became angry again.

"I don't support you smoking pot," I told him. "It may damage your etheric body."

He admitted that on the night of my dream he was smoking pot with a girlfriend.

"My hunch is that you were angry at me in your dream not because of your magnanimous concern for my etheric body, but because you sensed what I was doing that weekend and you were jealous. I was making love, laughing and having a wonderful time."

I was shaking as he spoke.

"Furthermore, I don't want you to meet me at the airport when I fly to England this summer. I don't need you to hold my hand."

Robert took me behind his workshop and pointed to a pile of

pots, explaining that he and Lisa had taken pottery classes and these were their failures. He told me to release my anger by smashing the pots.

"I don't know where to begin," I moaned.

"Begin at the beginning," he suggested.

"I'm angry with Akara," I confessed, picking up a pot. "I needed him to honour my decision to take final initiation instead of hanging on to me the way he did."

"Tell him."

"It was my destiny to take final initiation," I shouted, smashing the pot into a million pieces. "Why did you hang on to me?"

"I'm angry with my therapist too. I asked him to be my guide detective, and he happily agreed. Then, when something came up that he didn't want to deal with, he judged it and didn't bother to find out if I was telling the truth. He never even dialogued with Sheta Nut to test the accuracy of her story," I yelled, smashing another pot. I was remembering, with upset, what he had written to me in a recent letter:

"Akara died in Egypt a long time ago. Yes, he did a forbidden act by entering the temple, pleading for your life and seducing you, but you also had the power — and the responsibility — to say no to him, and you're the one who decided to proceed with the doomed initiation after being advised against it by the wise ones and after committing an act that you knew was against the rules and would lead to failure."

I was furious with Akara for making me promise to find him in the future, and even more furious with my therapist for denying my truth. Instead of helping me to integrate the extraordinary proof I had about the continuity of life, he had condemned Sheta Nut without a trial.

"Do you think I made it up?" I appealed to Robert.

In response, he took my hand and led me into his workshop. On his desk were a pile of books. He pulled one out, leafed through it and handed it to me.

The book contained a series of lectures given by Rudolf Steiner in 1908. In these lectures he talked about the ancient Egyptian practice of developing inner sight and knowledge of the higher realms through an initiation involving physical entombment.

"In the ancient initiations . . . for a period of three and a half days, the candidate was put into a deathlike condition in which the physical body was deserted by the etheric body while this latter, freed from the physical, united itself with the astral body. When the hierophant again awakened the candidate, the latter was illuminated. He knew what took place in the spiritual world, for he had made a remarkable journey during the three and a half days. He had been led through the fields of the spiritual world. He had seen what went on there, and he knew from direct experience what another person could learn only through revelation. A person thus initiated could, out of his own experiences, give knowledge of the beings who were in the spiritual world, beyond the physical plane."[5]

"This is what you are able to do," Robert told me. "It's what your writing is all about. How else did you acquire such a gift?"

"If it's true, why doesn't he recognize me?"

"If it doesn't mean anything to him, why is he reacting to it?" he asked. "Surely, if it was a figment of your imagination, he'd be neutral. His reaction is the proof you are seeking. Why does he have so much stuff on Sheta Nut? You can feel his anger in that letter he wrote to you."

"You're right," I agreed. "He has not behaved like a therapist."

"Rudolf Steiner said that the ancient Egyptian initiations were held for a specific purpose. The hierophants saw into the future to a time when humanity would be separated from its source. They sent the initiates into that future as torchbearers with a powerful message."

He handed me the book to read:

"I know there is a spiritual world ... I have lived in it ... and bring you the gifts of the spiritual world."[6]

"Isn't this what you're doing through your writing?"

I nodded.

"What else is making you angry?"

"I'm really angry that he told me I'm too stuck in my astral-emotional reactivity to address the world's pain. He's numb and stuck in his denial patterns, just like all the other people in this country. The planet would have to die before they felt anything. They produce twenty-five per cent of the world's carbon dioxide emissions, but they prefer to commit global genocide than give up their cars and their extravagant lifestyles."

"It sounds like you're angry with everyone."

"Yes, I am," I shouted, running outside and smashing the remainder of the pots. "Stop destroying the planet and wake up!" I screamed, as I ran through the woods.

"WAKE UP!"

"Let yourself explode!" Robert shouted, as he caught up with me and held me in his arms. My body was vibrating with rage and grief, and when I screamed it sounded like a mantra. Then we were spinning together in an explosion of light. Every atom in my body was dancing as I experienced myself as both male and female; alpha and omega.

Afterwards we walked slowly back to the house where Lisa was spinning beside the fire.

"I have to return to my class," I told them. "I walked out in a rage because nobody has the guts to say NO to the government. They are contributing towards the pollution, and maybe even Wormwood. I'd prefer to go to prison than pay someone to kill Gaia. The people in this country have tremendous power. All they have to do is say NO."

As I approached the sunroom, I heard them talking about me:

"I think there's a lot of truth in what she's saying," said Sharon.

"She's very evocative, but does she have the courage to respond to what she evokes?" Meara asked.

"Her writing will make a lot of people angry," Danny pointed out.

"I've asked her if she's strong enough to put her writing out," Vivian agreed. "It's going to create a tidal wave."

"She came here to give birth to the book," Sharon commented.

"It's not the book she's giving birth to," Shakura argued. "She's giving birth to herself. She is in transition between her inner world and the outer world. This is what the chaos is about."

"She's in labour," Meara nodded.

"She yells at us about paying taxes, but if she makes a million dollars from her book, she'll have to pay as well," they all agreed.

After I had returned to my usual seat by the door, I explained what was going on for me.

"I'm channelling some really serious material. I can't even share it with you or write it down. We are in grave danger. We're entering a planetary crisis, but we have the power to transform it into a planetary pentecost."

"When you yell at us, we feel helpless," Shakura told me.

"Your book is going to wake people up. Then you'll have to speak to them," Meara warned.

"I dread that," I groaned. "In Atlantis nobody listened to me when I told them what danger we were in, but now I'm talking about a global catastrophe."

"I also feel the danger," Patrick agreed.

"We need instant help for saving the planet," said Eleanor.

"We need an awakening pill," I joked.

"Not Nutra Sweet, but Cosmic Sweet," David laughed. "We are having to cross the abyss. We need guides who have painfully, but successfully, negotiated the abyss. The archetypal wounded healer is the hero who not only finds the Grail but brings it back."

1 *Esoteric Psychology* Vol. II, Alice Baily. Lucis Press, 1942.

2,3 *For Your Own Good*, Alice Miller. Farrar Straus Giroux, 1984.

4 *The Act of Will*, Roberto Assagioli. The Psychosynthesis and Education Trust, 92-94 Tooley Street, London Bridge, SE1 2TH, 2002.

5 *Egyptian Myths & Mysteries*, Rudolf Steiner. Anthroposophic Press, 1971.

Fifteen

Awakening

I arrived in the rose garden, where I was swept off my feet by the fragrance of the roses, and entered the Castle carrying Michael's flaming rod. As darkness descended, Robert lit the rainbow candles he had made, and later that evening the Omega Man, his daughter and I climbed the spiral staircase to the top of the tower where Gaia slept in the Bridal Chamber. The roses were still in bloom, filling the chamber with their aroma. I lit the white candles I had brought with me, and opened the door leading out onto a balcony. The stars were twinkling in the sky like winking spectators, the Moon was full, and nature appeared to be taking a deep breath and standing on tiptoe. The silence was tangible.

After we had meditated together, we saw movement in the sky, and cried out, unable to believe our eyes. Flying towards the Castle were millions of Guardian Angels, each one carrying a child. The children were being brought from all over the world. The Solar Angel had kept its promise. As they approached, we heard the flapping of their wings, and soon they were landing in the grounds of the Castle with their precious burdens. When the gardens were full, they put them through the doors and windows, and onto the balconies. The children flowed into the Castle, filling it with their gaiety.

"The children are coming home," I sighed.

We heard them running along corridors and into rooms which had not been used for centuries. They opened windows and invited moonbeams to play upon their faces. They climbed old forgotten staircases with the rainbow candles. Some of them ran up the stairs leading to the Bridal Chamber and stood wide-eyed in the doorway. A distant clock struck midnight. Mystery and enchantment were in the air.

We were standing on the balcony with our faces turned to the night when we saw what looked like a star approaching from far away. As it grew larger, we trembled. It was not a star. A gleaming blue orb, with an inner radiant fire, aligned itself with the Moon and cast a blazing plume of light across Gaia's bed. She stirred in her sleep, but did not awaken. As the orb approached, I recognized Ananda standing in a blazing chariot of fire, his face shining like the Sun, and his hair flaming out in a radiant halo. His being was so full of tenderness and love that the children, gazing at him in awe and fascination, burst into tears of relief. Ananda steered the chariot onto the balcony and stepped out. He was dressed in a blazing white tunic and carried a sword of glistening gold. He had a strong but gentle manner, and did not hesitate for a moment. He entered the Bridal Chamber, where we knelt with hearts racing.

Without looking at us, he stood at the foot of Gaia's bed and slowly lifted the drapes. When he looked into her face, he could not conceal his love. It shone from his eyes and played around the corners of his mouth. He walked to the side of the bed and leaned over, his Light shining directly across Gaia's serene face. Slowly he drew closer and left a lingering kiss on her lips. Now she stirred and slowly, slowly opened her eyes. Everyone in the room gasped. Her eyes shone like diamonds, and a tender smile lit up her face when she saw Ananda.

"It is I, Ananda, your Lord of Love."

"I had such a strange dream," she whispered.

He nodded: "You have been awakened from the dream, my Lady."

She smiled a long thoughtful smile, and looked around the room at us. Then back at Ananda. "How is the Kingdom?" she asked in a sweet melodious voice, ringing in our ears like tinkling bells.

He beckoned to us to come closer. Vivian and Paul had joined us in the Bridal Chamber, and stood with the children who had gathered around the bed.

"How is the Kingdom?" he asked.

"The trees are singing."

"And the Moon is smiling in the night sky."

"And listen . . ."

It was the song of a thousand nightingales.

Suddenly I remembered the Great Dragon. Whispering that I had to go, I crept out and clattered down the spiral staircase. Now that Gaia had awakened, I was afraid it would ascend and destroy the Kingdom. I did not notice that Paul was following me until I reached the dungeons.

"This is something I have to see," he told me, as we ran through the door where evil used to dwell, and through the collective unconscious. Caligastia's Caverns were empty, as was his throne. When we arrived at the boiling lake, to my surprise there were dozens of little red boats with black sails and the initial 'C' painted on them. They obviously belonged to Caligastia, and I was upset that he had failed to tell me about them. We climbed into one of the boats and sailed across the lake. As we glided over the steaming waterfall into the Pit and spiralled through the vortex, Paul cried out in delight.

More of Caligastia's boats, with children sitting in them, were also winding their way through the vortex to the cavern where the Great Dragon waited for us. Many children were already down there either playing in Noah's Ark or staring in awe at the Great Dragon who, to my horror, was already uncurling itself in preparation for its explosive ascent into the Kingdom.

"STOP!" I shouted. "I kept my promise. Now you must keep yours."

"Nobody really cares about Gaia," roared the Great Dragon, breathing fire.

"We care!" shouted Paul, myself and several thousands of children.

"You're only saying that because you are afraid."

At this point the four archangels appeared. They radiated amongst the children and surrounded the Great Dragon, who loomed up huge and flame red in their midst.

Raphael addressed the children: "I am Archangel Raphael. I have dominion over the air. Your parents have polluted the air almost to the point where it is too contaminated for you to breathe."

"What can we do?" the children cried out.

"The Beings you call trees are Gaia's lungs. They are dishonoured when they are cut down for profit. Live lightly on the Earth, do not pollute the air which gives you life, and honour the trees by replacing what has already been taken."

The children were silent for a long time.

"We did not know what our parents were doing," they whispered to each other.

Gabriel now addressed the children: "I am Archangel Gabriel. I have dominion over the water, which has been polluted with oil, sewage, chemicals and other toxic substances. The waters of life are essential for your existence on Earth, for the waters form seventy-five per cent of Gaia's body, and also your bodies."

"Our parents didn't tell us," the children wailed.

"I am Archangel Uriel. I have dominion over the earth. Gaia's body has been filled with poisons, pesticides and nuclear waste, which is lethal. The Earth is a living being, whose outer skin sustains you, but her skin is being eroded."

The children were distraught.

"I am Archangel Michael. I have dominion over the element you call fire, which is Gaia's life-force. Children of the Earth, take heed: when the atom is split, you are playing with fire and the destruction of your own life-force. Wormwood is more than just the physical death of a planet and its many life-forms. It is the death of your souls and the end of existence."

The children looked at each other in horror.

"I'm afraid," said a little girl, looking up at the Great Dragon.

"Snuggle up," it whispered in response.

As several children sneaked in beside her, it was obvious to me that the Great Dragon had a big heart.

"Now I understand," I said, with sudden insight. "Without our hearts we don't know when we're in danger. Our hearts help us to feel for each other and for Gaia, but we aren't encouraged to listen to the intelligence of the heart. The politicians and the Illuminati tell us to listen to our minds, but our minds are tricksters. Our hearts tell us when we're in danger, but we have all been numbed."

"Are we in danger?" Paul asked.

"Yes, you are," roared the Great Dragon. "The sooner you realize it, the better. Being numb won't help you."

All of the children started to cry, pleading: "We aren't really in danger, are we?"

"Do you want me to lie to you, like your parents and the politicians?" I asked. "Somehow we have to help everyone in the world to find their lost feelings. The politicians and the Illuminati use their power and their rationalizations like alcoholics use alcohol. We simply have to stop supporting their addiction. This is the most loving thing we can do. Just say NO to them. They can't throw all of us into jail. When we face the truth, we can take action. We must rise to the occasion."

"That reminds me," said the Great Dragon. "I must rise up."

"You promised you wouldn't destroy the Kingdom," I begged.

The archangels turned to the children and spoke:

"We know how hard it is for you, but you must heal the damage your parents have done. You can heal the Earth with your love, but you must also take action on Gaia's behalf. Plant trees, clean up the environment, and remineralize the soil. Then we will join with the nature spirits to help you create Heaven on Earth."

"Come on," said the Great Dragon. "Help me to rise up out of this pit. I have never before arisen in full consciousness. So you must all help me."

The children were discussing how to get the Great Dragon up through the vortex when Paul, who was exploring Noah's Ark, found the rope.

"We'll tie this rope around you and hoist you up to the next level," he said.

We tied the rope securely around the Great Dragon and pulled it behind Noah's Ark as we sailed through the vortex, setting it down in Caligastia's Caverns where it licked each child in turn.

We left Noah's Ark floating on the boiling lake and were walking through the caverns when I noticed the fourth locked door; the one Caligastia did not have a key for. I tried to resist my curiosity, but it was hopeless. I had to open the fourth locked door.

I used Paul's spell for opening locked doors, which still worked. The door creaked open and I found myself in a mysterious cavern with a beautiful crystal pyramid standing in the middle of a lake. It was the most beautiful pyramid I had ever seen, and I knew I had to explore it. I told everyone to wait, and then shut the door behind me.

When Michael's flaming rod shone on the crystalline structure of the pyramid, it sent rainbows bouncing around the walls of the cavern. It looked like a temple, and I longed to enter it, but could find no way of crossing the lake. As I explored, I found archways leading to other caverns, and then I noticed an opening in the ceiling, which appeared to be covered with a transparent film, like glass. Through this opening I saw dolphins swimming around, and realized that the collective unconscious stretched under the Lost Valley and terminated beneath the Pacific ocean.

I was wondering how to cross the lake when I noticed a familiar odour. It was the smell of pine forests, rotting leaves and stag musk. I looked up and saw Pan standing in front of me. I was so pleased to see him, I hugged him and buried my face in his fur. He took my hand and led me through the water, which to my surprise, was not wet. We climbed three steps and entered the temple, which had a prismed crystal ceiling. In the centre of the temple stood a rectangular altar emitting a mysterious blue flame. Pan lifted me onto the altar, where I was engulfed in the flame, and sat cross-legged in front of me playing a haunting melody on his pipes.

I closed my eyes and hurtled back through the centuries to a primordial time when rainforests covered the Earth and humanity had not yet been separated from its source. Akara and I were practising tantra on the altar Pan and I were now sitting on. Just as in my vision, the women danced clockwise in an inner circle while the men danced counter-clockwise in an outer circle. Beyond them stood the gods. All the gods were being honoured, and we were calling forth the separated ones to take form on Gaia's embodiment. My twentieth century mind recoiled in horror as we welcomed the Divine Opposites to dance within our souls to enable the separated ones to return home.

Then I had a terrifying insight: we were in danger because we had lost our dancing partners. The world had been taken over by the male aspect of the logos and was dancing counterclockwise. Logic, mental process and numbing rationalizations had taken control. Humanity now worshipped a male God and had forgotten the Goddess who is connected to feelings, heart and soul. We need to dance again with the feminine; not exclusively in either a clockwise or counter-clockwise direction, but in harmony and rhythm with each other.

"In Lemuria we cooperated with humans to create a garden globe," Pan explained. "When nature creates on its own, there is wilderness. When humanity creates on its own, there is desert, but when nature and humanity join forces, a garden is created. In Lemuria, which stretched across the Pacific ocean, humans respected nature and communicated with the nature spirits.

"In the rituals that you and Akara participated in you invoked the infernal hierarchies to incarnate, for these beings had separated themselves in darkness. Gaia's Mission was to offer redemption to the Light lost in darkness."

"Wasn't that a dangerous thing to do?"

"It has taken aeons for the danger to manifest. The infernal hierarchies will either be redeemed or they will attempt to destroy Gaia's embodiment. This is the meaning of Armageddon."

"This must be why Satan wants to destroy the world. If the infernal hierarchies are redeemed, he will lose his followers and his power, but what can we do?"

"You can befriend the darkness within your own souls, for that is where the drama is being acted out. The infernal hierarchies use human agents and can only be redeemed through them. You can also bring humans and devas into conscious interplay. As a seventh-ray soul, you are asked to renew human intercourse with the devas and the nature spirits to create a garden globe for the seeds of a New Humanity. It is also your dharma to assist in the transition of a large number of human beings from the fourth to the fifth world. Your special task is to unite spirit and matter.

"We ask you to carry this message to the world: if the destruction of the rainforests continues, humanity will exterminate itself, for all life sprang from these forests. As Gaia's lungs, they breathed you into existence.

"The nature spirits cannot tolerate the pesticides or the toxic materials now contaminating the soil, air and water. Many of these beings no longer wish to support humanity. They are retreating to the wilderness and will vacate the planet if the destruction continues. Without the help of the nature spirits, nothing can grow and the Earth will become a barren wasteland. However, if humanity recognizes its plight and calls to us for help, we will happily cooperate with you to create a garden globe. The choice is yours."

Pan looked deep into my eyes: "You are the gardener. We ask you to send our message out into the world and to plant the seeds of a New Humanity. Will you do that?"

Being too paralysed to speak, I nodded.

He held my hands and asked me to close my eyes. I found myself walking through a beautiful meadow full of wild flowers and fairies. The meadow was hidden in the middle of a forest and everything was in full bloom. The birds were singing, butterflies were dancing among the flowers, and bees were gathering pollen. In the distance I heard voices, and then saw a group of children running through the forest towards the meadow. They were laughing and playing with music bubbles.

We heard the sound of distant celebrations. Angels were gathering in the meadow as a procession meandered through the forest. It was led by Gaia and Ananda, walking arm in arm. Gaia was radiant and regal, wearing a crown of wild flowers on her head and a gown which reflected the grass, sky and trees. When they entered the meadow, the children threw flower petals over them, and then formed a large circle. Into the circle glided a group of Planetary Beings, which included Venus, her beauty veiled in swirling white mists. On either side of her stood Saturn, white-bearded and wearing an alchemist's robe, and Neptune, shrouded in mystery. Jupiter joined them, bearing gifts of sound and colour. All the planets in the solar system appeared with gifts of precious gems and ancient documents containing the secrets of the sky.

When Sanat Kumara waves the rod of initiation above Gaia's head to show that she is now a sacred planet, great rejoicing breaks out. Many Planetary Beings pay homage to Gaia, using her soul name, Sandolphon:

"Greater courage has not been known amongst us, dearest sister, for you chose to leave the Light to search for the Light lost in darkness."

Paul joins us in the circle.

"I was concerned when you didn't return. I saw you meditating on the altar, and then I found myself here."

I explain what is happening as Mercury, dressed as a winged messenger, and Mars, dressed as a warrior, kiss Gaia's hand.

Mercury and Mars step aside, and Caligastia is brought into the circle by a group of feminine deities calling themselves the Seraphim Sisters. They radiate love from every angle of their being and carry the energy of the Mother Goddess. All of us are instantly filled with an acute, inexplicable longing to be mothered by the Seraphim Sisters, who have totally transformed Caligastia. Already his scales are peeling off and he is beginning to sprout wings. He is presented to Gaia, who embraces him and shows no sign of resentment or unwillingness to forgive him for what he has done to her. Her love for him is so tender, embracing and unconditional, he bursts into demented sobs. She waits quietly until he regains his composure, and then calls him by his angelic name: Samael.

Immanuel, Michael, Gabriel, Uriel and Raphael now enter the circle, and after paying homage to Gaia they lead us out of the meadow and through the forest. We are soon standing in the rose garden where Gaia and Ananda look with delight at the roses, which are all in bloom.

"Ah, the roses," sighs Gaia. "How I love the roses. Each rose symbolizes the soul of a person."

Ananda smiles knowingly.

As they admire each individual rose as if it is the only rose in existence, Paul attempts to catch goblins, but he does not have much success. They are far too quick for him. He does manage to catch a couple of fairies, but they pop in his hand like soap bubbles and appear laughing on his shoulder, reminding me of Houdini, my escape artist subpersonality.

Maitreya approaches me, suggesting that I return to the temple. I have no desire to leave, and then feel guilty because I have totally forgotten about the Great Dragon.

When I open my eyes I am lying alone on the altar wrapped in a ram's fleece.

"Are you ready?" Pan asks, appearing at my side.

He lifts me off the altar and leads me down the steps, which I look at in amazement. When we entered the temple, there were three steps; now there are nine.

"You must hurry," he says, glancing up at the ceiling.

Then I realize what is happening. The crystal pyramid temple is ascending towards the ceiling. When it reaches the transparent film, it will crash through and the sea will gush into the cavern. As I grope for the door handle, I glance back at the pyramid's apex, which is now piercing the transparent film.

"We're going to be flooded," I stammer, slamming the door behind me.

"Don't panic," says Paul. "We have a boat."

We sit in the Noah's Ark, which is still floating on the boiling lake, and I try to explain about the crystal pyramid, but I am interrupted by a loud crash and the rushing of water. When the cold sea water runs into the boiling lake, it sizzles. Slowly, as the lake overflows, Noah's Ark floats through Caligastia's Caverns surrounded by hundreds of the small red rowing boats. We float past Caligastia's empty throne and through the black wrought iron demon gates.

As we are swept through the collective unconscious, I confess that I have somehow activated the crystal pyramid's ascent. When we reach the door into the dungeons, I try to figure out how to take the Great Dragon through it.

"How did you get here in the first place?" I ask.

"I think the Castle was built on top of me."

It is obviously an impossible task, and I feel desperate. I wade through the water, which is pleasantly warm, and make my way up into the main entrance hall. I am standing there wondering what to do next when I see Arthur running towards me. He is carrying several bundles of dynamite, and I now understand why Merlin said he was training Arthur to use his intuition.

We return to the dungeons where the children are paddling and swimming, and soon have the situation under control. Before blasting out the wall between the dungeons and the collective unconscious, Paul gathers the children and takes them outside into the garden. There is a loud explosion and the wall is down. The unconscious and the collective unconscious now run into each other. The Great Dragon wades through the dungeons and sits at the bottom of the stairs, but they are too narrow. After the staircase has been blown up, it is simply a matter of hoisting the Great Dragon through the hole into the main part of the Castle. It takes a lot of effort to pull on the rope, but at last we have it sitting in the hall smiling all over its dragon face and puffing out smoke rings. I open the main doors leading out into the courtyard, and with a lot of pulling and pushing we have the Great Dragon outside in the sunlight, where it sniffs the air and gazes up into the sky with a rapturous expression.

I find Vivian in the rose garden with the other members of our class. Sharon is sitting by the well, drinking the water and looking exhausted.

"I had your book photocopied," she informs me. "There's a copy for everyone."

I have been so busy, I forgot about Sharon's offer to photocopy my manuscript.

"I don't know how to thank you."

"Don't thank me," Sharon insists. "This book is a gift because it has helped me to accept my own truth. Now I know I'm not crazy."

"Didn't it occur to you that we might both be crazy?" I laugh.

It is time for me to go home.

I walk over to Vivian and thank her for keeping her promise, but she looks puzzled. "You were Akara's sister and my friend in Egypt," I explain. "Before I went into seclusion prior to final initiation, you promised to be there for me when I emerged from the underworld."

"Thank you for going into the underworld for us," she says as we embrace.

I hand her a copy of my manuscript to give to the Omega Man.

"You are coming back, aren't you?" asks Paul, who loves my stories.

"Yes, I've left my Shakti shoes in the Awakening Room."

"I'd like you to meet my half-brother," he says, leading me across the garden. "This is Marlon."

Of course, I recognize him immediately. It is Marlon with his dragon, who tells his child all about our meeting in the Lost Valley.

Paul and I walk into the Castle and climb the stairs to the Bridal Chamber, which is now empty, but from the balcony we see something glistening in the ocean.

"It's the crystal pyramid temple!" I exclaim.

As the Sun sparkles on its crystalline structure, it sends rainbows dancing across the ocean. Whales and dolphins gather and swim around the temple, as if to celebrate its reappearance. We also see the new lake which is forming in the Lost Valley, where trees and flowers are already beginning to grow. Paul and I are enjoying the scene when the Omega Man joins us.

"Vivian gave me a copy of your book, and I want to thank you for being so dedicated to the truth and your creative process," he tells me with tears in his eyes.

"Don't thank me. Thank Sheta Nut. She sacrificed her life for this process to occur."

"It's a profound teaching about the relationship between the human and devic kingdoms, between the reality of the human physical world and the inner planes of life," he continues with enthusiasm. "After reading the first part of the book, I went for a long walk in nature and was very sensitive to the devas. Your writing will inspire people to have a conscious relationship with the devic kingdom."

"I hope so," I comment.

"I see the book as one huge love letter to Akara."

"It is. Sheta Nut wants Akara to understand why she left him in Egypt. She kept her promise to find him in the future, and wants him to know that she will always love him."

"Maybe it's even a love letter to me," he adds, a little bashful.

"It is," I agree, blushing.

"It is the greatest of gifts, a profound inspiration in my life, and a blessing beyond measure. Thank you for being my friend, for the deepest of deep sharing, and for being a magnificent blessing in my life."

We are embracing when I feel a new presence. It is Maitreya.

"I did it," I sigh with relief. "I completed the Journey."

"All you have to do now is give a speech," he smiles.

My jaw drops, and when I look down everyone is gazing up at me with expectant expressions on their faces.

"Do you want the good news or the bad news first?" I ask.

I don't want to tell them the bad news, but decide to get it over with. "The Earth is in danger, and so are we." I give them Pan's message and repeat what the archangels told the children. "But we can heal the Earth with our love," I tell them, waving Michael's flaming rod. "And we can take our Light to the light lost in darkness. We can flood the world with Light."

"We are one Earth, and one people, with one destiny!" Paul shouts.

"We are all In Love, and love is all there is," I proclaim. "Armageddon will not happen. Instead we are creating a Planetary Pentecost, which is a mass movement of the heart. All we have to do is change our minds and commit ourselves to a life filled with love. Gaia has awakened. Now it's our turn:

"IT'S TIME TO WAKE UP!"

As everyone cheers, golden threads stretch out from each person's solar plexus to the Sun, which now resembles the Maypole I saw at the Love Feast in Shamballa. They all shout out in wonder as they touch each other's threads, which sparkle in the rays of the Sun. Then a miracle occurs: our Guardian Angels, whom I recognize as the singing dancing Solar Angels I saw in the Sun, take our golden threads and weave them into the Sun's Corona to create a gorgeous, intricately patterned lacy wedding garment for Gaia to wear, and as we reach out to her in love our Solar Angels shower us with Jewels of Light. I am so ecstatic, I do not notice Isis standing in the chariot of fire. She beckons to me to join her, but I hesitate and confess that I am afraid of fire.

Isis laughs: "After all you've been through, you are still afraid of fire?"

I laugh too. It is ridiculous.

As Maitreya lifts me into the chariot, I close my eyes and take a deep breath.

"Don't forget your backpack," he says, handing it to me.

"It's light and easy to carry, isn't it?" I reply, giggling, and then realize that it is not the backpack he is referring to, but Light. It is Light he wants me to carry into the world.

When I look at the balcony, Vivian, Paul, the Omega Man and his daughter are watching as Maitreya gives Gaia the wedding gown, which she steps into. Ananda takes her hand, like a proud groom, and dances with her as the angels sing and the children dance.

"Gaia, I love you and will sing your praises for ever," I call to her, and laugh when I open my mouth, for I am no longer singing out of tune.

Then I call to the Omega Man:

"I hope you will forgive me for leaving you in Egypt. I love you beyond measure and kept my promise to find you in the future, but my commitment is to Gaia and to our individuation process. These are the reasons why I took final initiation."

Everyone waves as the chariot of fire takes flight. When I look down I see the children dancing in a circle around Gaia and Ananda, while the Great Dragon suns itself on the lawn. As I watch, columns of light rise up out of the ground to surround them all, like the soaring spires of a great cathedral, falling back to Earth as fountains, and showering them with glistening silver dew. They clap their hands in delight and surround the Great Dragon, who looks up and winks at me.

Gaia's Castle sparkles like a precious jewel, its pinnacles gold-tipped, reminding me of the palace in Maitreya's garden, as we fly over it in the chariot of fire, which writes in huge fiery letters in the sky:

THE EARTH IS A TEMPLE OF LIGHT

"Phew! I'm glad I've reached the end," I gasp, collapsing in a heap.

"Good heavens!" Isis exclaims. "Do you really think this is the end?"

Triumph now with joy and mirth,
The God of Peace hath blessed our land;
We enjoy the fruits of Earth
Through favour of His bounteous hand.
We through His most loving grace
A king and kingly seed behold,
Like a Sun with lesser stars
Or careful shepherd to His fold.
Triumph then, and yield Him praise
That gives us blessed and joyful days.

Thomas Giles, *Songs from a Wedding Mask* (1607)

Epilogue

The Earth Awakens was written in1985/6 before cell phones and computers. I typed the manuscript on an electric typewriter and transcribed Vivian's classes from cassettes. We played vinyl records and when computers appeared they were cumbersome and used floppy disks. I bought a word-processor in 1990 and typed the entire manuscript onto small disks, which were later transferred to floppy disks in preparation for publication. By then I had a laptop.

Since then there have been rapid technological advances and we now have the World Wide Web enabling us to communicate with each other instantly across vast distances. In the 1990s I felt alone in my environmental activism, writing endless letters to companies around the world about the disappearing rainforests and the abuse of indigenous people's rights, unnecessary plastic packaging and the urgent need for recycling. Now we are recycling, signing petitions on line, and being heard. I no longer feel like a solitary voice in the wilderness.

We survived the end of the Mayan calendar on December 21st 2012, which according to Mayan elder Carlos Barrios did not signify the end of the world but its transformation. He says we are in transition between the World of the Fourth Sun and the World of the Fifth Sun, which calls us to unite in support of life. Whereas the elements of Water, Air, Fire and Water dominated past epochs, there will be a fifth element to reckon with in the time of the Fifth Sun – the element of Ether which represents spiritual energy. This is similar to what is written in *The Earth Awakens* and which I did not fully understand when I wrote it. We are entering the first age of conscious evolution in which we are required to co-evolve with nature and Spirit. It is our collective wake-up call.

Although the world did not end on the 21st December 2012, we cannot be complacent. Since 1990 carbon emissions are 58% higher. In 2012 North America experienced more extreme weather than any other continent, the UK was the wettest since records began, Brazil experienced the worst drought in fifty years, floods hit China, the Philippines, Australia and Nigeria. Hundreds died in sub-zero temperatures in Russia and Eastern Europe whereas in central Australia temperatures exceeded 50 degrees centigrade.

Buckminster Fuller suggested that it is not possible to change things by fighting the existing reality. Instead we have to build a new model that makes the existing model obsolete. This is already happening as towns move away from fossil fuels towards local economies as part of the Transition Town Network. We are now being asked to achieve the equivalent of building cathedrals in medieval times when the builders knew they would not see the finished product. What are we building for our children and their children? It may well be that, as Deepak Chopra points out: "the fate of the planet depends on a collective decision."

I am often asked if The Earth Awakens is true, and I can only respond that I experienced everything written within its pages. I found Vivian through an obscure encounter in New Zealand, and I had dreamt about her house six years earlier. On reflection, I do not know how I found time to write. I was cleaning, gardening and typing for Vivian as well as studying and taking her classes. I often had no idea what was going to appear on the pages and was amazed by what did appear. There were strange synchronicities and verifications that still take me by surprise years later.

"The New Epoch begins with a mass movement of the heart" proclaimed at the Galactic Gathering has been verified by the Institute of HeartMath which discovered that the heart's electromagnetic field is the strongest electrical field of the body conveying patterns of coherence out into the environment and being detected in the nervous systems of other people and animals. Heart coherence was demonstrated in September 2001 when two satellites orbiting the Earth showed spikes in the Earth's magnetic field fifteen minutes after the first plane hit the World Trade Centre and fifteen minutes before the second impact. Subsequent studies by Princeton University and the Institute of HeartMath found that the correlation between the satellite readings and the events of 9/11 were not mere coincidence. Satellites recorded similar spikes after the death of Princess Diana. Their conclusion is that the heart-based emotions of the world's population influence the magnetic field of the Earth. There is now no doubt in my mind that a "mass movement of the heart" could indeed bring in a New Epoch and change the world.

Other books published by Inner Way

Transpersonal Development
Roberto Assagioli

First published thirteen years after Assagioli's death, *Transpersonal Development* is a collection of his lectures, essays and notes. It would undoubtedly have formed part of the book he was writing which he planned to call Higher Psychology and the Self.

Transpersonal Development is divided into three parts: Part One describes the reality of the superconscious. Part Two delves into the problems and difficulties experienced on the spiritual path. Part Three deals with the everyday application of those insights gained in the process of spiritual awakening.

As Sergio Bartoli writes in the Preface, Roberto Assagioli was truly a 'scientist of the spirit' who dedicated his life to discovering the reality of phenomena beyond the evidence of verified facts.

The inspiring message of this book is that transpersonal development is not just for the exceptional few. It is possible for everybody. It contains practical guidelines to help people achieve the goal.

Assagioli's article 'Smiling Wisdom' has been added as a final chapter because when we step upon the spiritual path the quality that will help us the most is humour.

What a wonderful production! The new edition of Transpersonal Development is a great achievement. I had never liked the previous edition because the translation, for me anyway, made Assagioli's book seem rather uninteresting. Not so now! The new translation is fresh and brings the words alive in a new way, and there are real gems in here. Even though I've read it before in previous translations, it is like having a 'new' Assagioli book ... amazing!
Will Parfitt, Psychosynthesis Writer and Educator

ISBN 978-0-9530811-2-7

RACHEL SPRING AND THE PROCLAMATION

Marilyn Barry

Part One of an exciting new trilogy written for teenagers and enjoyed by adults, dealing with family relationships, environmental issues and romantic love.

When 12-year-old Rachel Spring is sent from England to California to live with her cousin, Hetty Slymer, she does not realize just how much her life is going to change. She makes friends with Aaron, Hetty's son from a previous marriage to Spike, an eccentric inventor, who is attempting to solve the world's environmental problems. Her other friends include Pearl, a homeless teenager living on the streets of L.A., and Gideon whose large chaotic family bring warmth and Rachel's first experience of falling in love.

Rachel talks to nature spirits and her deceased mother who teach her the true meaning of life. Her inner world both nourishes and bewilders her as her outer world changes and presents her with many challenges, but this is no ordinary coming-of-age story.

On a camping trip with her friends to the mysterious mountain behind Spike's ramshackle house, their lives are changed for ever after an extraordinary encounter.

Some readers' comments:

'A wonderful world of fantasy mixed in with teenage and pubescent realities. Magical but with no sentimental slush, this is the perfect book for younger readers.'
William Bloom, author of *The Power of Modern Spirituality*, *The Endorphin Effect* and *Working with Angels, Fairies and Nature Spirits.*

A wonderful book filled with everything you would want your teenager to know: family relationships, environmental issues and the love of nature...all bound together in an engaging story that creates a really enjoyable read.

A great message for young people wanting to know how to help the earth and create a better future...

It's a whole combination of friendship, young love and some fantastic magical/ spiritual ideas that are totally believable and really well thought out and put across...the style of writing keeps you reading and I just loved the characters...

ISBN 978-0-9530811-5-8

Being Here When I Need Me – An Inner Journey

Vivian King Ph.D.

Inspired by Psychosynthesis, Vivian King invites us to take a journey into the heartland of ourselves where we will meet our inner healer, creative genie and beloved Self who is always here to love, understand and support us. With its unique combination of mysticism and science, this book helps to bring us home to the Self.

Vivian King writes: 'As you rest in the meadow by the brook, make your way through the forest, and climb the mountains of your mind, you will discover what is profoundly meaningful and holy.

'Learning to be here for yourself, you will no longer be dependent on material things or other people. You will have the inner strength to be with others without losing your sacred centre. You will never need to walk alone again.'

Described by its readers as down-to-earth, comprehensive, clarifying and powerful – a simple, pragmatic way to open up to the Higher Self.

ISBN 978-0-9530811-1-0

"Being Here When I Need Me *provides a natural way to open to your higher Self. It is down-to-earth, comprehensive, clarifying, and powerful. Vivian King's approach to Psychosynthesis is both inspirational and scholarly. I highly recommend this book to those committed to personal and spiritual growth and to all humanity."*

Edith Stauffer, Ph.D., Founder / Director of Psychosynthesis International
Author of *Unconditional Love and Forgiveness*

Some readers' comments about ***Being Here When I Need Me:***

"I began underlining with a marker until I realized I was marking the whole page."

"A simple, practical, pragmatic way to open to the Higher Self."

"Your writing helps me regain my faith in myself, in life and in God's presence."

"A blend between prose and a literary novel. It doesn't have an arid feeling like most structured material has."

"This book is not for wimps."

Inner Theatre – Unmasking the Human Spirit
Vivian King Ph.D.

On the corner of Imagination Street and Adventure Avenue, in the theatre of your mind, you will find a cast of characters as rich and varied as actors on a Broadway stage.

To produce a successful play – perhaps even a divine comedy – it is necessary to claim your director's chair, become acquainted with your players and playwright, and discover the secrets of directing.

Welcome to the rich and innertaining world of your inner theatre!

Inner Theatre Playbook – Vivian King

Welcome to the Inner Theatre – the private world of your personality where you are the playwright, the director, and all the players; in short – the whole play.

Inside the theatre, you will be given an entertaining way to recognize and develop the many aspects of yourself. You can expect to explore the unknown regions of your mind, to broaden your emotional repertoire, and to strengthen your centre of inner authority. You can take off your masks and be your natural self.

In the beginning, you will meet a guide who knows her way around the Inner Theatre. First, she will take you behind the scenes and give you a tour of the set. Then she will encourage you to explore your director's sanctum and to find your director's chair. Your guide will introduce you to prominent members of your entourage, audience, and supporting cast She will reveal the profound, yet simple, secrets of directing and will stand beside you as you learn to recognize, accept, and direct your inner actors.

The principles you learn in this programme will not fail you. You will find them useful throughout life. By taking responsibility for your own act and giving the best of yourself, the world will become a better place to be – or a better play to see.

Becoming A Star – Reviewed by Ralph E. Melcher
The Journal of the Association for Humanistic Psychology

Vivian King has produced a wonderfully innovative tool for supporting the intrapersonal development of children from the ages of 8 to 12.

In *Becoming A Star* she addresses the needs of children on a myriad of levels, providing them with an entertaining way to develop self-awareness, self-acceptance and self-responsibility.

Based on the premise that children are inherently playful and creative, and that they respond readily to love, acknowledgment and understanding, the programme is designed to build a strong sense of self that includes the clear perception and acceptance of the child's unique desires, feelings, and talents. The child also gains an ability to contact inner sources of guidance and wisdom in order to express 'star' qualities.

The Leader's Guide involves as much trust in the child's own emerging 'inner curriculum' as it does a thorough familiarity with the material. The 'Preparation' is a careful walk-through to set the stage, involving the use of props, music, mood, and work materials. The 'Programme' is then carefully scripted, with each section annotated with the corresponding section in the child's Playbook. There is enough material to provide room for flexibility, and suggestions are offered for additional activities that children may pursue with the group or on their own. A set of illustrated visual aids completes the leader's package.

The Playbook is full of pictures and exercises, including many pages for children to engage their budding creativity. As the programme unfolds, new territory is continually unveiled as children explore first the theatre, then their inner actors, and eventually their own inner playwright and director. The programme touches on virtually all of the essential aspects needed to achieve self-reliance in a constantly changing world.

Claiming Your Director's Chair – Reviewed by Ralph E. Melcher
The Journal of the Association for Humanistic Psychology

How do you get a teenager's attention and hold it? Vivian King has developed a course of activities that is both engaging and entertaining. Designed for those who are poised between childhood and adulthood, it helps and encourages them in facing this time of deep challenge and growth.

In *Claiming Your Director's Chair*, Dr King's programme applies the methods and metaphors of the theatre to bring teenagers in touch with their inner wells of creativity. The skills and insights unveiled in the chambers of the Inner Theatre can be of immense value in helping them to make the choices that will shape their lives and help them arrive at a true sense of self-awareness, self-acceptance, and self-mastery.

Dr King outlines her understanding of the sometimes overwhelming drama that modern teenagers must learn to face, and vividly outlines the possibilities of either Tragedy or Divine Comedy. Her stated goal is to support these amateur actors in producing an individual and collective drama that can be see as 'The Greatest Show on Earth'.

Plenty of resources are provided in both the Leader's Guide and the Playbook. Each lesson plan is carefully laid out, with a clear explanation of its purpose and a bit of theoretical background, followed by suggestions for props and setting the stage. The exercises themselves follow a series of activities that include readings, role playing, and the use of audio and visual aids. Scattered throughout are teaching tips based on the a author's extensive experience of working with similar groups. The segments are somewhat open-ended, offering numerous suggestions for optional activities and encouraging students and teachers to create their own exercises.

The Playbook is a workbook with text and spaces for writing and drawing. It is filled with illustrations and a feast of quotes, cartoons, and potent words of wisdom. Players who pass through this course will become acquainted with the depths and heights of themselves, and will have an entertaining way to handle the complexities of life. Those who continue to use these principles will develop a rich inner life, and will be able to contribute positively to the larger World Play.

About the Author

Vivian King, like Dorothy in *The Wizard of Oz*, grew up on a farm in Kansas. Along the yellow brick road, she was trained as a psychiatric nurse and a psychotherapist, specializing in Psychosynthesis, a transpersonal psychology. Her experience as director of Psychosynthesis education and counselling programmes for over twelve years inspired her to write her book *Being Here When I Need Me*. She travelled throughout the USA, the Baltics and Russia, where she conducted workshops on Psychosynthesis using the metaphor of the 'Inner Theatre', before a tragic car crash ended her physical life in 2000.

Inner Theatre books only available from Inner Way Productions: www.innerwayonline.com

www.ingramcontent.com/pod-product-compliance
Lightning Source LLC
Chambersburg PA
CBHW072113270326
41931CB00010B/1545

9780953081196